CONGREGATION
OF THE

VOICES
AGAINST
THE DEATH
PENALTY

CONDEMNED

WITH ESSAYS BY EDWARD KENNEDY,
MARIO CUOMO, TOM WICKER,
MIKE FARRELL, CORETTA SCOTT KING,
PETER GABRIEL, AND OTHERS . . .

EDITED BY SHIRLEY DICKS

PROMETHEUS BOOKS • BUFFALO, NEW YORK

Published 1991 by Prometheus Books

98 97 96 95   5 4 3 2

Library of Congress Cataloging-in-Publication Data

Congregation of the condemned : voices against the death penalty / with essays by Edward Kennedy . . . [et al.] ; edited by Shirley Dicks.
    p.   cm.
Originally published: 1991.
ISBN 0-87975-970-4
    1. Capital punishment. 2. Capital punishment—United States. I. Dicks, Shirley, 1940–   . II. Kennedy, Edward Moore, 1932–   .
HV8698.C69   1995
364.6'6—dc20   94-39969
                                                        CIP

Printed in the United States of America on acid-free paper.

This book is dedicated to my son Jeff Dicks who sits on Tennessee's death row for a crime he didn't commit; for my two daughters, Tina Thomas and Laurie Dougherty; for my youngest son, Trevor Dicks; and last of all for my granddaughter whom I adopted, Maria Dicks.

A Mother's Torment

A mother sits alone and cries
For the son that she has lost,
And she vows to get him back someday
No matter what the cost.

For you see they took him from her
And she found out far too late
They only wanted a sacrifice
To satisfy their hate.

She searched for truth and justice
But was met with hostile stares,
And she faced the ugly fact
That no one really cares.

And as they take her son away
She hangs her head to cry
For the jury made a decision:
They've sentenced him to die.

But still she's searching for the truth
Though no one hears her plea
And knows she'll never give up her fight
Till the day they set him free.

—Laurie Dicks

The Life He Lives

He sits alone inside his cell
As his tears silently fall.
He hates this life he's forced to live
And wants to end it all.

For he did nothing wrong.
Can't they understand?
They've closed their ears to him
Yet believed another man.

He doesn't know how this can be
And asks the question why.
They turn their heads and walk away.
They've left him there to die.

No one else has listened
So he turns to God, to pray
For comfort and understanding
Till they learn the truth someday.

—Laurie Dicks

My Daddy

My name is Maria, and I'm thirteen years old
And already I've been through a lot
But the thing that hurts me the most
Is that my daddy is locked up.

He hasn't held me since I was born
And I long for him to be home
So I can tell myself and all my friends
This is *my daddy*, and mine alone.

I never get the chance to kiss him
And tell him I love him so much.
Is that too much to ask for,
Just to feel my daddy's touch?

They lied about my daddy
And took him away from me,
And I cry and pray that someday
They'll set my daddy free.

Then I can tell him how much I love him
And he'll kiss me and hold me so tight,
And tell me we'll never be parted,
Daddy's home, everything is all right.

—Laurie Dicks

The Execution

They bound my hands and chained my feet,
They led me through death's door.
I looked for a moment
At this world I'd see no more.

My daughter cried in pain.
She didn't understand
Why it was my mother
So tightly held her hand.

My chest began to heave,
My mind began to burn,
All the voices around me
I just could not discern.

The tears began to tumble
As I looked at my mother's face.
She had strongly tried to handle
What was fixing to take place.

In an instant it is over
The pain for me is through.
Yet it's never ending
For the ones I've bid adieu.

Why must the innocent suffer,
Their lives forever unhinged?
So you have your satisfaction,
You have your sweet revenge.

   —Michael Orndoff, Death row, Tucker, Arkansas

    (dedicated to Shirley Dicks' efforts
    to help the innocent families and
    death-row inmates who suffer)

Introduction

Shirley Dicks

In 1978, my oldest son, Jeff Dicks, found himself in trouble with the law. He turned himself in to authorities and gave a statement about a crime that he had knowledge of but had taken no part in. We never got an attorney for him; he just told the truth in a statement to detectives. The case came to trial, and in the end he was given the death penalty along with the boy who committed the crime.

I couldn't believe that this could happen in the United States, and so I began to research the death penalty by talking to the experts on the subject. It was only then that I became interested in capital punishment. I had never before considered the death sentence or given those who were on death row any thought. I figure that's the way of everyone. Unless it happens to you, or a loved one, you don't think about the death penalty or the innocent people who are being killed in the name of justice.

The purpose of this book is to inform the public about how the death sentence is given and perhaps bring about a change in attitude regarding capital punishment. The death penalty, because it involves the deliberate taking of a human life, has always been an important issue. People have committed murder since Cain and Abel, but that doesn't mean they are inhuman. I believe they are still the children of God.

In the Bedau-Radelet report on "Miscarriages of Justice in Potentially Capital Cases,"* it was reported that 350 people have been wrongfully sentenced, twenty-three of which were actually killed by the state before they were found to have been innocent. England did away with the death penalty after one person was executed who was later found to be innocent. How many innocent people will the United States execute before we stop this barbaric punishment?

People have been sentenced to death and executed, not because they have been found to be uncontrollably violent, but because they are hopelessly poor. Most were represented at trial by court-appointed attorneys, many of whom had never handled a capital case before. They are the unlucky victims of prejudice, the losers in an arbitrary lottery that could just as well have spared them as killed them, the victims of the disadvantages that almost always go with poverty. You won't find a wealthy person on death row because they get excellent legal defense. Justice is for the rich in this society. A system like this does not enhance respect for human life; it cheapens and degrades it. However heinous murder is, the system of capital punishment does not compensate for or erase those crimes. It only tends to add new injuries of its own to the catalogue of our inhumanity to each other.

Capital cases are very expensive and there is no doubt that it costs more to execute a person than to imprison him for life. The increased costs are a result of the need to house each death-row inmate in an individual cell, to separate him from the general population, to provide separate recreation, and to increase security. Thus, a state with capital punishment is required to spend millions on housing just those convicted of capital crimes. The estimate for housing a capital offender for twenty years is $800,000.

The Supreme Court has ruled that states can execute the mentally retarded and juveniles. At least six mentally retarded people have been executed. No one argues that the retarded should not be punished for their crimes, but clearly, the justice system cannot continue to ignore the disabling effects of mental retardation if justice is to be genuine for them.

Having the death penalty does not deter others from committing

---

*Hugo Adam Bedau and Michael L. Radelet, "Miscarriages of Justice in Potentially Capital Cases," *Stanford Law Review* 40: 21–179.

murders, and in some instances, it makes violent crime more prevelant. For example, in Louisiana, during the summer of 1987, eight people were executed. In that same time period, the murder rate in New Orleans rose 16.9 percent. States that do not have the death penalty have lower crime rates than states that have it.

Most murders are committed in the heat of passion or while the person was under the influence of drugs or alcohol. Murderers do not expect to be caught or to be sentenced to death, so the threat of the death penalty has no deterrent effect on them. Yes, it will deter that person from ever committing another murder, but so would a life sentence. A life sentence is just; capital punishment is revenge.

I was once asked whether I would still be against capital punishment if it had been my husband who was murdered. I answered, "If it had been your child who killed my husband, would you still be for it?" I know what it's like to be on the receiving end of the violence. Last summer my youngest son was robbed at gunpoint in Knoxville, Tennessee. The robbers forced him to strip and then one of them started beating my son on the head with a gun. If he hadn't started running and escaped, my son would have been killed.

As I watched him lying in the hospital with his jaw broken in three places, I felt great anger at those responsible. I know what it is to watch my closest family member violated. I felt his pain, yet could do nothing to help. It seemed so senseless to me that people could hurt another human being for the sake of money. I would have liked to get my hands on those boys who made my son suffer so badly. But even had he died, I wouldn't have wanted the robbers to get the death penalty for the simple fact that the authorities might convict the wrong person. I can understand revenge, but I know something else. I know society should strive for something better than the death penalty. It has never worked since the beginning of time, and it won't work now.

Mario Cuomo spoke very eloquently when he said:

Where would it end? You kill my son, I kill yours. You rape my daughter, I rape yours. You mutilate my body, I mutilate yours. You treat someone brutally, and I, the established government of one of the most advanced states in the most advanced nation on earth, will respond by officially and deliberately, treating you brutally, by strapping you to a chair and burning away your flesh, for all to see, so the barbarians will know that we are capable of official barbarism. We will pursue this course, despite the lack of reason to believe it will protect us, even if it is clear, almost with certainty, that occasionally the victim of our official barbarism will be innocent.

Camille Bell, one of the contributors to this book, whose son was killed in Atlanta said:

I don't necessarily think of killing someone as punishment. When a person is dead, you're no longer punishing him. You're punishing only the people who love the person you've sentenced to die. That being the case, why would I want to have any mother go through what hurt me so much? . . . If a person ends up in prison and has to live each day just trying to survive, he will think of why he is there. That, in my opinion, is punishment. . . . I don't want the person who murdered my child to be killed, but that doesn't mean I don't want him punished. If you can't give me back my child in life, don't kill in his name.

Part One

The Men on the Row, Their Families, and Friends

1

Jeff Dicks

Death Row, Tennessee

Jeff was born in Concord, New Hampshire, on December 6, 1957. He was the oldest of four children in a closely knit family. While they weren't rich by any means, the kids had everything they wanted and plenty of love. When Jeff was ten years old, his family moved to Ashville, North Carolina, to live away from the cold winters up north. Since the family was close, his grandparents soon moved south also. Then it was only a matter of time before the rest of the family—aunts, uncles, and their families—all moved to the Ashville area. Their life was normal with weekend barbeques spent together with the family.

When Jeff was fifteen years old, he went to work selling Fuller Brush products with his mother. They would work together trying to see who could sell the most in the three-hour time limit they set for themselves. Most of the time Jeff came out the winner because he had a charming way about him that people liked and trusted. His two sisters and a brother tagged along whenever they could. Most of the money he earned he would give to his mother to help with the kids and to pay the rent on the new home they had moved into. Jeff's father was a mechanic and did not earn that much money, so they all had to work to get by. Life was going along well and they were all happy.

When Jeff was eighteen, he met a girl named Betty and fell in love for the first time. She was a year younger than Jeff and wanted to get married. They had a small wedding with just the family present. They moved into an apartment, and a couple of months later Betty found out she was pregnant. She wasn't happy about it because she had been raised in an orphanage and didn't want to be a parent. She felt she was too young, but Jeff was happy at the thought of being a father, for he loved children. He and Betty moved to Kingsport, Tennessee, and Jeff continued working for the Fuller Brush company.

While in Kingsport Jeff befriended a boy named Donald Strouth. He felt sorry for him and let him stay at his apartment until he could find work. Strouth would just hang around day after day not bothering to look for work, but Jeff was too soft hearted to tell him that he would have to move.

One day Jeff and Donald Strouth, whom everyone called Chief, went out in a car belonging to Chief's girlfriend, Barbara Davis. Jeff was driving and Chief told him to pull over in front of a used-clothing store just around the corner from Jeff's apartment. Jeff did as he was told, and when Chief said he was going to rip the store off, Jeff just laughed, sure that he was only fooling with him. Chief went inside the store and when he came out a few minutes later, Jeff saw blood on his jeans. Chief's hands were full of clothing and he dumped them in the back seat.

"I asked Chief what he had done in there, but I was afraid of the answer," Jeff said.

Chief told him that he had robbed the old man and had hurt him. It wasn't until much later that Jeff found out that Chief had killed the shopkeeper. He told Chief that he wanted no part in the robbery. He did not want any of the money and said he was going to call his mother to come and get him and Betty.

My mother came to pick Betty and me up. She asked me what had happened and I told her that Chief had killed a shopkeeper. I didn't take any of the money and I did not go inside the store. I told her that I would never hurt anyone and I never really thought that Chief was going inside that store to rob it. Mom said that she would take us to South Carolina and hide us out until she could think of what to do.

My mother found us a small apartment within walking distance from the town. We didn't have a car and would have to walk to work. I found a job with Manpower and Betty got a job as a waitress not far from our place. For the next month we stayed there with mom coming every week to bring food and just to visit.

It was only a few weeks later that she told me that the police had questioned her about my whereabouts. They told her that they had Strouth in custody and only wanted me as an accessory to the robbery. It was then that I decided to turn myself in. I didn't think I would have to serve that much time for I had not taken an active part in the crime.

Jeff turned himself in to the Buncombe County Sheriff's department and gave a statement without an attorney present. The detective from Tennessee had told him that he would not need one since he was only an accomplice. This was the first of many mistakes that Jeff was to make.

Chief had been caught and during his trial witnesses linked him to the murder. His girlfriend, Barbara Davis, testified that Chief had told her that he had done what he knew best. He had hurt the old man and slit his throat. She took the police to the spot where they had buried his blood-stained jeans. Chief's friend, Jeff McMahan, told the jury that he got a call from Chief the day of the murder. Chief had told him that he had killed an old man in a robbery. Chief had gone to High Point, North Carolina, in a car that he had bought with the stolen money.

Jeff McMahan said he saw the blood-stained jeans that Chief was wearing. Betty also testified that when she got in the car with Jeff and Chief that day, she saw the clothes in the back seat. She also noticed the blood on the jeans that Chief was wearing, and when she asked what had happened, Chief replied, "I had to hurt an old man. I slit his throat."

The used-car salesman testified that Chief had given him the money for the old used car that he had sold to him. He pointed Chief out as the one he gave the title to. Chief stood on the Fifth Amendment and would not clear Jeff. He told Jeff that he would tell the truth later on after their appeals ran out. It didn't take the jury long to give Chief the death sentence and he was taken to Nashville prison.

Jeff was taken to Blountville, Tennessee, where he was put in jail to await his trial. The attorney wanted $100,000 to represent him and he knew that the family could not come up with that kind of money. Bond was set at $100,000 and even with a bondsman it would take $10,000.

My mother went to a lot of attorneys to find one to represent me. But they all said the same thing, that I should not have given a statement without an attorney present. The police did not have any evidence against me except the statement that I had given them. It would make my defense harder as I had admitted to being there. I was appointed a court-appointed attorney, James Beeler. He had never handled a capital case before and felt that he was not qualified to do so. Mom still wanted to get me another attorney. She had found out that they were going for the death penalty on me too.

My mother became desperate when she could not raise the money for an attorney and decided to break me out of this jail. It was not a successful attempt and the authorities decided to move me over to Brushy Mountain Prison in Knoxville where security was tighter.

When my mother could not break me out and could not raise the money for an attorney legally, she decided to write worthless checks. She was able to get some money by selling the house and the checks to hire Larry Smith of Asheville, N.C. He had never handled a capital case either, but mom felt that he would be better than a court-appointed attorney. As it turned out, this lawyer was worse than any that I could have gotten. All he wanted was the money. Mr. Beeler felt that I was innocent and did all in his power to represent me. But Larry was the lead attorney, so what he said was what they had to do. Even though Mr. Beeler had never tried a capital case, I believe that he would have done a much better job than Larry did.

Jeff's attorney did not call on the witnesses who had testified at Chief's trial and who may have been able to clear him from getting the death sentence. The prosecution made it sound as though Jeff needed the money and had gone inside the store with Chief. He never called the Fuller Brush manager to prove that Jeff was still selling in Kingsport and did not need the money. If he was short one week, his mother would get whatever they needed. They were not told that Chief alone spent the money on a used car for himself. Barbara was not allowed to tell the jurors anything that Chief had told her about the crime or that he had committed it alone.

When Strouth was brought in, he would not tell the jury that Jeff had not taken part in the crime and had not gone inside the store with him. If Jeff had gone inside the store with Chief, it would have made him guilty in the felony-murder rule. If a murder is committed while a robbery is going on, then all present are just as guilty. It does not matter who actually committed the murder.

The jurors came back with a guilty verdict and the death sentence.

My mother was taken out of the courtroom by the sheriff because she yelled out during the argument. She was trying to tell the jurors that I had not taken part in the murder and the judge yelled for the sheriff to put her in jail. It tore me up to see the pain she was going through and I wished there was something that I could do for her.

During this time Betty had a baby girl whom they named Shirley Maria. She decided that she did not want to be a mother and was going to give it to the orphanage in Knoxville.

My mother talked to Betty and decided that she would raise Maria. She said that she would not allow my child to be given away to strangers. Betty just felt that she could not be a good mother; she couldn't take the responsibility. I felt sorry for her and I still love her today. Not everyone is cut out to be a mother.

Jeff was taken to Nashville where he was put on death row. Every day is spent in a ten-by-eight cell, which contains his bed and every item he owns and is allowed to have. The prisoners are only allowed out one hour a day to the yard for exercise. Noise is constant and loud, radios and TVs blaring, each trying to outdo the other. Shouting goes back and forth between the inmates and the guards and the inmates. There seems to be so many people always around, yet each man is lonely.

The routine stays the same day after day. There are no activities whatsoever. You're always walking straight ahead without really seeing. There is always something missing. It's like there is a hole right through you. You can't figure out what it is, but you always have that empty feeling. All your eyes can focus on is tomorrow. You know tomorrow is only going to be a rerun of today but that doesn't seem to matter. You're always striving for that next day and putting another one behind you.

Jeff spends most of his time listening to cassette tapes. "My music is my last link to being on the outside," he says. "Through it I can go back in time and enjoy the good times over and over." When he isn't listening to his tapes, Jeff reads a good deal. He takes advantage of the hour a day in the exercise yard to get a breath of fresh air. The rest of the day is spent in the cell.

He knows that he is innocent and feels that one day it will be proved and he will get a new trial. He feels he certainly didn't have a fair trial the first time around. During that first year he was alone. His mother, daughter, and younger brother had to flee North Carolina because of the check charges against his mother.

My sister Tina worked hard to pay off the charges against mom and had the authorities sign a paper stating they would not prosecute her when she turned herself in. I didn't want her to come back because I knew what they had done to me and I knew they would give her a jail sentence. I didn't want my mother to be put in prison.

She was lucky and received a year's probation. She was allowed to visit once a week with me. The first time I saw my daughter she was a year old. I can't tell you the feelings of love I experienced as I held her in my arms. She would put her arms around my neck and say, "I love you daddy." It was a three-hundred-mile trip one way from North Carolina to Nashville, so mom decided to move her and Maria over here to be able to visit me twice a week. I look forward to those visits and have watched my daughter grow up. She is nine years old now and so pretty. I couldn't have made it without their love.

Jeff's attorney, Larry Smith, was disbarred on perjury charges a few months ago and is no longer on the case. Jeff represents himself because the family cannot afford an attorney. While in prison the past nine years he has taken many Bible courses, gotten his graduate equivalency degree, and has taken an eighteen-month law course from the Blackstone School of Law.

All through the years his grandmother and grandfather have made the trip every other month to see him. They live on a pension and money is tight, but love for him keeps them coming every time they can. His sisters come when they can get off work. Now that his younger brother is twenty, he also comes over when he can to visit. The inmates agree that it means a lot to anyone in the isolation of death row to be able to visit with their families.

I guess the hardest thing for me is to know that sometimes the kids at school make fun of Maria about me. Kids can be cruel and I hate that she has to go through it. One day she put her arm around me and asked when I was coming home. How do I answer that question to her?

When people usually think of death row, they envision the likes of Charles Manson and other notorious mass murderers there. They are taken aback to see that the men on Tennessee's death row are not that much different from people you meet every day. There is no crazed glint to their eyes, no foam coming from their mouths. They are sad and frightened. And they are human beings. The saddest thing about the death penalty is that innocent people are sometimes sentenced to die. There have been cases in which it was officially proved that the men were not guilty of the crimes with which they were charged. It is already too late for these men; they have been executed.

Mom

The mind of man the years may span
With thoughts of early days
When mother called him "little man"
In tones of loving praise.

The queen was she of all the earth,
The princess of the dawn,
And none can ever beat her worth
Though childish days are gone.

For she still lends those helpful hands
As in the days of yore.
Her tender heart still understands
As e'er it did before.

And she's the queen of mother love
To little hearts now grown
Who ask the blessings from above
On her for good they own.

—Jeff Dicks

2

Shirley Dicks
Mother of Jeff Dicks

I remember the day I got a call from my oldest son, Jeff, who lived with his wife Betty in Kingsport, Tennessee. He sounded scared and asked me to come to Tennessee to pick them up, saying he would tell me what it was all about when I got there. I lived in Asheville, North Carolina, just over the Mountain from Johnson City where they were waiting in a hotel. I felt dread as I drove the miles over the winding, twisting road that led me to my son. When I finally pulled into the hotel, I could see Betty waiting for me and I followed her into the room to where Jeff was waiting. As soon as I saw his white face, I knew that something bad had happened.

Jeff told me how he had been driving around with his friend, Donald Strouth, who was also known as Chief. He had instructed Jeff to pull over in front of a used-clothing store and said that he was going to rob it. Jeff thought he was joking and waited inside the car, never dreaming that Chief would actually go inside and hold it up. When Chief came out with blood on his jeans, Jeff knew that something had happened. It wasn't until hours later that Jeff found out on the news that Chief had gone inside and killed the elderly shopkeeper and stolen two hundred dollars.

All Jeff could think of was to get away from Chief, so he called me to come and get him and Betty. He refused to take any of the robbery money that Chief offered him. He wanted nothing to do with the crime.

I moved Jeff and Betty to Greenville, South Carolina, until I could decide what to do about it. I knew hiding them was wrong, but I was afraid of Jeff being put in jail. I would just have to think of some other way to handle things. After finding them an apartment and seeing that both of them had jobs, I went home to think about all that had happened.

About a week later five detectives came to the Holiday Inn where I was a cocktail waitress. They questioned me for six hours in the back room, sometimes shouting loudly at me to tell them where my son was hiding out. Detective Keesling was a tall, hard-looking man who told me that if the police should find Jeff, they would shoot to kill. He assured me that they only wanted him to come in and be tried as an accessory to a robbery. They had Chief in custody and knew that he alone had killed Mr. Keegan, the shopkeeper. I told them that I was not going to tell where Jeff and Betty were, but that I would tell Jeff what they had said and if he wanted to turn himself in, then I would let them know.

As I left the motel that night my knees were buckling and I was afraid I would not make it to the car. Tears blinded my vision; I could barely see the road as I drove. As I screached to a halt in front of the house, I screamed to my husband, Nelson. I began telling him what had happened, crying all the time and hardly taking a breath. He assured me that the police were right, that Jeff should come in and take his punishment, but there was something about the way the detectives had treated me that made me leery. I just had a feeling that something wasn't quite right. I wanted to trust Nelson and the police, but just couldn't.

I called Jeff the next day to tell him what had happened. He said that he wanted to come in because he knew that he was not guilty. Even though he had taken none of the money from the robbery and had stayed in the car, he was willing to come in and face the charges.

To our horror, when Jeff turned himself in, he was charged with murder one. Fear overwhelmed me; my mouth went dry as I asked the detective why he was charging Jeff with murder. I started crying and reminded him what he had told me, that Jeff would be charged as an accessory to a robbery. Detective Keesling told me that the charge would be changed during the trial. Jeff gave a statement, without an attorney present, that he had been there with Chief and had waited in the car.

Jeff was taken to the jail in Blountville, Tennessee, not far from Kingsport. I went there to find an attorney who was experienced in handling capital cases. Each attorney I visited told me it would cost $100,000 to represent Jeff. The fact that Jeff had given a statement without an attorney present was going to make it hard to represent him. A lawyer would never have let Jeff say that he was at the scene. The police had no evidence linking him to the crime.

As I drove home that night, I wondered how I was going to raise the kind of money that was needed to insure Jeff a fair trial. I felt as if I hadn't slept in a month, and all the news I had heard only made matters worse. We had a new home but had very little equity, so I knew that selling it would not bring enough money. I would have to borrow it somehow. My husband, Nelson, was home and I told him what I had found out about the cost of a good attorney. He told me that Jeff would be given a court-appointed one and that was good enough. He didn't seem worried, and I started yelling at him that he didn't love Jeff. "I will raise the money with or without you," I shouted, running to my room.

Betty was living with me and my other three younger children. She was expecting a baby in August. Earlier I had found out that I was also pregnant and didn't know where it would all end. How would we cope? The whole world was crashing down on top of me and I didn't know where to turn for comfort.

In the weeks that followed, I worked two jobs to raise the money to find legal counsel. In the meantime, Jeff was appointed James Beeler from Kingsport. He had never handled a capital case before and he looked worried as he explained what was going to happen. He said Jeff's statement would be used against him and that he should never have been allowed to give one. All I knew of the legal system was from watching Perry Mason on television, where the bad guy always got caught and the innocent one was set free.

Mr. Beeler said the state was going for the death sentence for Chief and Jeff. I felt faint and had to blink back the tears. This was a nightmare I was having and soon I would wake up to normal day-to-day living. But this nightmare went on and on. I knew I could not afford a good defense attorney, so I decided to find witnesses who might clear Jeff.

Betty and I went to Kingsport to the scene of the crime. I began to question the people in the stores directly across the street from where Jeff had waited in the car. Suddenly, a policeman came over and told us to leave town. I tried to tell him that I was only trying to find someone who could testify that my son had waited inside the car that day. But again he yelled at us to leave town and not return.

Instead of leaving town, we went to the hotel and there I called the local television station. I told them what had happened and they sent a television crew out to interview me. I told them I needed to find someone who may have seen Jeff sitting in the car that morning. I gave them a picture of Jeff, which they flashed on the screen as I talked into the camera. That night we saw it on the six o'clock news. It was supposed to run at ten o'clock, but I got a telephone call from the man at the television station. He said he was sorry, but so many people had called in and said they did not want the mother of a murderer to be pleading for her son that they would not run it again. The people of this town had already tried my son and found him guilty before he even came to trial.

The next morning we drove back to Asheville. I was discouraged and could do nothing but cry. How could I save Jeff when they all thought him guilty? My pregnancy was making me sick all the time and I had to take care of the other children. Nelson was always there, but I could not talk to him about my feelings. He just said that everything was going to be all right. I heard that phrase over and over until I was ready to scream.

Chief's trial was held in Kingsport and they needed Betty to testify against him. The first to testify against Chief was his girlfriend, Barbara Davis. She described how Chief had come to her place of work that day in a newly purchased car. She asked him how he could afford the car since she knew he didn't have any money that morning. He told her he had robbed the shopkeeper and slit his throat.

I felt sick listening to her testimony, but also glad that the jury was hearing how Chief alone had committed the murder. It never dawned on me that Jeff would have a different jury and they would not hear all this evidence. Little did we know that the prosecution had planned it this way. By trying them separately, Jeff's jurors would not hear all the evidence. Had they been tried together, Jeff would not have gotten the death sentence. They wanted to make an example of him.

Barbara also testified that Chief called her to pick him up when his car broke down. When she got there, he was still wearing the bloodstained jeans. Barbara told him to rip them up and bury them in the woods. She later took police to the spot where the jeans were buried, and they were used as evidence.

While listening to the testimony, I saw Chief look back at me with a smirk on his face, and again I felt faint. I felt the evil coming from him and I shuddered. Jeff had been so naive to befriend this boy; he had told me that Chief wasn't bad, that he just didn't have a family who loved him.

The next to take the stand was Jeff McMahan, a friend of Chief who lived in High Point. He testified that Chief called him the day of the murder and asked him to meet him at a convenience store. When McMahan arrived, he saw blood on Chief's jeans and Chief confessed that he had killed an old man in a robbery, and that his partner had froze up on him and waited in the car.

I was beginning to feel better now that I heard McMahan's testimony. Surely they could not give Jeff the death sentence when so many people had testified that Chief alone committed the crime.

The next to testify was Betty. She related that Chief and Jeff had picked her up that day and that she had asked Chief how he had gotten blood on his hands and jeans. He told her that he had slit a man's throat.

The used-car salesman also testified that it was Chief who paid two hundred dollars cash for the used car.

That night at our hotel, Betty brought McMahan in and I asked him if he would testify at Jeff's trial. He said that the state was paying his week's wages and his hotel room. I told him that I would do the same thing if he would just testify at Jeff's trial about what Chief had told him. Offering him money would be one of the many mistakes I was to make.

It didn't take the jurors long to come back with the guilty verdict and the death sentence. Chief didn't say anything; he just looked back at his mother in the courtroom. I looked up and saw Detective Keesling looking at me with a self-satisfied grin, and I had a sinking feeling. Suddenly I just knew; they were going to do the same to Jeff. I felt stifled; the walls were closing in on me. I had to leave the courtroom and run outside to get some air.

I decided that there was no way I could raise the kind of money

I needed to hire a good attorney. I was desperate and time was running out. The jail they were holding Jeff in was a small place that only had two guards there during visiting hours on Sundays. I thought that the only way to save his life was to help him break out of jail. When I told Nelson what I was planning to do, he looked at me as if I had lost my mind. There were times when I wondered if I had.

"You're crazy," he yelled. "You're going to be sitting up there with Jeff. You can't get away with something so ridiculous. What if someone gets hurt?"

I assured him that we were not going to use bullets in the gun. I had a small .22 pistol that I carried in the glove compartment of my car when I traveled. Sometimes I would go 1,000 miles to New Hampshire to visit relatives. Only the children and I would go, so I felt comfortable knowing that I could scare off anyone if my car broke down. I had never bought bullets for the gun as I was afraid one of the children would accidentally set it off.

I know now that I was bordering on insanity. Fear was driving me to do things no sane person would contemplate. At the time, it seemed the only answer. Nelson told me that he would not help in my crazy plan. I figured I would need three other men to hold the guards in the jail until Jeff and I had left. But how was I going to find someone to help me?

Betty and I went to the roughest bar in Asheville. We were scared to death just seeing all the hard-looking people inside. We sat down, and a couple of Hispanic-looking men came over to the table. They didn't speak English well, but it was evident they were trying to make a pass. I asked the one sitting closest to me if he wanted to make some money. I had saved $3,000 and I figured that would be enough. He said sure, but when I said I needed some help in a jailbreak, he looked at me as if I were crazy. Together they got up laughing, and then they yelled out what I had asked him to the others in the bar. This wasn't going well. Betty and I got up, quickly walked to the door, and all but ran to the car.

How do you go about finding someone to help, I wondered. I was beyond all reason now, and even my family was trying to talk me out of it. No one was going to kill my son, I vowed, not while I was alive. I did find someone who said he would help me. Instead, he went to the police with my plans, and when we visited the jail the following Sunday, there were guards and police everywhere. We had noticed a state police car following us from the North Carolina border, all the way to Blountville, but we didn't realize what was going on. When we went inside the jail for our visit, there was a huge female guard. She could have been a lady wrestler, and I noticed that she just kept staring at me. I was beginning to feel nervous. I knew something was going on. The atmosphere was too quiet, not like it usually was. When we left the jail, we noticed that the police car was again following us back to the North Carolina border. It wasn't until we saw the newspaper the next day that we knew what had happened.

"Deputies head off planned jailbreak," I read. They said that ten extra deputies spent seven hours stationed around the jail. They had increased security because someone had tipped them off about a jailbreak that was to occur during the visiting hours. They said that Jeff Dicks was the center of the attempt and as of yet no arrests had been made.

They moved Jeff to Brushy Mountain Prison where security was tighter and not many people had escaped. Now I knew that the only way Jeff had of winning was to hire a competent attorney. It seemed as if everything was going from bad to worse but I had to keep trying, I had to hold up and stay strong.

I put my house up for sale, even though I knew it wouldn't bring enough money. Day after day I thought of new ways to get money, and finally I decided to write fraudulent checks. I would buy merchandise and then take it all to the flea market and sell it. It seemed to be the only answer. I just could not think of a legal way to raise the kind of money needed to defend Jeff. It was wrong to put such a high price on representation, and I cursed myself for not being wealthy.

I went to another city and opened a checking account using a different name. I knew that what I was doing was wrong, but at the time, I didn't care what happened to me, if I could only get the money Jeff needed. Next, I got a driver's license using a phony birth certificate and waited for the money to come in.

My mouth went dry as I placed the items on the counter of the first store I went to. I was shaking as I wrote the check. I just knew everyone was watching me and that I would be caught at any minute. The salesclerk just smiled and gave me the bag. Quickly I ran outside, my heart pounding in my chest. I had made it. But at the next store the clerk questioned me more closely. He wanted to see more identification. I told him that I didn't have any on me, and that I would come back later, but he called the manager over. I didn't wait but ran out of the store and sat in the car for five minutes until my breathing was normal again. For weeks I went from state to state opening bank accounts and buying merchandise.

Back home again I felt safe, but I was getting weary. All the traveling back and forth was beginning to have its effect on me. I was tired and had lost weight even though I was five months pregnant. I started crying over everything and just didn't know what to do. Nelson tried to help me, but I pushed him away. He didn't understand my feelings. I loved Jeff and knew he was going through hell in prison. I had found out from a guard that another guard had thrown hot boiling water on him as he sat helpless in the cell. Another guard, when taking Jeff to the hospital, put a pistol to his head and begged him to make just one move so he could save the taxpayers the money of a trial. I felt so helpless and didn't know any more what to do or where to turn.

The days we went up to visit Jeff were the hardest. He had gotten so thin that he looked like a skeleton. His eyes were dull and sunken in his face. It just tore me up to see him like that. We could not hug or kiss, but had to talk through a small hole in the door. In order to hear, you had to put your ear to the hole and listen, then look up to talk again. I couldn't say anything, just cry. Hard as I tried to hold myself together in front of Jeff, I couldn't do it. My heart was breaking, and I couldn't control my emotions. I wanted to kick the door down and take him away with me. Each visit he looked at me worriedly and said he was doing fine. I knew he was only saying that to ease my mind. He was being mistreated and I was helpless to help my son. I prayed to God to please spare his life; he was a good boy; he had just been in the wrong place at the wrong time.

My oldest daughter, Tina, was working and she gave me all her money to help Jeff. She pleaded with me not to do anything else against the law. She was afraid that she would lose me too, and she could not bear that. I knew the pain I was causing the other children, but I was helpless to stop. I had one thing on my mind, and that was to save Jeff, no matter what I had to do. I explained to the kids that what I was doing was wrong, and I knew sooner or later I would have to pay for my crimes. Deep within me, I felt it would be worth it to be able to hire an experienced attorney for Jeff's defense. That's all I could think of—ways to get money. I couldn't eat or sleep and it became an obsession to me.

I remembered that my grandmother, who lived in Massachusetts, had a Visa card. She had good credit and her limit was high. I decided to travel the thousand miles and steal it from her to buy more merchandise. I knew she would not have to pay the charges once she reported it stolen.

I visited with my grandmother for two days and had her Visa card in my wallet when it was time to leave. I felt guilty, but again I rationalized it by saying she would not have to pay the money back. I would have to face the guilt once it was known that I had stolen the card. Still, I wondered if there wasn't another way. But if there was, I couldn't think of it. I left Nana's that day feeling terrible, physically and mentally, yet determined to get on with the buying of merchandise.

I hadn't gone far when I started bleeding. I checked into a hospital, and that night I lost the baby. Nelson flew in to be with me, but I signed myself out the next day. I had to start buying again; that's all I could think of. Time was running out.

Barely able to stand, I went to the first store and used the card. My knees kept buckling under me but I had to go on. All the way to Asheville, I stopped at store after store.

Betty had a baby girl, whom they named Shirley Maria, after me. We called her Maria, though, to avoid confusion. She was a beautiful little girl, and as I held her, I thought of the child I had lost. Pain filled me and I blinked back the tears and cuddled her close.

The warden gave us permission to bring Maria to the prison for one hour. We were allowed to visit in a room with a guard present. At least we could give Jeff a hug and kiss. They also permitted us to bring in a camera and take some pictures of them together. I watched as Jeff very tenderly held his daughter. I knew the love and pride in his face and I knew the feelings he was having. He would want to protect his child, just like I was trying to protect him. When we left, I gave him a big hug and thought my heart would break as I felt his bony body close to mine. He was suffering, and I couldn't do anything for him. I would have gladly taken his place if I could have.

My family kept telling me to let the justice system work, that I was going to get myself in so deep that I would be in prison along with Jeff. But nothing they said could penetrate my mind. All I could see was the state trying to murder my child. I loved him and I would die before I would let anyone kill him.

My unlawful pursuits finally caught up with me in a small town in North Carolina. The clerk suddenly said she had to call the card in. I knew they didn't call the cards in if the amount was under fifty dollars, so I knew she suspected something. I told her never mind, that I didn't want the merchandise, but she was already on the phone. I ran out of the mall. Just as I was getting to my car, I saw the security car come flying around the corner and stop in front of the store. That marked the end of the credit-card buying.

With the U-Haul full of merchandise, I went to a fleamarket in Florida each weekend and then came back to visit Jeff on visiting day. Life was a roller coaster with no end in sight until I was able to hire an attorney in Asheville, named Larry Smith. After telling him the facts, he assured me that Jeff would get probation. I told him how I was getting the money and that I would send him a money order every weekend from Florida.

Around this time Betty decided that she was going to give the baby up for adoption. She felt she was too young to raise the child and didn't want the responsibility. I told her I would adopt Maria. I had the attorney draw up the papers and she signed them.

Larry had given me hope, which I clung to desperately. Mr. Beeler, the court-appointed attorney, was hesitant to tell me that Jeff would only get probation. He felt that Jeff would get time, a lot of it, but would not comment further. I felt uneasy and the fear was still there as much as I tried to push it aside. The trial was scheduled for February 5, 1979.

Larry explained that anyone testifying at a trial would have to sit outside the courtroom. Since I was going to get on the stand, I would not be allowed in. The jurors were finally picked, but they excluded all those who said they were against the death sentence. I felt weak and scared and knew Jeff was in for a big fight. I asked Larry where McMahan was and also the Fuller Brush manager. I had given him the telephone numbers so he could call them as witnesses. He told me he had everything under control and not to worry.

The prosecution brought in Chief's bloodstained jeans and tried to make the jurors believe Jeff had worn them. After questioning from Larry Smith, they conceded the pants were the ones Chief had worn. They said that Jeff was not working and needed the money from the robbery. Larry never called Mr. Clayton, the Fuller Brush manager, to disprove it.

Barbara Davis was called to the stand, and with the jurors out of the courtroom, the judge told her she could not repeat anything Chief had said to her about the crime. It was called hearsay evidence and was not admissible. She could not tell the jurors that Chief had said he slit the man's throat or that he had spent all of the money on a used car.

I was getting tired of sitting outside and hearing about the testimony from family members. I asked Larry when he was going to call me to the stand. "I decided not to call you," he said. "I think you would fall apart and that would look bad for Jeff."

Larry didn't call on Betty and didn't put on much of a defense. The jurors had not heard half of the evidence. Mr. Beeler said he would have called on McMahan and the Fuller Brush manager but he was not lead counsel, so he had to go along with whatever Larry said. I was really worried now; the trial was over and it was time for the closing arguments. We would be allowed in the courtroom for that part of the trial and I sat down with my family.

The prosecution began by saying that Jeff and Chief had both gone inside the store that day and slit Mr. Keegan's throat. I jumped up in my seat and began yelling that it was not true. I wanted the jurors to know that Jeff had not gone inside with Chief that day. On and on I went. Through a fog, I could hear the judge rapping his gavel and telling the sheriff to put me in jail.

I was put in a room with two other girls. From my cell I could see the room where the jurors were deliberating. I could hear their laughter and felt rage surge through my body. My son's life was at stake and it was as if they were laughing about it. The hours ticked by as I sat by the window watching and waiting.

I heard footsteps coming to the room and my heart stood still. It was Mr. Beeler. I walked slowly over to where he stood patiently waiting for me. I couldn't read his face, but when he said, "I'm sorry," I screamed. Jeff had been found guilty of murder. I covered my ears and backed away from the door crying. The girls put their arms around me but I couldn't be comforted. The next part of the trial was to decide if Jeff was to get life or the death sentence. Again I waited by the window watching the jury room. I wanted to plead with these twelve people to please have mercy for my child. Where was God, I wondered. How could he let this happen?

Suddenly the back door of the courtroom opened and I could see my daughter Tina coming slowly out in the yard, her head bent low, her long brown hair covering her face. I knew in that instant the jurors had given Jeff the death sentence. Time seemed to stop, and I couldn't catch my breath; darkness was coming over me.

"No!" I screamed over and over. "You can't do that to my son. He's innocent! You can't send him to die. Oh God, no!" The screams went on and on as I held onto the bars. The room was spinning around and around. I could hear my mother's voice yelling up at me to hold on. She was begging me to stop, saying we would fight it, but I had no mind left and the screams continued.

The door opened and my mother and a nurse came in. She gave me a shot and then I went off into darkness. The next morning, the guard came up and told me I could leave if I promised to be quiet. I agreed and was led down to the sheriff's office. There my family was waiting, and we were told to leave Tennessee and not return.

A police car escorted us to the city line and one of the officers came over to the car. He told me that he couldn't believe Jeff had gotten the death sentence. He had been in the courtroom and heard all the testimony. He said he was sorry, but he had a job to do.

I knew I would have to leave North Carolina with my two youngest children, Trevor and Maria. The State Marshall had come during Jeff's trial to question me about the checks and the credit card. I was supposed to come to his office as soon as I came back to Asheville. Jeff had been taken to Nashville where death row was located and I would not be able to see him.

Nelson was going back to New York and would take our daughter Laurie with him. She was sixteen years old now and did not want to go on the run. Because of all the turmoil, we had filed for divorce and it was almost final, but Nelson told me to call if I ever needed anything.

I kissed my parents and daughters goodbye. We were all crying and I said I would get in touch with them as soon as I was settled.

Now I had lost Jeff and also my family. I was alone and thinking of just ending it all. I couldn't do that, my mind kept telling me. I had Trevor and Maria to think of and the rest of the family. They all loved me and I couldn't do that to them.

Texas was the first place that seemed to be friendly, and I found a trailer for us to live in. Calling my family before the police had the phone tapped, I gave them my phone number so they could call me from outside pay phones. I knew it wouldn't be long before the warrants were out for my arrest.

I was only there for a month when I broke all the bones in my ankle. I was taken to the hospital where I had surgery to repair the damage and had to stay for two weeks. The surgery was painful but somehow I welcomed the pain. It took my mind off Jeff. My mother told me he was doing all right and they had driven the three hundred miles to see him. The FBI had questioned Jeff about my disappearance.

For the next year I was in a cast and a wheelchair. Trevor took care of Maria and did a lot of the cooking. I couldn't seem to get myself together and constantly wondered how Jeff was doing. I had gotten cassette tapes from him, sent by my mother in another state. I received a Mother's Day card from him, and I felt the tears starting as I read the words he wrote:

Mom, tho I don't say it very often, I want to say I love you. I'm very lucky to have such a special mother. I wouldn't trade you for my freedom. Thank you for always being there for me. I've never been good at showing my feelings, but always know that I love you mom and you make me proud.

Finally, I called my mother and told her to talk to the FBI and tell them I would turn myself in if they would guarantee that I could visit Jeff one time before they sentenced me. My daughters, Tina and Laurie, didn't want me to come in. They had paid back the credit-card charges, but were still afraid I would spend years in prison. I knew I would have to face up to the crimes I committed, and I could not go on any longer without my family. I had to see Jeff again, no matter what price I had to pay.

The FBI agreed that I could go to Tennessee and see Jeff if I came in. I packed up Trevor and Maria and we came back to North

Carolina. I was taken to the courthouse and after waiting awhile, the officer came to talk to me. He said if I pleaded guilty, the judge would give me a fine and a year's probation. I readily agreed to this and was released.

The first time I saw Jeff was just great. I couldn't hold back the tears as I held him. He hadn't known that I was turning myself in because I didn't want to worry him. He looked down at me and said he loved me. How I loved this man-child of mine. He held his daughter and she didn't appear to be afraid of him.

For the next year, I traveled back and forth every weekend to visit Jeff. The trip took six hours each way and was tiring, not to mention the expense, so I decided to move to Nashville to be near him. I found a small trailer and we moved in. This way we could visit twice a week with Jeff and get him out of his cell.

I wrote to F. Lee Bailey and all the famous attorneys I knew of, hoping to get help from a lawyer who could find a mistake in the trial and have Jeff's sentence overturned. Some time after the trial, Larry Smith had been disbarred for perjury. I finally found Bart Durham of Nashville.

He arranged for a postconviction hearing. The same judge and prosecution were there. Bart tried to convince the judge that Smith, as lead attorney, did not provide adequate counsel. I had to go on the stand and apologize to the judge for my outburst in the previous trial. I didn't want to apologize, because I felt the judge knew Jeff was innocent. He was the same judge on Chief's trial.

Mr. Beeler said he disagreed with Smith's approach and defense of Jeff because he had not subpoenaed the witnesses that we had given him, and because he had put Jeff on the stand unprepared. He said Larry did not discuss a strategy with him and he had not been made party to the case preparation. He said Smith would not return his calls about the case, and that friction developed between them during the trial.

Others testifying were state's witnesses who said they were not interviewed by the defense lawyers. Smith responded to those allegations by saying that no witnesses would talk to him and he could not find any beneficial witnesses. Larry then accused me of offering money to McMahan to change his testimony. McMahan had spoken with Mr. Beeler before I even met him, so he couldn't change his story. I never wanted him to change his testimony, just to come to Jeff's trial and testify.

I felt like slapping Smith in the face as he stood on the stand making accusations. I had offered to pay McMahan way over the cost of the hotel room and food. He could not afford to come over otherwise and I felt his testimony was important. I didn't want him to change anything he had already testified to.

McMahan got on the stand and said I offered him money to come and testify for Jeff. "I can only tell you what Chief said down at the bridge. And he said his partner froze up in the car. I don't give a damn whether she sends me the money or not. When he said 'froze up,' that means the guy stayed in the car," he said.

Back in Nashville we waited for the outcome of the hearing. It came back upheld. The judge would not agree that Jeff should have a new trial. Bart said to keep my spirits up, that the fight was not over. He assured me that Jeff would get a new trial at the federal level. I wanted to believe him with all my heart, but my head told me different.

The years went on and Maria was starting school. She had grown up suddenly and I felt a pang as she went off to her first day at school. We took pictures, so Jeff could see the things she was doing. He wanted to participate in her life as much as possible. She loved playing with him when she visited the prison, often making him carry her piggyback around the small room in which we had our visits.

The judge and district attorney took themselves off the case and yet they are still on Strouth's case. This is very unusual and it only means one thing to me: that they feel guilty knowing they sent an innocent man to death row.

I started reading all I could on the death sentence and discovered how unjust it is. I would see others on the row getting their sentences overturned, some who had admitted their guilt in the crime, but because an error had been made at the trial, they had their sentences changed to life. I was glad for the men, but sorry that Jeff hadn't gotten a break yet. Here he was, innocent, and he was still on death row. Chief was up there, but still would not tell the truth and free Jeff.

Tina and Laurie would come over to visit with Jeff when they could get away from work and stay with me. I was lonely and hadn't made many friends. The few people I talked to looked at me with disdain and fear when they found out my son was on death row. Children were not allowed to play with Maria once word got out. She began to have headaches and was ill a lot. It made me angry to know that people could be so cruel and take out their hatred on us. Mostly, I stayed inside and kept to myself.

Jeff had an execution date but we didn't know it because Bart had resigned from the case. I wasn't able to keep up with the monthly payments, so after five years he just quit without telling us. Larry Woods, an attorney in Nashville who fights the death sentence, stepped in and stopped the execution.

The years have been tough, but I've found the strength to go on. I knew I had to be strong for Jeff and Maria. Without their love, I couldn't have gone on this long. I finally put Maria in our church school and the headaches stopped. She is at the age when she knows the state wants to kill her daddy and she wonders why?

I have met many new friends in a writing group that I started, and I hope I have changed many people's ideas on capital punishment. These people have accepted me for what I am, and not judged me on what I've done. Our church members are also getting interested in the prison. I gave them the names of inmates who needed someone to write to them. Now a lot of inmates have found new friends through the mail. I started a prison ministry for the guys on the row and am able to get things like fans and TVs for them, and to find people willing to visit them.

I sold my first book on capital punishment and hope that it will inform people about how wrong capital punishment is. I'm proud to be Jeff's mother and no matter what happens, we'll stick together.

Through the writers club, I met a wonderful woman named Elaine Neel, who has always been there for me. She even went to visit with Jeff and really cares for him. I had given her the name of another boy on death row who needed someone to write to, and she began to write to him and visit also. Whenever I get discouraged, which happens a lot, Elaine will pick me up and keep me going. Sometimes I feel like giving up, but I know I can't. I can't let the state win and murder my son.

Jeff had his teeth pulled out by the so-called dentist in the prison. The dentist accidentally cut Jeff's tongue and it began to swell. By the time I went to visit a couple of days later, his tongue was sticking out of his mouth and he couldn't even talk. I couldn't stand to see my son in that condition and I burst into tears. Another friend, Zel Morris, took me outside and then we called the warden. Zel told him that Jeff needed immediate attention before his breathing was cut off. He assured her that he would see to it.

The next day, the only thing they did for Jeff was send him to the nurse, who simply gave him some aspirin. He couldn't even swallow it because he couldn't get anything past his tongue. She sent him back to the cell to die. The other inmates began making nosies on the bars and finally after Jeff was gasping for breath, they took him by ambulance to an outside hospital. He did recover, but with the kind of care they give inmates, he could have died. The attitude of the prison staff is: Why should they get medical care? They are going to die anyway.

I see him suffer so much and I wonder if it's all worth living for. Some people have been real cruel and say he shouldn't have been with Strouth that day. Of course he shouldn't have been there, but he didn't know what his friend was like. No one can tell what a friend could do in certain times, and because he believed Strouth wouldn't do anything, Jeff was sentenced to die. I don't think he should die for believing in a friend. Just look around and see how many murders are committed each year and most get off.

Maria is now thirteen years old and she has been stricken with rheumatoid arthritis. She is confined to a wheelchair and I wonder how it will all end. Will our family ever know happiness in this lifetime, or are we condemned to a life of trials and tribulations? Jeff has made all the appeals over the years himself, because we still cannot afford an attorney for him. No one wants to help a poor, innocent man. After my first book came out in 1990, I again wrote to a few attorneys and asked if they would take my son through the federal court, which is the last one we have left, but no one will so far. I offered all the money that would be made on the book, and any other books that I might sell, but so far no one wants to take it.

What is so sick is that right after Donald Strouth's trial, he told the district attorney that Jeff did not take part in the crime. It was typed up but Strouth's attorney told him not to sign it, as he would hurt his own appeals. The DA knew at that time that Jeff had not taken part in the crime, but still he sentenced him to die.

Bart Durham tried to get this letter, but was unable to. Donald Strouth has told many people over the years in there that Jeff is innocent. Jeff Blum of the Death Penalty Resistance Project wrote Jeff a letter in 1986, in which he states, "I know from Chief's own mouth that you were not involved in the murder for which you are condemned to die. I also know that if you don't get some competent legal help, you will die whether innocent or not."

I watch my son in prison, suffering every day, and I watch his daughter suffering with the pain of arthritis and the pain of knowing the state wants to kill her daddy. Jeff was taken out of Judge Nixon's federal court and no one seems to know why or how they could do that. He was the first one in there, yet he was taken out and sent to the federal judge in Greeneville. Judge Nixon is against the death penalty and Jeff might have stood a chance with him. The judge over in Greene County is for the death penalty and will not care that Jeff is innocent.

All we can do is pray that God will show us mercy. Maria prays every night that God will let her daddy come home where he belongs. Until that day, we will keep on hoping and praying.

3

Maria Dicks
Daughter of Jeff Dicks

I'm thirteen years old and for as long as I can remember my mother and I have gone to the prison to visit with my daddy every week. My grandmother adopted me when I was born, but I call her mommy because she is the only mother I ever knew. My mother didn't want me and was going to give me away.

When we visit with my daddy, we go into a cage with a table and have cokes and candy while we visit. Some people don't realize that I know the state wants to kill my daddy. I don't know how they can say it is wrong for someone to kill someone, then they turn around and do the very same thing. My daddy never hurt anyone in his life, but they still want to kill him.

We play cards when we visit and I win a lot of the time. I love my daddy so much and he's so good to me. When I was little, he gave me his color television, the only one he had. He told my mother that he still had his, that he had bought me that one. Then a long time later we found out he was using a small black-and-white one. He didn't care that he couldn't watch television in color; he just wanted to give me something of his because he loves me so much. That's the way my daddy is, always thinking of someone else even though he goes without things a lot of the time.

We used to live in a mobile-home park and I had a best friend there, named Vallie. One day I gave her a box of clothes that I had outgrown. They were all good clothes, but the next day she brought them back to me. She said her grandmother told her she couldn't have them because my daddy was in prison. Then her mother said that my daddy deserved what he got, that he was no good. I was so mad at her, but I couldn't talk back to an adult. I didn't tell mommy for a long time because I didn't want her to get in a fight with Vallie's mother. I don't know why some people can be so mean to other people just because they have someone in prison. They just don't care that he's innocent.

Some of the kids at school used to make fun of me because my daddy was in prison and I was sick a lot. Most of the time I said I was sick so I wouldn't have to go to school, but then momma put me in the church school. The kids there are so nice to me, and some of them even write to some of the men on death row.

For Father's Day this year I bought a real gold chain for him to wear. He loved it and gave me a big hug and kiss. My best friend, Kandy, goes to the prison with me sometimes to visit with daddy. Her mother lets her go and we have a good time. We usually go to Shoney's after our visit so we can eat before heading home.

Sometimes I hear my mommy crying and I cry, too. It hurts that my daddy can't be home with us. It hurts to think that someone wants to kill him, and we can't do anything to get him out of that place. I ask mommy why. Why do these people want to kill him? To kill my daddy won't help anybody and it won't bring anybody back to life.

We pray everyday for my daddy and I know that Jesus will hear our prayers. Jesus was put on death row and they executed him for something he didn't do, so I know he loves my daddy. Another man committed the murder, but they said my daddy went in the store with him. Chief will never get to heaven because he won't tell the truth and free my daddy. Jesus tells us to forgive those who do wrong to us, but I don't think I can forgive Chief for what he has done to my daddy and us.

I wouldn't trade my daddy for the President or anybody else. I'm proud that he's mine and I know I have the best daddy in the world. But Jesus will save him and one day he will come home to live with mommy and me, and that will be the happiest day of my life.

4

Zel Morris

Married a Death-Row Inmate

I don't feel any different from any other married woman, with the exception that Tim does not share my bed. I met Tim while tending bar in Florida. I remember his sad, blue eyes the first time I saw him, and that's what first attracted me to him. I wanted to wrap him up in my arms and make him happy. We spent many days and nights together, talking and laughing, and finally falling in love. We were the best of friends, but we didn't know that we were really in love until Tim was arrested for this crime and snatched away.

Several police cars, county sheriffs, and other law-enforcement officers surrounded the small trailer where we lived. They took Tim down to the police station to question him about a murder committed in Tennessee. He was later released, but several weeks later he was arrested again and this time was taken to Greeneville, Tennessee, to await trial for the murder. I went to Greeneville and worked there for three months so that I could visit Tim every day. Then I went back to Florida and worked for another three months to keep the payments up on my mobile home. This went on for a year, and I just ran back and forth between Florida and Tennessee until Tim went to trial.

I believe the death penalty is wrong. I never did believe in it, but until this happened to Tim, I assumed that everyone who got the death penalty was guilty. That didn't make it right, but it did make me think about it less. I believed that our justice system was perfect, that it didn't convict innocent people. I found out the hard way, and during the trial I learned that in reality the state didn't have to prove Tim's guilt, but rather, we had to prove his innocence.

The attorney appointed to represent Tim was inexperienced in capital cases. But without money, and lots of it, an experienced attorney was not available to him. Tim was expected to provide proof of innocence, beyond a reasonable doubt, to a jury composed of death-penalty proponents.

I also learned during the trial that you don't have to be guilty beyond a reasonable doubt to be convicted; circumstantial evidence is enough to send you to death row. The state then has the lawful power and privilege to commit the very same crime for which you were unable to prove your innocence—premeditated murder. The state can and does kill people to show that killing is wrong.

After Tim was sentenced to death, I remember running from the courthouse, my heart breaking, and tears streaming down my face. I kept thinking about what had happened and decided that I could not spend my life waiting for a man condemned to die.

I moved back to Florida and tried to forget Tim, but it was useless. I loved him more than I ever thought possible and decided that right or wrong, I was going to be by his side.

Once again I moved, this time to Nashville, where death row was located. I found a small apartment and a job as a waitress near the prison. I was allowed to visit with Tim twice a week and that's all I lived for.

It wasn't common knowledge that Tim was on death row but the fact that I was in love with someone in prison wasn't anything I was ashamed of. I shared the fact that he was on death row with my closest friends.

People assume that Tim is guilty just because he was convicted. They don't believe that the innocent can be found guilty and sentenced to die, but it's been proven in a study by Hugo Bedau and Michael Radelet that 350 wrongly convicted persons were sent to death row.*

I think our society has come to the point where you have to prove yourself innocent instead of the state proving you guilty. The biggest injustice is that so many innocent people are convicted of crimes they

*Hugo Adam Bedau and Michael L. Radelet, "Miscarriage of Justice in Potentially Capital Cases," *Stanford Law Review* 40: 21–179.

didn't do, and are lumped with those who admit their guilty. The state seems to arbitrarily select who will get the death sentence and who will go free. There's nothing right with the system starting with the jury. You cannot even sit on a jury if you do not believe in the death penalty. The prisoners on death row are caged like animals with nothing to look forward to, without a reason to live. That leaves us victims on the outside gasping for air just to breathe, to get along without the people we love, and to fight for their lives.

Half of the people I meet feel sorry for me but don't want to get too close; the other half come right out and ask me if they are going to fry him. This scares me, and it hurts that people can be so cruel. They're either scared of me or they act like I have something contagious, so most of my closest friends are other women who also have a loved one on death row. We have to stick together until the rest of the world really can learn to accept the fact that we didn't do anything; we're human like everyone else.

After a while Tim and I decided to get married. We ran into trouble because the state of Tennessee had never allowed a death-row inmate to be married. For a year I had to fight the system and finally the warden gave permission for us to be married.

Our wedding was on the front page of the local newspapers, and the story was picked up by papers around the rest of the country, too. I got a lot of death threats, and many nosy people wanted to strike out and hurt me. And it did hurt. But after a while, the publicity died down and people realized that it wasn't just something I had been going through, that I really loved Tim. There's still cruel people around, but I've found out that there are a lot of good people, too. Those who have someone on the row are like family. We're all one and the same, and can share and relate to one another. We're victims just like the families of the persons who were killed. The only difference is their loved ones are dead and buried in the ground, and our loved ones are the living dead.

I was finally able to quit my job as a waitress when I got a better job with the Coalition on Jails and Prisons. The men on death row would call me daily with problems, which I did my best to help, or I would just listen to those who were lonely. I worked there for four years and during that time I learned how unjust our so-called justice system really is.

The public in general needs to be more educated about the death penalty. If people got more involved, not necessarily with death-row inmates, but with prisons in general, the whole community would be improved. People don't think that it could happen in their families. If they would go and visit a prison, or just talk to an inmate's family, I feel that they would get a little insight on what we are going through and it would bring a better understanding among all of us.

I have spoken out several times publicly against the death penalty and my feelings about it—about how we as family and friends are treated. It's very unfair. A lot of times we are mistreated by the public as if we were the ones who committed the crimes. When we visit men in prison whom we love and care about, we're discriminated against by the very same people who are supposed to be there to protect our rights.

Some guards are very nice, but there are others who shouldn't be working in the system, because they let their personal feelings get in the way of how they do their job. I've never been personally harassed by the guards but have seen it done to many other people. We've been made to wait outside in rain and snow for as long as six hours just to get inside the prison itself. Then, once inside, we may get an hour to visit.

We're allowed to take three dollars in change for the snack machines we pass on the way to death row. It depends on the mood of the person in charge that day if we are allowed to take a soda or candy bar over with us.

You're not allowed to have much personal contact, like touching, with the men on the row. You can hold hands but kissing and any kind of sexual contact are forbidden. I suppose that's for everyone's protection, but sometimes that's carried a little too far. The guards stand and watch you during the visit through a glass door and its like visiting in a fish bowl.

There was a time when we were allowed to occasionally share a meal with our loved one. I remember we used to be able to have a dinner four times a year with the death-row inmates and families. The Prison Ministry would bring in hamburgers and french fries, and we would all sit down and enjoy just having a meal with our husbands and sons and fathers. There was never any trouble, but prison officials stopped that. Now we're lucky if we can sit down and share a cup of coffee together.

One major gripe I have is the inmate cannot use the restroom during a visit. The visitor can use it but we have to terminate our visit if the inmate should have to use the bathroom. This to me is cruel and inhumane.

It's hard to survive when you have a loved one on death row, especially if you are a woman alone. You have only one salary instead of two to live on. I've worked as many as three jobs in order to keep food on the table and a car to drive and a halfway decent place to live in. It's a very lonely life if you're not surrounded by family and friends. Loneliness is a major thing I fight.

I married Tim because I love him. I married him for the same reason any woman marries a man. I don't feel any different from any other woman who is married. Why would I marry a man on death row? I've had this question asked of me many times before and the only thing I can say to you, the reader, is I'd rather have a day, a week, or a year with Tim, even under these conditions, than I would a lifetime with any other person.

I always have to say that there is a possibility that he won't get out, but I know in my hear that he will come home. That's all I live for. We are very much in love and where he is I'll be, and where I'll be, he will be. The only thing separating us is the bars. We're just people, like everyone else and we've got the same feelings.

5

Sarah Easley

Mother of Executed Prisoner

I have never felt such pain as I did the night my son Jimmy Wingo died. I didn't think I would live through it, and I'm not sure that I wanted to, but somehow I found the strength through God. I just felt that I couldn't bear that kind of pain, but when Jimmy died, there was such a sweet spirit that came into the car. A friend and I were driving away from the prison and were on the way home after spending time with Jimmy. He didn't wanted me to stay outside the prison until it was over; he wanted me to be home when it happened. By Louisiana law, the family members had to leave six hours before the execution, so we couldn't stay at the prison with him.

We cried so hard we had to pull the car over to the side of the road, and we just sat there, crying and talking about Jimmy. I was hoping for a miracle, but I knew in my heart it wouldn't happen. I sincerely hope no other mother will have to go through that kind of pain again, and, praise God, maybe they won't. At ten minutes after twelve, the lady who was with me said that something was happening. I could feel the peace that surrounded us. I can't describe it, but the car was filled with peace, and we didn't shed any more tears that night. It's as if the Lord said to us, "It's all right. Jimmy is home with me." So that's how I handled it. I know that the Lord blessed me. He was there with me, and I was never alone.

On the last day we went in at eight A.M. and spent the day until six that evening with Jimmy. Jimmy talked to his children telling them

53

not to let this make them bitter. He was innocent but he told them that he would be with the Lord soon and away from all the pain. It was so hard to visit knowing this was the last time I would see my son alive, and it took all I had not to break down. All too soon it was time to leave and we said our goodbyes.

Jimmy had been in jail on a burglary charge. While there, he found out that his girlfriend was in trouble, and he called me and asked if I could bring her there to visit with him. I told him that I had no way to do that, so he said he would just leave, that he had to see her. My son and an acquaintance, Jimmy Glass, were trustees and were allowed to walk around at will; so they just walked out of jail that day.

When I hung up, I started to call the jail and tell the jailer not to let Jimmy out. My husband told me to let him grow up and stop making his decisions for him. I thought, well let it fall where it will. He was only in there for simple burglary. Since it was his first offense, we expected him to get probation. My husband and I had gone up to his son's house for the Christmas holidays. It was December 23, so Jimmy couldn't get hold of me anymore.

Once outside the jail, Jimmy gave Glass his shirt to wear because Glass had tatoos on his arms and no shirt to cover them. Then Jimmy started thumbing a ride and Glass went the other way. Jimmy walked for a long time before he could get a ride. He stood in the rain and waited for a car to come by. Then a car stopped, and Jimmy Glass was driving. My Jimmy knew the car was stolen, but he got in anyway. Glass still had Jimmy's shirt on and there were traces of blood on it.

They drove on to the house where the boys changed clothes because they were wet. Jimmy and his girlfriend went on to the motel to talk things over so they could decide what they were going to do, and Glass went somewhere else. They were there when they heard on the news that Jimmy was wanted for the murder of an elderly couple.

When he found out he was wanted for murder, he and his girlfriend hid out in the woods for twelve days. They had no food or water and were scared to death. I felt fear because I knew they were hunting him like an animal with guns and dogs. They had him surrounded but couldn't get him. Finally, he just gave himself up and no one was hurt.

I was terrified about the whole thing when I heard about it. I had this terrible dread, like doom was impending on me. I had told Jimmy not to do anything rash when he called me and said he had to get to his girlfriend.

When all this happened, my husband began acting funny and wouldn't come home or comfort me. Jimmy wasn't his son, and he blamed me for the trouble he was in now. He kept telling me over and over that they were going to kill Jimmy this time. I don't know if he realized how much he was hurting me with his cruel words. Jimmy was my son and I loved him. I didn't want to hear that he was going to be killed. I wanted to feel the comfort of my husband's arms around me. I wanted him to hold me and let me cry on his shoulder, but he didn't. I had to go through it all alone. It got so bad I was afraid to turn on the television or listen to the news, afraid of what I would hear.

Once in custody, both boys were finally convicted and sentenced to die. I thought my heart would break. I knew my son wasn't capable of killing anyone and I prayed that God would save him, that he would somehow have Jimmy Glass tell the truth, that my Jimmy wasn't with him when he killed the couple.

On Saturday, October 8, 1983, Jimmy wrote me a letter that almost broke my heart. I'll share a few parts of it with you.

My dearest Mother,

I love you, mom, more tonight than I ever knew before. I hope that you can understand all that I'm about to say. God showed me tonight how much He truly loved me. I want to ask you to forgive me for all the pain and sorrow that I have brought into your life through the years. I know that there's no way I can take back all the nights that you must have lain in tears, trying to figure out what you did or didn't do to keep me from showing you how much I loved you. I could never be close to you the way I should have been, and I really don't know why, for God in heaven knows that a more loving and caring mother never lived in this world like you. I can't remember telling you while I was growing up that I was proud of you for being the beautiful lady that you truly are. I never realized until tonight how foolish and blind I'd been for so many years. I've never felt the sorrow and pain before that I live with tonight. I suppose the hardest thing for any of us to do is to admit that we were wrong and evil. God showed me what it means to suffer and love someone, for He revealed unto me the many times that I persecuted Him, and tore the heart and soul that I know He has. I felt like I died tonight inside, my heart felt as if it would explode and I couldn't bear it another minute. All I can do is say I'm sorry and ask that you forgive me, as I know God has, and I'll not make promises anymore that I can't keep. All I can do is hope and pray that I never cause anyone else to suffer the sorrow and pain that I felt this night, ever again. I love you, mama, with all my heart, and I'm very proud of you. I'll close for now. God bless you and be with you all, as He is now with me. Be sweet, and take care, love always,

Your son,

Jimmy

The Lord let me know that Jimmy and I weren't alone. He was there with us, and it was that faith that sustained me throughout this whole ordeal.

My husband walked out about that time and didn't even try to contact me. He had nothing to do with Jimmy either. He didn't send money to help me out, didn't ask if we had enough to eat, he just stayed gone.

The first thing that Jimmy said to me when I was finally able to visit with him was "Mama, I didn't kill anyone." The prison at Angola, Louisiana, was a six-hour drive, and I just didn't have any way to get there. I already knew in my heart that Jimmy hadn't killed anyone and I asked him how I was going to prove that? Jimmy had a court-appointed attorney who sold him down the drain. He was friends with the DA and didn't put up a fight to save his life.

It was so hard to raise the money to get to Angola to visit with Jimmy. It was so far we had to stay at a motel overnight and it cost about one hundred dollars. For someone who just gets by, we couldn't raise the money very often, so we didn't get to visit with Jimmy as much as I would have liked to do.

James Allison would take me and the grandkids over to visit with Jimmy and pay out of his own pocket for us to do this. He wanted the kids to see their dad and be able to visit with him. He was a wonderful man to do this for someone he didn't even know.

James began to read everything on the trial and he came to the realization that my Jimmy was innocent. He saw that the trial was a farce and Jimmy didn't stand a chance.

After the trial I got statements from some of the people who testified at his trial, which said they had lied on the witness stand, but that didn't do any good either.

Jimmy Glass said that he had killed those people, but he said that my Jimmy made him do it. He said Jimmy held a gun on him and just made him kill these people. We know a man who knows all about these murders, but he's afraid to talk to clear Jimmy's name. He's afraid of what may happen to his family if he were to speak up. These things happen sometimes, and I don't blame the man for not speaking up. He has to look out for his own family members. It wouldn't be worth it for one of his children to be killed because he tried to clear my Jimmy's name and it wouldn't bring Jimmy back.

People weren't very friendly after the trial. Even people that I had known for years would turn and walk away when they saw me coming and wouldn't say anything to me. I had one person say that I should have been able to save my son's life, that I was his mother and it was up to me to take care of him. She was trying to put a guilt trip on me and she was supposed to be my friend. These things hurt me a lot and I decided to change churches. I came across a little country church that I started to go to and the people accepted me as I was. I had done all I could to help my son, God knows I did. I loved my Jimmy, and there wasn't anything I wouldn't have done to save him.

Jimmy Glass was mistreated as a child. His parents were alcoholics, and the kids made fun of him. I think that's why he did what he did. When he got a gun on the Browns that day and saw they were scared, he loved it. He hated people because of the way he had been treated all his young life and he just killed them. He told someone that he had the thrill of his lifetime that night. He felt good inside because he had made someone suffer.

This is why I fear for my oldest grandson. He has that hate inside him. He loved his father and knows he was innocent. I've tried to talk with him and make him see how wrong it is to hate so much. His father wouldn't want him to feel that way. He would want him to go on with his life and make something of himself. My grandchildren are still suffering from all of this. I worry about them something awful. I don't get to see them very often, but I've heard how they are being tormented by the other children in school. They yell out, "Your daddy was burned. They burned him up." My grandkids just cry. The oldest boy is fifteen, and he hates the system so much for killing his father.

He wants to beat on these kids who say cruel words to him and his younger sister. I can understand that because sometimes when people make sly remarks to me, I feel like lashing out myself. I hate that they have to go through all this, but kids will be cruel and there's nothing we can do. Some of the kids even call him "killer Wingo."

Their mother is an alcoholic and has been for years. She just refuses to try to help these children, and I can't do it. I don't have any money left over to help them and I just make it by working at the nursing home. I wish I could help them, I really do, but I can't. I'd like to take them away from here where people wouldn't know them or their father. I've begged their mother to do so, but she won't do it.

I'm not trying to put this lady down because she needs help too, but I just wish she would take more of an interest in the kids.

My life has been tough since Jimmy was murdered. People still avoid me, not like they used to do, but still they do it. My own family is closer to me now and we've stuck together. I cry over Jimmy once in a while, but the Lord has helped me through it. I don't know how I'd have made it if my faith hadn't been so strong.

I'd like to warn other mothers not to use a court-appointed attorney if your child gets into trouble. If you can't afford one, you might as well forget it because your child will die, like mine did—not because he's guilty, but because he is poor. Anybody can be in that situation. It doesn't just happen to certain individuals. It can happen to you like it happened to me.

6

James Allison

Minister to Death-Row Inmates

Just a few years ago, I was completely uninterested in anything to do with prisons or inmates, and if anyone had asked me about the death penalty, I would have answered that I believed in it; that I believed it was a deterrent. Four years later, I am actively involved in prison ministry, and have felt called to minister especially to those on death row. And I hate the electric chair.

What caused this change? Primarily one man, Jimmy Wingo, who was executed in Louisiana's death chamber on July 15, 1987. I had known Jimmy some fifteen years earlier, when he was a student at the high school in North Louisiana where I was a counselor. I had lost touch with him over the years, but when I heard on the news in December of 1982 that he was being hunted as a suspect in the killing of an elderly couple in north Louisiana, I remembered him.

The things I read about Jimmy didn't fit with the young man I had known. But when he was tried and found guilty, I assumed he was guilty. In early 1985, I contacted Prison Fellowship in response to their plea for pen-pals for prison inmates, and I was sent the name and address of K. C., a young man in Illinois, to whom I began writing. When I would write K. C. or pray for him, the name of Jimmy Wingo came to my mind and I would pray for him. I told K. C. this, and that I felt I should write to Jimmy if he would like to hear from me. I did this, and a couple of days after writing the chaplain, I had a letter from Jimmy, saying he would like to hear from me.

In his first letter, he told me his trial had been a farce and that he was an innocent man, and invited me to look into his case. I thought, Yeah, everyone on death row says he is innocent, I'm sure, but I'm just going to ignore that and write him a letter. Little did I know then how my life was going to change, as well as my outlook on the death penalty and the men on death row.

Letters began to flow between me and Angola's death row, and since Jimmy had a death date set soon after I began writing to him, and he wanted to see his children, I took his mother and children down to south Louisiana to visit him while I waited. He sent word that I could probably get a special visit if I would contact the warden, and the next week the warden granted me the first of five special visits before I was approved as Jimmy's spiritual advisor. In Louisiana, six hours before an execution, the family must say goodbye to the condemned man, and only his attorneys and/or his spiritual advisor may stay with him for the remaining time. I was happy to be approved as his advisor, since this meant I could visit Jimmy regularly (twice a month) instead of asking the warden for special visits.

On our first visit, Jimmy and I had instant rapport, and every visit I ever made to him while he was on death row was a joy. We became the best of friends, and as time went on, I came to consider him the son I had never had, and he considered me his father, since his real father had died some years before.

After I got to know Jimmy, I felt certain that this man could not be guilty of the horrible crime he had been convicted of, and I began to look into his case. I found that he was right when he said he was not really defended at his trial; when I read the actual transcript of his trial, I was sick that a man could be put to death on purely circumstantial evidence, and that a jury could sleep at night after such a farce of a trial. The District Attorney who prosecuted him was a master of the game; he had five men executed in a short span of time. Jimmy's attorney put on no defense at all, and Jimmy's story was never heard, though he begged his attorney to let him get on the stand.

During the slightly more than two years that Jimmy and I were close, he had several death dates, but received stays. During that time I tried every means possible to get someone to listen to his story and prevent such a great miscarriage of justice. I could fine none. The news media seemed to love to show the worst pictures of Jimmy they could, making him look like some kind of monster, and always calling him "convicted killer Jimmy Wingo."

I took them recent pictures of him, but they were never used. I became more involved with prison ministry, and began to visit other death-row inmates, and my opinion of them changed completely. I discovered they are not all monsters, even though the public generally perceives them that way, and the state treats them that way in the way they are confined.

As I befriended men on death row in other states, I found that, although conditions were not perfect, almost every other state had better living conditions and privileges for their death-row inmates than Louisiana. Jimmy had come back to God after his arrest for murder, and for two years he prayed for a prison fellowship seminar for death row, as there had been one offered the first year he was on the row. In the fall of 1986, nine of the thirty-nine men attended a death-row seminar, and I was happy to have the opportunity to assist in it. When Jimmy's best friend, John Brown, made a decision to give his heart to Jesus Christ at the end of the seminar, Jimmy was beside himself with happiness. He was suffering terribly with an ear infection the prison seemed helpless to do anything about.

This was the only religious activity for the men on death row for two years, and it would be another year before there was anything else offered them. They had had no services, no communion, no Christian fellowship at all except a "one-on-one," when one inmate was allowed to leave his cell for one hour a day and could stop in front of another cell and discuss the Bible or pray with a fellow inmate. Since that time, there have been very few services provided for those who want to attend, and they must attend in handcuffs and shackles.

Jimmy had been convicted of taking part in the murder of a man and a woman. Jimmy Glass, the man who had actually killed the couple and admitted it, was executed a few days before Jimmy. Since the executions, one of his friends has voluntarily come to me to say that Glass had told him that Jimmy was never in the house with him, but that Jimmy had "ratted" on him, and "if I'm going to hang, so is Wingo."

I have heard that he told others the same things, but unfortunately he did not tell anyone in authority the truth, and another innocent man died. I have come to hate the electric chair, and believe there is a better way to handle the punishment of men who are convicted of first-degree murder.

Many who have studied the history of executions say that at least 10 percent of those executed have been innocent. Death is final, and we simply must not take the chance of executing any more innocent men. Nothing shows that execution acts as a deterrent. If it did, then certainly Louisiana should be murder-free instead of having one of the highest murder rates in the nation. My study of the Bible has done nothing to convince me that Jesus is an advocate of capital punishment, and I can not imagine Him "pulling the switch" on Jimmy Wingo or any other man.

Jimmy's final date drew close, and I kept a diary of the last four days of his life, as we sought desperately to save him from the execution chamber. My diary entries were published in our local newspaper, and my prayer was that it would touch people and help us rid our land of this terrible evil.

Friday, June 12

I left my sister's house at 8:30 and drove to north Baton Rouge to the motel where Jim McCloskey and Richard Reyna were staying. Jim and Richard are with Centurion Ministries and have been working feverishly for the past ten days gathering evidence to get Jimmy a stay, so he can get a new trial and prove his innocence.

Since Jim McCloskey got national exposure on "60 Minutes" and the "Today Show" for his work in behalf of the innocent in prison, he has had over 600 requests for help, so the fact that he took Jimmy's case is a minor miracle in itself. I've worked closely with him and Richard for over a week and have nothing but admiration for them.

We visited for a few minutes and then Jimmy's lawyers came in and we watched together the tape Jim had made of one of the state's witnesses. We all felt confident that if anyone would look at this tape, Jimmy would have no trouble getting a stay, and Jim and Richard could continue to gather evidence to prove him innocent. We didn't have much hope that the Pardon Board would do anything for us but we felt we needed to go through with the hearing. I talked a little with Bob Selcove and Ward Oliver, Jimmy's young attorneys, about the type of questions they could ask me at the hearing, and then we left in separate cars for Angola and the hearing.

I stopped by the motel in St. Francisville and picked up Sarah, Jimmy's mom, and we drove the 25 miles out to Angola, which seems like it is at the end of the world.

When we got to the gate, I went inside the reception building, where I had arranged to meet Rev. Ed Rowe, who had come out to the prison earlier to see Jimmy. Brother Rowe is president of Christian Mandate for America, a conservative organization in Washington, D.C. He had become convinced some time ago that Jimmy was an innocent man, and he had flown down, at his own expense, to attend the Pardon Board hearing and do whatever he could to help. He had spent the morning with Jimmy, whom he had never met, and was tremendously impressed with him—as is everyone who meets Jimmy.

A driver took Sarah, Ed, and me over to the training academy where the hearing was to be. Shortly after we got there, Jimmy was brought out in shackles and cuffs. A guard took Jimmy's cuffs off after he was seated at a table near the front of the room with his lawyers beside him.

These attorneys look so young, but they have spent a lot of time working on Jimmy's case, at their own expense. I'm sure this must be their first capital murder case, and they are going up against a master of the game, Henry Brown.

Jimmy looked tired, and I'm sure he was. For the past nine months, he had suffered from an ear infection, accompanied by throbbing headaches and earaches and ringing in the ear, and for the past two months he had had acute bronchitis. He had been getting only a few hours of sleep at night for some time.

Members of the Pardon Board came in and the hearing started with testimony from Sarah, who told them that Jimmy had always been a good father to his children, and that his family needed him. The board questioned her briefly and then it was my turn.

The attorney asked me questions about how I knew Jimmy and how well I knew him, about my prison-ministry work, and why I believed Jimmy should not die in the electric chair. After his questions, each member of the board questioned me. It was obvious from their questions that they were very unsympathetic. Many of their questions were asinine and they hammered at insignificant little things.

Among other things, I told them that in the past two years, I had never met anyone who knew Jimmy who had not told me that they never believed he could have been involved in something like the crime he had been convicted of, and that I had letters from other death-row inmates who told me what an influence for good he had on their lives when they got to death row. One man had written that he had made a profession of faith in Jesus while he was in the parish jail, but it wasn't until he got to death row and met and talked to Jimmy that he really dedicated his life to the Lord, and that Jimmy was a real inspiration to him.

Jim McCloskey was our third witness and he did a superb job of telling about his work to find and help the innocent in prison, how he had become convinced that Jimmy was an innocent man, and what had been found to show that witnesses had lied during the trial plus other irregularities that should show the board we needed more time to gather material for a new trial.

Again, from the hard line of questions about immaterial things, it was evident they were against us. Reyna and I took a break, and out in the hall we asked a TV newsman what he thought and he said, "You want to know what I think? I think they had their minds made up before they came in today." That's exactly what I thought, too.

At least, though, they did listen to all but the first part of Gwen Hill's tape. They had told us they would look at the highlights but they didn't have forty-five minutes to look at a tape. (A man's life was at stake and they didn't have forty-five minutes to look at an important piece of evidence! Someone told me the governor appoints these people, and they get $60,000 a year to "serve the people.") Richard ran it forward a little, and once they started looking at the tape, I believe they were spellbound as Gwen alleged she was manipulated into giving false testimony at Jimmy's trial. We have other tapes confirming the things Gwen said on her tape. The tape they did see was powerful, but again their minds were made up before they came in.

Jimmy was the final witness and he did a superb job of telling his story. He told them why he was in Webster Parish Jail in the first place. He had always been truthful about what he did wrong and he always said he was never with Glass in the Brown house, and there is no evidence that he was there.

Again the board took a hard line of cross-examination, then Henry Brown spoke and presented one witness, Jimmy Morgan, who said most of Gwen's tape was a lie.

The lawyers were given ten minutes to sum up. Then Jimmy asked to speak. He accused the DA of lying and challenged the board to make Henry Brown produce the tapes of his statement when he was arrested, because he never had said the incriminating things the DA quoted him as saying. The board said they had a transcript, and Jimmy pointed out transcripts could be altered, and again demanded that they listen to the actual tapes. The board refused, and took a ten-minute recess before coming back in to say Jimmy's request for clemency was being denied. This was nothing less than we had expected, but at least Jimmy was at last able to tell his story, and I felt the media were impressed.

Saturday, June 13

I was at the prison by 8 A.M. and by the time I got to Camp J (death row), they had brought Jimmy into the visiting shed. I gave him a big hug when he came in, since this was the first contact visit I had with him since his execution date was set last August. Usually we had to visit with a screen between us, and today they still left him in shackles and cuffs.

The time flew by as it always did when I was with Jimmy, and after about an hour and a half, his mom and a friend arrived to visit, so I left them and went to visit another friend in Camp J, and then spent two hours with Jimmy's good friend.

I talked to Jim McCloskey that night and I believe at last I began to accept the fact that Jimmy would probably be executed Monday night. The Fifth Circuit had declined to look at the evidence and denied Jimmy's appeal for a stay. All we had left was the U.S. Supreme Court, and they usually voted 7-2 to deny stays. Our governor didn't offer us much hope, either.

Sunday, June 14

Again I got to the prison at eight and drove to Camp F, the death house.

Jimmy had told me the day before that the warden wanted him to move over there a day early since he was expecting so many visitors, so he thought he would move about 7 A.M. Captain Arnold was there and said Jimmy was on his way, and about 8:15 I saw him coming into the lounge area where we were to visit, with only shackles on his legs and no cuffs. We gave each other a big hug and sat down at a table to talk.

Two guards stayed in the room with us, and one of them put on a big pot of coffee for us to drink. I know the coffee tasted good to Jimmy, since he had to drink instant coffee most of the time the last few years, when he had the money to buy a jar.

About half an hour later his family began arriving, and he was so happy to see his children that he gave everyone big hugs. I had talked with him about having a short worship service in the afternoon after the family was there, and he liked the idea.

About 10:30 I left them to visit while I went over to death row to visit three of Jimmy's best friends. All of them seemed to be holding up well, and all sent messages to Jimmy.

I went back over to the death house around 2 P.M. and called Jim McCloskey in Houston from the office there. Jim wanted to talk to Jimmy, too, so they let him come in to talk. The warden and the officers could not have been any nicer to us during this difficult time. Primarily, Jim wanted us to know how he was progressing with plans to get in to see the governor, and I promised to call some friends of the governor when I left the death house in the afternoon. We were not trying to get a commutation from the governor, but wanted him to give us a thirty-day stay, so Jim and Richard could continue their work on Jimmy's case, and we felt sure if Edwards saw the evidence they had, he would order a thirty-day stay.

At 3 o'clock we all gathered around the tables and I read Exodus. Jimmy and Sarah joined me in urging everyone there not to be bitter about the injustices done to Jimmy, but let Jesus Christ turn any bitterness into sweetness. I listened as Jimmy talked to his children. He gave them a beautiful talk on what he wanted them to do. He told them they have a right to be angry about what has been done to him, but they mustn't seek revenge and must not be bitter, as bitterness would only hurt them. He encouraged them to read the Bible and do their best to live by the teachings of Jesus, and to turn their lives over to Him.

I tried to get some rest during the day and kept in touch by phone with Jim and talked to some other concerned friends who loved Jimmy. When I got to the gate, the guards asked me to park my car and Assistant Warden Peabody took me over to the death house in his car. On the way he talked to me about my being a witness to the execution. Jim had asked if he could take my place, as he felt it would help him in his ministry if he could tell people he watched an innocent man being executed. I wanted to be with Jimmy as long as I could. He said I could walk with him from the cellblock to the door of the chamber and then Jim could step in and take my place. I decided this would be the best thing to do and later I told Jimmy my decision. He was relieved that I wasn't going to watch him die, and said he knew I would be with him in spirit.

Jimmy's mom left at six and I stayed to visit. We talked about a lot of things, and were interrupted a few times, once by Warden Butler to let him know the U.S. Supreme Court had refused to review his case, and so that hope was gone. We never did hear from the governor, but since I understand he was having a party at the mansion that night, I suppose he had more important things on his mind and didn't want to think that a man was getting ready to be electrocuted.

Jimmy told me twice during the last couple of days that he didn't want to leave us, but that he was a little excited about the prospect of seeing the Lord and heaven, and kidded me that he would get there before I did.

They took him away to get ready and I told him to give me a big bear hug, because after they shaved his head he might be too ugly for me to hug. I didn't know then that I wouldn't have a chance to give him another hug. They had told me when he was ready I could walk with him to the door of the chamber.

When he was ready, I pulled a chair up close to the bars and we clasped left hands and talked for the last half hour he had to live. He smoked a little more but didn't display a lot of nervousness, and I kidded him about having no hair, no beard, and no eyebrows and about wearing a diaper. He was wearing a pair of jeans with the left leg cut off. He sat on the end of the bunk and put his foot up on the bars as we talked.

We tried to tell each other what each had meant to the other. He asked me to keep an eye on his mother and children for him. At just past midnight, I saw the death squad at the door and told him they were coming. We only had time to tell each other that we loved each other, and then they were at the cell and I was asked to wait outside the cellblock. In about two minutes the door opened and I expected to walk with him to the chamber as the warden had told me. But he was surrounded by the death squad and they rushed him past me so fast I couldn't even speak to him.

I followed behind and watched him as he went into the chamber. About 12:17 the door burst open and a couple of guards rushed out yelling something. My heart went into my throat because I was afraid something had gone wrong and Jimmy was suffering. Immediately they ushered out of the witness booth a young reporter who had fainted, and by that time Jimmy had been with the Lord for a few minutes of our time.

During the last half hour of our time together, Jimmy had asked a guard to mail some letters for him. I told him that I would and he said, "No," that mine was with them and he didn't want me to read it on the way home. When I did get my final letter from him, I wept. I will not share it all, but among other things, he said:

> I don't want to leave you physically, and I wish with all my heart I could remain in this world with you . . . but I am not afraid or apprehensive about what I face, for the Lord has given me an unbelievable inner peace about it all. I suppose a lot of my peace is because after death I know I will be totally free, no more pain, suffering, or sorrow. For death is but a stepping stone into eternal life for the Christian. I do worry and hurt for you all though, for as my pain, suffering and sorrow end, yours will be at its worst, and that tears my heart out. One day you will see me in Heaven, and when you get there, I will have a big bear hug waiting for you and proudly show you around.

I don't know why Jimmy had to die like he did, but I am confident of his salvation and that at last he was free of all pain and suffering. I miss him, but I know that one day I will see him again and will proudly let him show me around.

7

H. Edward Rowe

President, Christian Mandate for America

To Those Who Murdered Jimmy Wingo:

The Jimmy Wingo story has a familiar ring:

- an arrest under questionable circumstances

- a small-community District Attorney seeking to build his image and career by securing convictions

- a court-appointed defense attorney who is a buddy of the DA

- a shoddy defense that is more appropriately termed a non-defense

- intimidated witnesses

- a conviction based on purely circumstantial and inferential considerations

- appellate-level reviews of the original trial transcripts, which could not possibly have presented a full factual record of events

- a futile clemency hearing before a morbid panel of professional deniers, whose role is to uphold the "system" rather than be swayed by compelling evidence

- rejected reprieves by the Supreme Court and by a gutless wonder governor who talks out of both sides of his mouth with respect to capital punishment, and who would rather have innocent blood drip-ping from his cruel hands than run the risk of offending the inhabi-tants of redneckville

- all this ending in the murder of a young man within a total vacuum of hard evidence that he had ever in his life been present in the home of the murder victims

It is a sad day for Louisiana, for America, for civilization, when truth is on the scaffold and wrong on the throne.

Any state that demonstrates a propensity to kill human beings on anything LESS than complete substantive evidence of murder is itself a murderous entity and is not one shade better than the most ruthless and brutal elements of "murder incorporated."

The misuse of human power structures for the self-aggrandizement of tyrants is as old as history. It is also a very serious violation of the moral laws of the righteous God of the universe, who will ultimately judge and smash every wicked system. The public thought Jimmy Wingo was on trial, but from a far more pertinent perspective, Louisiana was on trial in the Wingo case.

Louisianans, how many more humans are you going to murder on the mere shadow of suspicion supported by non-evidence and based on discredited and/or altered testimony?

State representatives, when will you ever develop the moral con-science to enact laws strictly forbidding executions pursuant to flimsy though often reviewed courtroom trials producing much verbiage and speculation but no real evidence?

You deputies who threaten witnesses with dire consequences unless they "cooperate" with you, then "program" them to give false testimony in the courtroom so as to convict innocent people—do you really think the Almighty is too blind to see, too deaf to hear your insidious ways, and too lacking in justice to deal with your wickedness in His own way and on His own schedule?

You judges who appoint inadequate and compromised counsel for the penniless accused, who take bribes from the wealthy, who wink at courtroom improprieties, who suppress truthful testimony and encour-age falsehoods, who sit passively while prosecutors brazenly manipulate juries, who uphold those objections that would support deceit and overrule those that would discover truth, who instruct juries so as to pre-determine an unjust outcome of trial proceedings—when will you elevate assured evidence and objectively established truth above your own career goals and obligations to the murder machine? Do you really expect the righteous judge of the universe to wink at your sins in that approaching day when you will stand before His bar of justice?

You appellate and review-board panelists who entertain without con-science the most obvious of fabrications; who allow circumstance, con-jecture, and mere inference to justify your murderous intent; who would rather maintain your power-position than exonerate the most innocent of men—do you really expect your wickedness to flourish forever?

District Attorneys, when will you climb above the selfish and short-sighted goals of career advancement and develop the moral stature to advocate just penalties dictated by impeccably founded truth rather than unconscionable schemes designed to get another scalp on your belt?

Governor Edwards and Counsel Bill Roberts, you were given all the facts concerning the serious possibility of Mr. Wingo's innocence—yet you chose to murder him rather than grant even a few days' delay so that further investigation of last-minute new evidence could be made. Were you so concerned about covering up the possible crimes of the "good ole boys" of the system, who allegedly resorted to threats to intimidate witnesses into telling lies in court in order to convict Jimmy Wingo?

Warden Butler, do you really value your job so much as to oversee a possible murder, in spite of all the question-raising facts you heard on the afternoon of June 12?

You, veiled executioner, who prefer to hide behind a pseudonym, you who told the press you don't worry about whether you're pulling the switch on an innocent man—when will you make it your business to study these cases and to attempt, at least, to keep your hands clean? When will you decide for a pure conscience in preference to a $400 job that may bring you under the judgment of God for the sin of murder?

Citizens of Louisiana, how long will you be governed by brutal peo-ple who—in spite of changed testimonies, newly uncovered facts, and a total lack of any real evidence of guilt—are able to go to bed at night and sleep serenely while the precious lives of the innocent are destroyed by the lethal voltage of the electric chair?

When will you realize that your hands are stained with blood too, so long as you remain silent in the face of these outrages? When will you awaken from your slumbers to elect District Attorneys whose first commitment is to truth rather than tyranny, to God rather than government?

When will you realize that if Jimmy Wingo can be murdered within a vacuum of evidence and pursuant to a woven fabric of lies and distortions, you can be murdered by the same system?

No, I wouldn't want to share the guilt of the murderous tyranny of Louisiana or of any other state. That's why I raise my voice in outrage. I swear eternal hostility to all forms of tyranny that would entertain the slightest risk of murdering the innocent.

Show me the blood of the victim on the hands of the killer before you talk to me about killing the accused.

Yes, I am indignant. From the rooftops of America I shout, STOP THE KILLING ON LESS THAN TOTAL EVIDENCE!

I convey the firm resolution of my soul to fight to my last breath the murderous ways of politicized human systems. And with all sincerity I affirm that I would a million times rather have walked to the electric chair in Jimmy Wingo's shoes than to have stood, for one moment of decision, in the shoes of Henry Brown, Lawrence J. Hand, Sr., Oris C. Williams, Faye U. Brown, Johnny Jackson, Sr., Edwin W. Edwards, Judge Bill Roberts, Warden Hilton Butler, or that anonymous and sleazy man who manipulates the death-switch in such an unconcerned manner.

People who murdered Jimmy Wingo, take no comfort in the apparent delay in the implementation of divine justice. It rushes swiftly to meet you at the crossroads of time and eternity. Its coming is as inexorable as the tide. Your wicked devices will yet be brought to light. Your evil days are numbered.

Just as Jimmy, his loved ones, and friends ran down the clock on that final night, the clock that will deliver your doom ticks away the remaining hours to that inescapable event. The cup of your iniquity will soon overflow. A fate far worse than one you imposed on Jimmy awaits you.

Only genuine repentance and regeneration can spare you now, and it is a consummation devoutly to be recommended.

8

Vietnam Veterans on Death Row and Post-Traumatic Stress Disorder

Shirley Dicks

Wayne Felde was convicted and sentenced to death for the 1978 killing of a Shreveport police officer. While there was no question of Felde's guilt in the case, signficant debate about his culpability has been raised.

Felde voluntarily joined the army and was sent to Vietnam in 1969. When he returned to the States he was suffering from nightmares, flashbacks, and other symptoms of a disease now recognized by the American Medical Association as post-traumatic stress disorder (PTSD). PTSD is blamed in similar symptoms in over half a million Vietnam veterans and is treatable. But when Felde returned, the disease had not yet been recognized, and Felde received no treatment.

Testimony at Felde's trial strongly suggested that Felde was attempting to commit suicide when the victim tried to wrestle the gun away. In the struggle, the gun went off, fatally injuring the officer.

Felde's trial attorney based his defense of Felde on his symptoms of PTSD. But the defense, the first of its kind in the United States, failed. After his conviction, both Felde and his attorney asked the jury for the death sentence. The jury tearfully obliged, returning a death sentence with the following statement: "We believe the trial of Wayne Felde has brought to the forefront those extreme stress disorders prevalent among thousands of our veterans."

PTSD is now a recognized and treatable illness. Just two weeks after Felde's execution, the California Supreme Court unanimously overturned the death sentence of a death-row inmate in that state, citing the presence of PTSD. In this case, the Court wrote: "As his patriotic duty, he killed our enemies efficiently. Unfortunately, after returning home, he irrationally killed again. . . . There is macabre irony in the fact that the society on whose behalf Lucero took an undetermined number of lives is now seeking to take his life."

According to Dr. Joel Brende of the Veteran's Administration, Bay Pines, Florida, over 500,000 Vietnam veterans have been in trouble with the law, in prison, on probation, or on parole nationwide. The major responses of veterans suffering from PTSD to their experiences during and after the Vietnam War are: intrusive thoughts and flashbacks, isolation, emotional numbing, depression, unexplainable or inappropriate anger, substance abuse, guilt, suicidal feelings and thoughts, self-destructive behavior, anxiety, and emotional constriction that obstructs the ability to achieve intimacy with family, partner, or friends.

Our technological society of the '90s has forgotten the deaths of more than 50,000 young men—3600 tons of bone and flesh; 154,000 pounds of brain matter; and 65,000 gallons of blood in Southeast Asia. But for many who returned from the hostile jungles of Vietnam so many years ago, the agonizing memories continue to linger on.

Gary Cone, who now sits on Tennessee's death row in Nashville, is one such veteran. Like Felde and Lucero, the emotional stress of the war and his subsequent episodes of PTSD led him to commit an act of violence, for which he has been sentenced to death. The following is his personal account of the events leading up to his imprisonment.

Gary Cone: Death Row, Tennessee

There's little to say about my life before Vietnam. I remember my father as a harsh and unlikable man. He was stationed overseas. At such times, my mother would take us kids to southeast Arkansas to live. She would make our clothes and, while we had plenty to eat, there never was much left over for some of the extra things in life.

In 1966 I graduated from high school and later joined the army. After basic training, I was sent to Germany. I then requested to be sent to Vietnam.

Before I arrived in Vietnam, I had to wonder if I'd act like a coward when I saw my first battle. Would I turn and run, and would I make it back to my family? All these thoughts kept running through my head.

When I got to Vietnam, I found that the atmosphere was very loose in regard to getting something done. I first started taking drugs there, when they were given to me by the army medics. You could buy opium for ten dollars a bag and anything else you wanted to take.

Vietnam wasn't a pretty place by any means. The emergency-room tent looked like a slaughterhouse with blood everywhere. You couldn't mop it up fast enough. I'd see men with stumps where their arms should have been and I felt horror. Some had brains seeping down their faces and stark terror in their eyes. I knew they were conscious of how bad they were wounded and it was like watching a horror movie back home with all the blood and gore.

I dreamed of a hot shower, sheets on my bed, and a decent meal in a dry place. Pretty soon these pictures faded as we struggled just to stay alive. The horrors of war were too much for me to cope with. Women and young children, who were frequently befriended, were often caught hiding grenades in their clothing. We couldn't trust anyone and had to be constantly on the alert. The children seemed innocent, but the Cong would use them by hiding bombs on their little bodies. They had no respect for human life, not even their own children.

I rose to the rank of Staff Sergeant and earned a commendation. Taking body bags from the fields, some of which contained the bodies of my friends, was one of the many things in the line of duty I had to do.

My visions in sleep were clouded by the sight of a buddy's head being blown off, and dying women and children I had seen left in the fields. The Vietcong would often torture and cut the children in half. Women didn't fare any better, and it was a gruesome sight to see the tortures these people had to endure.

I started taking speed and opium. They were inexpensive, and it made life there easier to cope with. At times they felt like a necessity to me, such as when I pulled fifty-three straight nights of guard duty on the base perimeter and had to stay awake. I would smoke grass and other drugs all the time. It seemed like everybody over there was nineteen years old, and we all did drugs to stay sane.

After a year in Vietnam, I was honorably discharged and went home to go to college. I was twenty years old and had to use fake identification to buy beer. I was old enough to fight and kill for my country, but not old enough to buy beer. It's pitiful, but that's the way it was.

At home, I soon noticed that people often treated me badly, so I tended to stay away from them. When I was in Vietnam, that's all I cared about, but now that I was home, I wanted to forget being there. In retrospect, I'm proud that I did the right thing in going to Vietnam, that I didn't try to get out of going and fighting for my country.

I looked for work but couldn't find a job anywhere. It seemed like no one needed me. To survive, I made a decision to buy a pistol, so I could start robbing stores. I had never robbed anything in my life until then. Nonetheless, I went out and robbed a checkout stand at the grocery store. This is what I continued to do, even though I had already decided to attend law school at the university using my GI bill to pay the cost. During this same time, I met and fell in love with Glenda Cale, a student at the University of Arkansas, and we soon became engaged.

Vietnam still stuck with me, and I found it difficult to talk about my problems with my friends. Since I always seemed to have money, Glenda suspected that I was dealing in drugs. I was, however, getting the money to support my drug habit from robberies of gas stations and convenience stores. Two months before I was to start school, I was arrested and sentenced to twenty-five years in Oklahoma prison for armed robbery.

I hadn't been in prison long before my father died. Then, my girlfriend was raped and killed by an escapee from a mental hospital. The world had stopped for me, and I took more drugs to erase the pain. I began to mainline and I couldn't find any reason for straightening out my life.

Once paroled, I tried to put my life in order. I had a few months before school would begin, and I tried unsuccessfully to find work. There were no jobs that I could find with a record. So, I turned to the only trade I knew: robbery.

I chose drug stores, as I needed drugs as well as cash. I never wanted to hurt anyone and if something should happen to go wrong, I planned to just run away. On August 8, 1980, I robbed a grocery store. The next day I went into another store and filled a bag with over $100,000 worth of jewelry. I was seen leaving the parking lot and was soon chased by the police. They followed me at speeds of over 60 miles per hour through residential areas. I finally abandoned my car and ran on foot, with the police fast behind me. Gunfire was exchanged, and an officer was wounded.

I eluded the police and spent the night in a burned-out building. Police closed in and fired tear gas into the structure, but I hid in the fireplace and they soon gave up. The long night of fear from the police, the shooting, and the tear gas brought my mind swiftly back to the jungles of Vietnam. It was over 100 degrees that day, and the sweat poured down into my eyes. I had not eaten in several days and I actually thought I was back in the war.

I broke into a house, entering from the back door. When I left the house that day, two people were dead. I don't remember killing them, but I know I must have. I remember thinking I was in the jungle of Vietnam, with the Cong chasing me, trying to kill me before I was arrested.

I stood trial and was given the death sentence. I don't think I was represented very well with my court-appointed attorney. I liked my lawyer at the original trial, but he committed suicide, which made me wonder about his mental health all along.

He talked a lot about the things he was going to do in my case, about Post Traumatic Stress Disorder, which he never brought up other than mentioning it in the opening arguments. He didn't adequately present the drug problem I had.

Since I robbed drug stores and always had a bunch of drugs on me, they assumed I was a drug seller instead of a drug user. I hadn't bought drugs from anyone who could get on the stand and say I used them. They just assumed I was selling the drugs I stole. If I could have proved that I was a drug user in court, I believe I wouldn't have gotten the death sentence. The attorney just didn't bring up these important issues. I would still be in prison, but I don't think I'd be on death row.

I think the fact that the Vietnam War was the high point of my life is sad. I didn't come home in a body bag, I didn't come home in a wheel chair, and I'm not missing limbs or anything. But even though I thought I had come home a complete person, it's evident that I didn't. I don't think I deserve to die for my crime because I know the state of mind that I was in at the time of the murders. It certainly wasn't lucid or sane in any manner.

Today I sit on Tennessee's death row. Because no one believed that Post Traumatic Stress Disorder was real, the men who returned from the war didn't receive help to get over the horrors they had seen and done. Maybe if help had come earlier, two people wouldn't have died that day and I would not be sitting on death row. Is it my fault that I became hooked on drugs in the jungles of Vietnam and later thought in my mind I was back there? I don't know the answer. I just feel the government didn't do enough for us who fought for our country.

For many Americans the Vietnam War is over and long forgotten, but for thousands of veterans the horror of this war lives on. In flashbacks, nightmares, and other symptoms, we relive the time we spent in the jungle. Some turn to alcohol, others turn to drugs to blot out the inner agony that has no name but many faces. Some mistreat their wives and children. Some withdraw from society altogether.

Everyone faces crises in their lives but these are not usually severe enough to bring on Post Traumatic Stress Disorder (PTSD). The symptoms of PTSD are of such magnitude, horror, or duration that they overwhelm your emotional and physical coping mechanisms.

Some veterans, like me, have ended up on death row. We were taught to kill women and children and that life wasn't important. One day we were in the jungles of Vietnam, the next day we were back in the States. We were never debriefed after coming home. One veteran said:

> I felt sick as I heard the cries of the dying that day. I could see the faces of those who died at my hand, innocent faces begging to live. I was angry because I had orders to kill everyone. Now, I may die for a crime that I didn't commit, but I'm not bitter. This may be my just punishment for all those innocent faces. Then I'll be released from all my guilt. So many faces, oh God, so many faces.

9

Johnny Garrett

Sentenced to Death as a Juvenile

Johnny was born in Oklahoma City on December 24, 1963. His mother had just divorced his real father, and there wasn't much money to go around. She couldn't seem to come up with the money to pay for the birth of her son, so the welfare people decided to step in and take Johnny away from her. She went to her parents and begged for the money so she wouldn't lose her child, and they agreed to pay it off if they could have the child to raise.

For the first four years of his life young Johnny lived with his grandparents. During this time his mother had remarried and she was living in Amarillo with her new husband and first son. She decided that she wanted her son back and went to her parents and asked them to give Johnny back to her. They said no, that Johnny was better off with them and they were not going to give him up.

They fought over him and he was in the middle of the battle. He loved his mother and his grandparents. Why did everyone have to fight over him anyway? He became a very unhappy little boy and by the time he was five years old, a court battle was going on between his mother and grandparents for his custody.

I remember one time when I was visiting with my mother and her second husband (who some say is my real father), I guess I had been crying about something. I don't remember what it was, but it made him mad. He set me on one of those old fashioned wood stoves to punish me.

I screamed for help and the pain was unbearable. I didn't know why he would do this to me just because I was crying or being bad. No one should be treated this way and I still have the scars today on my buttocks.

Johnny's mother had just divorced her second husband and remarried her third one when she was granted custody of him.

I remember when mom took me to her home with Weaver, her new husband. Granny was crying and I started crying and tried to get to granny. I wanted to stay with my grandmother but I was carried to the car and taken away. I remember how scared I was when we got to Weaver's house. I couldn't eat or talk. I was devastated and I missed my grandmother. She had been mother to me for as long as I could remember and I wanted to go home, back where everything was familiar.

Mom tried to be nice to me and asked if I wanted to sleep with her and Weaver. I said I didn't and for the first couple of nights, I slept on the recliner chair in the living room. This was when I started to wet the bed. I guess my nerves were shot by then with all the turmoil over mom and granny fighting over me.

While I was very young, my mother bought a couple of dogs for my older brother Junior because he didn't have anyone at home to play with. I loved those dogs as much as if they were my own and would play with them every time I went over to visit. One day I found one of the dogs dead and I ran crying to my room. My mother took the dog to the vet to find out what she had died from. It seemed that someone hadn't liked her and had put broken glass in her food.

I found myself crying all the time. I would cry over the smallest things and not know why. I remember one day a kid from down the street came riding up on his bicycle. He told me that my mother didn't love me because she hadn't bought me a bicycle like all the other kids on the street had. I remember hitting him with a stick in the face. My mother did so love me and he wasn't going to say she didn't. The kid got to his feet and headed home.

My mother wasn't home, just my brother and I out in the front yard. I saw the kid's big brother coming at me to hit me. I've always been small and skinny and I knew I didn't have a chance with him. I screamed for my brother and he came running to help me. He was younger than the other boy but he fought him anyway to help me. He won and the boy ran off. I never did have any more problems with those two boys again.

The first time I ever stole anything I was in the first grade. I had gone to the store to get some things for mom and I started looking around at all the good things in there. I saw this play doctor kit and I wanted it. I wanted that kit real bad and knew I couldn't get the things mom had sent me for and the kit. I picked up the things mom wanted and then walked back to the toy area. I looked around and saw that no one was looking, so I grabbed the kit and stuffed it inside my shirt. Turning around I walked out of the store. Looking back I saw two men running after me.

I started to run and saw a car with the window open. I threw the kit inside and kept on running. When the men caught up with me they took me back to the store. They wanted to know what I had stolen and I told them I hadn't taken anything. They didn't believe me but they couldn't find anything on me that I hadn't paid for. They wrote a note and told me to give it to my mother.

After leaving the store, I threw the note away and got the kit; then I hurried on home. I had gotten away with it this time. I supposed the next time would be easier still.

I remember when my aunt, my mother's sister, moved in with us. She was sixteen years old and I can't remember why she had to come to live with us, but she did. We were very close and I remember one day when we were in a little store I saw her steal something. I told her that I could do that too, and soon we got real good at it. I would keep the cashier busy and she would steal something. Then sometimes we'd do it the other way around; she would keep the cashier busy while I stole some things. It was fun, especially with someone to do it with. It was exciting to put something in your pocket and walk out without paying for it.

I would dread the weekend as I got older. Weaver would come home and get drunk. When he was drunk, him and mom would fight all the time. I couldn't understand why she didn't just buy his beer and leave for the weekend. Then there would be peace, but she never would. She had five of us kids by then, and I guess it was hard on her too.

One time Weaver slapped my mother and as he went out the door she threw a bottle at him. It connected with his forehead and he was mad. But that's the only time I remember him physically doing something to mom. Sometimes I was glad when they were fighting because I could sneak some of his beer for myself.

I remember the first real beating he gave me. I guess I deserved a licking but not what he gave me. I was sick that day and hadn't gone to school. I found this can of black paint and decided to paint the old garage that was now Junior's room. I thought it looked old and worn out, so this is what I did. When I went in the house mom was real mad at me and wouldn't let me change my painted clothes. She wanted Weaver to see me with all the evidence still on me. When he came home, I hid under the coffee table so he wouldn't see me. He found me anyway and began to whip on me. He hit me with his belt over and over again until I thought I couldn't take anymore. The belt wasn't just landing on my butt, but he was hitting me on the back and anywhere else it might fall. My brother finally came in and told him that was enough.

Weaver told me to go to the bathroom and clean myself up. He wasn't talking about the paint either; he had scared me so bad I had gone to the bathroom in my pants. I hated him more and more. But how I loved my brother Junior. It seemed like he would come to my rescue all the time. I felt so confused during those years because I was being pulled toward my grandmother, my mom, and my brother. It seemed like they were always fighting over me. I felt like everything that went wrong was my fault and I began to hate myself. I felt left out because all my stepfathers and my real dad were always wanting my brothers and sisters and not me.

I feel bitter that I never had a real father to call my own, but I guess it made me closer to my brothers and sisters. I guess my mom's third husband treated me good in the beginning. Then after about a year he began to get mad when I continued to wet the bed. He'd rub my face in it and beat the hell out of me. He would accuse my mother of not teaching me to go to the bathroom and being a bad example for us kids.

I began running away and mom finally stopped reported me. She felt that I would come back when I wanted to. I was eleven years old when I left home and would sleep in cars at night. I was scared but I also felt more at ease. I knew I'd get a beating when they caught up with me but it didn't matter anymore.

My mom's fourth husband was the one who sexually abused me and I felt scared and ashamed. All of them except her fifth husband physically abused me. I thought it was a normal life, but now I don't think so. I started to look to older kids to hang around with, like bikers and truck drivers, and of course my big brother. I felt like I didn't belong with kids my age and they seemed to be immature compared to the way I acted.

I was drinking before I even started school because all the male figures in my life did. I drank to get drunk and forget the kind of life I was living, but it didn't work. I still remembered what my life was like and I hated it.

I don't think I blame my mom for the way I was brought up. She had her own troubles with the men she married. They would beat her and it was hard on her. I know she loves me and did the best she could to raise me and my brothers and sisters. I do blame her for the fighting between her and granny because she should have let my grandmother keep me like she promised.

I was seventeen when I was arrested and convicted of murder. I was sent to death row here in Texas and that is where I am right now. I read a lot, anything I can get my hands on, and I listen to my radio. I watch some television when there is something good on, which isn't very often. The televisions are bolted on the wall in front of our cells so I have to watch whatever is on at the time. We're not allowed to have our own in the cells.

My cell is twelve feet long and I have a bunk, sink, and toilet in it. I have my personal items such as photos, books, shoes, radio, fan, and things like that. The walls are colored a sickly white/grey and are very depressing. The bars are painted an ugly blue color and have a screen welded against them. When we watch TV, we have to look through the screen to see anything.

I never thought I'd end up on death row, but here I am. I hope all the kids out there will remember that it can happen if you choose the wrong path in life. It's so easy to take the wrong path, by going with friends who ask you to do something you know is wrong. But just remember: you may be the one in thousands who will get the lottery ticket to death row.

10

Marvin Amell, Sr.

Death Row, New Hampshire

I was born in Bethany, Israel, on January 2, 1953. I was an unplanned child, as my father only wanted one son and he had that in my older brother. I feel that I was kind of pushed aside at an early age from family life. I always had the feeling that no one really loved me or included me in the family fun.

When I was six years old, we came to the states to live and I was placed in a private school for boys, while my brother was able to attend a public school near our home. I didn't like this and thought they were playing favorites with my brother.

My parents used to pick me up on weekends when they had the time and when they wanted to. I felt so left out and I wanted so badly to be a part of our family. I needed to be a part of my father's life and know that he loved me. I never felt that love, not like he cared about my brother.

As a result, I would get into all kinds of trouble just so he would pay attention to me. Punishment was swift and severe, but at least they knew I was alive. It was better than being ignored all the time, I thought at that time.

As I grew, I watched my brother build a bond with my father that I plainly and simply hated. I was jealous of the feelings of love between them when I was just an outsider looking in. I wanted my father to love me. I needed his love so bad but never received it.

Finally when I was sixteen, I asked him to let me enlist in the army. I was hoping he'd tell me no, that he wanted me to stay home, but he agreed, and I was sent to Fort Dix in New Jersey for my basic training and then on to Virginia for flight-training school.

I think that's where I learned that by being cold and cruel to people I could, and did, gain respect. Later I found it was fear and not respect that I was getting.

I became a co-pilot engineer in eight months and I signed up for overseas tour, which at the time was Vietnam. That's where I became a one-man killing machine. Within a few months I became a pilot of a helicopter with a crew of eight. We became one of the best fighter crews, making over two hundred flight missions in a year.

After eighteen months on tour, my crew and I were shot down and six of my crew died, while I was held captive for six days. I don't remember much of it because I suffered a lot of injuries to my head, back, and legs. I found myself in a rehab center in Germany where I stayed for about nine months. Then I returned to the states to finish my therapy.

It was during this time that I began praying a lot. I noticed a young nurse's aid at the hospital in Laconia, New Hampshire. We dated and soon fell in love and were married. We settled down to be near my family, but nothing had changed; they still didn't care about me.

It was late in 1984, when I told my wife Robin we were going to have a honeymoon and we left for Kentucky. Robin had relatives there that we would visit. While there, we were robbed by a would-be thief. I was carrying a licensed hand gun and felt the need to use it. The man died and I was charged with murder one. I think the words used by the judge were "extreme violence and recklessness." Those words that I thought gave me respect earlier in life also will end it. I received the death penalty by the state of Kentucky in October of 1984.

I was lucky enough to be allowed to wait my sentence here in New Hampshire where I thought I had family. Through all this I found myself praying and it turned into a deep belief and respect for Christ.

After telling my parents and family of my new belief as a Christian Jew, I again found myself abandoned. I'm now a disgrace to my parents for being here on the row and for my faith.

I learned quickly that this was no place to be playing Mr. Tough Guy. When you're a bad ass in prison, you find yourself in the hole a great deal of the time, so I settled down and looked back at my life.

I came to realize that the lack of love and attention by my parents led me to find it elsewhere, which proved to be useless.

I use my time here as a learning experience where I build my faith and character out of the beatings I received while behind the wall. I took the lack of human companionship and turned it into time to see that people out there cared for me. I realized that if I would just be myself, people would see me for what I am and would either stand by me or leave me. Very few people have left my side and I'm cared for, worried about, and truly loved, and most of all I'm actually respected because I'm Marvin.

I've looked back at my early years and at all the pain I had to put up with. The problem is that you have to realize this early on in life. Don't see your hard times as someone pushing you back. Plant your feet on the ground and look inside yourself and focus on where you want to go in life. Understand that the road of life isn't always paved. I pray that anyone who reads this will understand that once you become embittered by life, you must quickly heal the wound. There's no way out once you're on death row. The path ends here.

11

Arthur Lanier
Death Row, Mississippi

I was born in 1957 and am the oldest of six children. My mother and father were together for the first five years of my life. But then my parents divorced because my mother was tired of being abused. Life certainly wasn't a bed of roses for any of us during those years.

We went to church all the time, and although I didn't really like going, I had to. I grew up believing in Jesus Christ and even when I was doing things I had no business doing, the Lord was right there with me. I didn't believe in fighting and didn't want to do it even though the other kids would pick on me constantly. Most of the time I would talk my way out of fights or just run. My brother Johnnie always stuck up for me.

I failed the third and fourth grades because I couldn't read or write very well. Since I couldn't understand what I was trying to read, I mostly just looked at the pictures in the books to know what was going on.

We lived on welfare and my mother worked as a maid. We had all the things we needed, and when she could, my mother would get some of the extras. I guess that took the place of her hugging and kissing us, or telling us that she loved us. Deep down we knew our mother loved us, but felt like she didn't at times. We got beatings when we did something we shouldn't have, and I got the worst of them, I guess because I misbehaved the most.

In junior high school I played football and tried out for band.

I remember making the honor roll once. I was sixteen when I got my first paying job and it was kind of fun to be out working. I also accepted Jesus Christ in my life and started going to church regularly again.

But when I turned seventeen, life took a bad turn for me. I didn't fight hard enough to live the life of a Christian and I let myself go back into the worldly life like everyone else I knew. I began living a life of sin, and once you let yourself open to its influences, to choose to live life without God, then you become a sinner. I let myself take the wrong turn in life, with worldly evil. The streets were calling me and I went. I was hooked on the ways of the world.

I didn't care about anything any more and began to get high, stay out late, and drink. All I cared about was running around with girls, getting high, and not working. I began stealing. Every time I needed money, I would just go out and steal it.

Finally, when I was eighteen, I got arrested and got nine years in prison. In prison I became involved with some sick people. The prisons are full of evil, sick-minded people, and I hung on to them. You have to decide to change your life and the way you want to live. Most inmates don't want to change and they learn even more ways of committing crime. After a while, I decided that I wanted to live the right kind of life, that I would get a job once I was released.

I went back out into the world and tried to keep a job and keep myself from stealing. I even went back to school to work on getting my graduate equivalency degree. But it was hard and I soon tired of it all. Thoughts of easy money came to mind and I stole a few times just to see if I could still do it.

Then it happened. The shooting was accidental. I was only protecting myself that day, but a life was taken. I never wanted to take his life, but we were both at fault. Within my heart and mind, I am truly sorry—sorry that a man was killed, sorry that it was me that caused it, sorry that both of our families had to suffer. We say that the truth will set us free, but I'm still waiting for the truth to be known while I sit on Mississippi's death row. I was always told that it was best to tell the truth. But is it better to tell the truth knowing you'll get punished or to tell a lie and get away with something? I say I shouldn't have the punishment of death for an accidental shooting. If he had followed the rules, he would still be alive, and if I had done my part and followed my right mind, it wouldn't have happened and I wouldn't be sitting on death row. I'm also sorry for all the people who are so willing to kill me, a man that had no desire to kill.

The only people here on death row are the poor, the blacks, and other minorities. Some have killed out of fear, for being afraid of getting caught in a robbery, and some of them are mentally retarded. The devil is working, using us to kill in order to get our souls. We let the pleasures of life take control over our lives.

Life here on death row is hard. People don't like to see a man on death row fighting for his life. I've had people tell me that they'll be glad when I'm dead; some say they wish they could pull the plug. They think that putting a man to death is justice, and to kill children and the mentally retarded is all right. The Supreme Court just passed a law that says states can kill those who are mentally retarded and all those juveniles who may be fourteen or fifteen years old.

God says, "Thou shalt not kill"; and Jesus said, "Let he who is without sin cast the first stone." It is man's law that says it's all right to kill each other in the name of justice. Twelve God-fearing people put man's law above God's law and sentenced us to die. I'm sorry for the way the world has become, for all the hatred and evil that people possess today. I wait and pray, and I have faith that there is going to be a better world. I hope that people will realize that they are murderers too, and it's a sin to kill those in the name of justice. Our blood is on their hands just as much as on mine when they sentenced me to die.

I want to tell the kids of the world, don't let anyone talk you into anything that isn't right, or that you feel is wrong. There are a lot of things that may seem to be fun, but can get you into deep trouble. Drugs will take over your mind if you let them. Don't do evil things just to have friends or to make yourself look cool. Always try to do better and make something of your life. Learn all you can about God and try to live the life He wanted. Obey your parents and teachers. Do all you can to fight the evil thoughts that come into your mind. Death row isn't a cool place to be; it's a living hell. You're dead, but they haven't buried you yet. Killing is wrong and although I am living on death row, I still live my life and deal with the things that are around me.

I forgive those who want to kill me by law. It was an accident that I killed someone. The man shot at me first and I shot back and killed him. I hurt a lot and if I die, I'll go down fighting for my life and praying for those who kill me.

12

Gary Graham

Death Row, Texas

A Kinder and Gentler America

There have been hundreds of state-sanctioned executions in the United States since the reenactment of the death penalty in 1976. Currently there are over 2,200 unfortunate, condemned American citizens nervously facing the cruel and unusual punishment of being executed by their fellow Americans.

The political, social, and moral fabric of our nation appears to be corroding more quickly than the ozone layer, and as a result, the delusioned members of the Supreme Court are becoming more and more reluctant to block executions.

At this time, there is one issue before the High Court that I find hard to believe we are even considering in such an advanced and civilized nation.

The issue is whether or not the execution of a mentally retarded person, who has the reasoning ability of a seven-year-old kid and an IQ estimated between 50 and 60, constitutes "cruel and unusual punishment" in violation of the Eighth Amendment to the U.S. Constitution.

Under consideration is the fate of Johnny Paul Penry, 32, who was convicted and sentenced to death by lethal injection, for the rape and murder of Pamela Carpenter, of Livingston, Texas, in 1980.

Following Penry's arrest for the murder of Ms. Carpenter, Penry made a verbal admission, and the police reduced his confession into a written statement, which Penry, a retarded illiterate, signed. Based on his statement alone, Penry was convicted of capital murder.

During the punishment stage of Penry's trial, his overworked, inexperienced, state-appointed attorney presented a considerable amount of evidence proving without a doubt that Penry was mentally unstable and could not have been responsible for his actions. Before the jury left the room for deliberations, the District Attorney asked the jury to give Penry the death penalty, a verdict "that you could go home and be proud of." Penry's attorney then made the following argument:

> I am somewhat amazed that Mr. Keeshan [district attorney] told you that you ought to return a verdict that you could go home and be proud of. Is there pride in taking the life of any person, much less a person which the evidence has shown here was an afflicted child at the age of nine? The records show that this boy had an afflicted mind at the age of nine, and we can't get around that. . . . And then at the age of seventeen, we again find the condition of this boy as being mentally retarded.
>
> And even now, these doctors say that he is mentally retarded, and then they ask you—Can you be a party to putting a man to death with that affliction? I don't think you could sleep with yourselves, with your conscience. . . . I don't think there is any question in any one of you jurors' mind [sic] that there is definitely something wrong, basically, with this boy. And I think that there is not a single one of you that doesn't believe that this boy has brain damage, as they found at the University of Texas when they ran those tests and formed those conclusions. . . . And I say to you, you have heard the evidence, and I think that Mr. Keeshan was in error when he told you: I want you to render a verdict that you can be proud of.

In spite of the overwhelming evidence showing Penry's mental retardation, the jury was unsympathetic and sentenced him to death. His attorney immediately appealed his conviction.

Upon appeal, after reviewing the case, the Texas Court of Criminal Appeals made the following observations:

> There can be no question that petitioner (Penry) does not think like a normal person, but then no normal person would have committed a crime like the one of which Penry was convicted. The blame for Penry's condition probably lies at several doorsteps. There was evidence sug-

gesting he was frequently and severely beaten by his mother, spent much of his life in state schools and mental institutions, and in his teens was victimized by other men (sexually and otherwise), who treated him like a slave.

The ultimate doorstep must be Penry's, however, because he is the one who stands convicted of taking Pamela Carpenter's life. Although Penry may be mentally abnormal, his upbringing was also abnormal. He has treated others as they have treated him. It may never be clear what role societal factors played in causing Penry's condition.

And while the Court acknowledged Penry's abnormalities, his cry for mercy fell on deaf ears, and no relief was granted.

Penry's attorney then took the case to the U.S. Fifth Circuit Court of Appeals, assuming justice had abandoned Texas and moved to New Orleans. But the Court summarized the facts by stating:

Penry introduced evidence of his mental retardation, and his inability to read or write. He had never finished the first grade. His emotional development was that of a child. He had been beaten as a child, locked in his room without access to a toilet for considerable lengths of time. He had been in and out of state schools. One effect of his retardation was his inability to learn from his mistakes.

It would be funny if this were not true, but again, the court refused to grant Penry any relief.

I believe if Penry could have afforded an experienced attorney, who specialized in capital cases and fully understood the complexities involved—like the attorney who represented John Hinckley after his attempted assassination of then President Reagan—Penry would have been placed in a mental institution long ago for some much needed treatment. Instead, the system viewed Penry as a "nobody," and locked him away on death row in Texas, where the odds of his mental condition improving are slim to none.

The case is now before the Supreme Court, which will have the final say on the fate of Johnny Paul Penry. The Court may decide if current standards of decency and fairness, as expressed in the concept of cruel and unusual punishment, permit the execution of someone whom doctors have consistently found to have a very limited ability to reason, plan, control his impulses, or follow instructions. Doctors suspect not just retardation but brain damage, perhaps resulting from severe child abuse. One attorney familiar with Penry's case recently stated:

> The question before the High Court today cuts to the core of the moral justification for the death penalty. Only the worst, the most culpable murderers are to receive the ultimate form of punishment. Using that standard, it is difficult, if not impossible, to view a mentally retarded individual as among the most blameworthy, the most accountable of killers.

A decision is expected in mid July. But the court could sidestep the main issue of Penry's retardation and choose the narrow issue of whether Texas's capital-punishment statutes allow a jury adequately to consider mental retardation as a mitigating factor.

I have known and befriended Johnny since my arrival on death row in 1981. Often I have stood back at a distance and watched Penry walk around and around the recreation yard, appearing to be lost in a world he cannot understand. I can conceive of no other condition that places greater depression and hardships on one's mind and soul than the horrifying and dehumanizing conditions Penry is forced to deal with here on death row.

Often I can feel the pain that Penry feels. I guess this is because, unlike the American justice system, I cannot willingly be indifferent to what has and is happening to Penry. If the Supreme Court allows Penry to be executed, it will be a very miserable spectacle I hope I will never live to see, for it will cast a dark shadow on every American citizen. And the words of Thomas Jefferson—"Indeed I tremble when I reflect God is just."—will echo across the land.

If the High Court can find enough compassion to save Penry's life and allow him to receive the proper medical attention, which will allow Penry to one day become more productive rather than destructive, then indeed we will be on the road to a "kinder and gentler America."

Editor's note: Since this article was written, the Supreme Court has reversed the death-penalty sentence imposed on Penry. The Court ruled that Penry's retardation was relevant to the issue of his personal responsibility for his acts.

13

James J. Wilkens, Jr.
Death Row, Texas

I understand that one of the main issues used to maintain the form of legalized murder known as the death penalty is the relief and comfort an execution (murder) will dispense to the family and friends of a murder victim. Well, let's take a look at some victims and their families and friends.

First of all, I cannot comprehend how the family and friends of a victim can derive any comfort from the knowledge that another human being has been murdered for their sake and the sake of their loved one, at least not with a clear conscience, unless there is the sensation of having one's thirst for revenge quenched. Surely, they must be able to realize that their loved one will not be returned to them as a result of the death of another. The way I see it, the only way anyone can derive any comfort from the knowledge of another's death is if they have a feeling of satisfaction. This is nothing less than revenge.

Once the victim's family has revenge and is satisfied, what about the new victim's family and friends? Oh yes, victim. For anyone who is executed in the name of justice is a victim, for there is no justice in murder, and willfully and knowingly taking the life of another is murder. Read any law book and you will find that this is the basic criterion for murder, unless it is in self-defense, i.e., killing someone who has placed you or a member of your family in immediate danger of bodily harm or death. There are variations from state to state, but the basic criterion for murder is the aforementioned.

So if you look at this issue from a realistic perspective, you will find that there is no way any state with the death penalty can justify itself to the families and friends of its victim. The state is, without a doubt, taking these lives knowingly and willingly. People have a tendency to "ooh" and "ah" at the pain and suffering of the victim's family and friends; so let's take a realistic look at all the families and friends of all the victims. Let's look at the pain and suffering that occurs when a state murders someone with electricity, gas, or an injection. Do these victims not have families and friends? What clearly defines an execution as murder is the fact that it is carried out as revenge and nothing less. To take the life of another for satisfaction is revenge pure and simple.

Has this system really pulled so much wool over your eyes that you can't tell that what it is doing is murder? Have you allowed the system to make you an unwitting accessory to murder? If you believe in and support the death penalty, then that is exactly what you are. How many times have you gone to bed with the knowledge that there was to be a "legal" murder held at the penitentiary in your community? Did you sleep well? Did you realize that the state was about to commit the exact same crime that the condemned was found guilty of? Did you know that they were committing this vile act in your name? Whenever you hear about a murder in the streets, you naturally feel compassion and sympathy for the victim and their family and friends, and you are appalled and saddened that something so senseless and uncalled for happened. Now let me ask you this: When you hear that there is to be a legalized murder under the guise of justice, are you just as appalled, just as saddened, and does it seem just as senseless? It should. Do you feel compassion and sympathy for this victim and his family and friends? Think about it. For there is no separation between the two events; they are both murder. And there is no separation in the feelings of pain and sorrow felt by the families and friends of each victim.

If we are so appalled by murder, why do we continue to advocate, and by our inaction, implicitly support murder under the guise of justice, especially when it is not justice, but murder/revenge? What is the difference between one life and another? You and I and all of us are just mere humans. Who are we to decide who should die and who should not?

It is an atrocity the way this system has painted up the death penalty. The pretty packaging is nothing but a facade that is used to cover up and sell the truth hidden behind it. But cut away the outer trappings, and you will find the naked face of capital punishment—revengeful murder.

14

M. E. Marrs

Death Row, Texas

I am currently imprisoned and have been sentenced to death in Texas, a state that has conducted more than its share of executions this past year. When I was asked to contribute to this book, at first I doubted that I had anything unique or original to say. Why do we kill people who kill people to show that killing is wrong? That question seemed to sum up all opposition to the death penalty. But that unremarkable question has continued to nag at me. I was unsure how I really felt about the law's view of capital punishment, and I needed the soul searching required to write about it.

I've always thought that many who favor execution believe that infliction of the punishment of "an eye for an eye" is simple conformity to the fixed will of God, as revealed in the Holy Scriptures. They should compare Jesus's explicit denunciation of that ethic in Matthew 5:38–40. Others seem to be programmed, conditioned by mass media, as so many of us today are. Exploitation by the media of the deep emotional response to violent crime may serve as an advertisement for violent solutions to crime. Nevertheless, heinous crimes are committed that outrage all of us, moving even the meekest to yell, "Get the rope." I needed to purge myself of the preaching and programming of others and uncover my true feelings.

While I have been an observer here, nine men have been executed. In my opinion, two had been convicted of horrible crimes; six were caught in the middle of desperate circumstances; and one was innocent.

I say that he was innocent, not because of his claim of innocence, but because of the undisputed facts of his case. At the trial of Doyle Skillern, the court heard uncontroverted testimony from the admitted trigger man that Doyle was innocent of the murder, that he was not even present at the actual scene of the murder, and that he had no foreknowledge that a murder would occur. This is not an isolated case. There are a number of such cases on death rows.

I currently share a cell with M. D. Crawford, who as a teenager robbed a convenience store with another youth who admitted that he, not Crawford, accidentally shot the store clerk. It is apparent that the court believed the shooting was accidental, because it gave the admitted trigger man a sentence of life imprisonment. So why is Crawford on death row? The irony of both his case and that of Skillern is that the trigger man in each instance received a life sentence. I wish to see no person condemned to death, but where is the consistency of the law when lives are at stake?

Suppose the courts were required to take a closer look at capital cases than is evidently required now, weighing the facts more carefully, demanding stricter standards of proof, enforcing more substantial procedural safeguards. Is this not what was promised when the current death penalty statutes were adopted, following the Supreme Court's 1972 ruling that previous statutes had inflicted unconstitutionally "cruel and unusual punishment" because of capricious and arbitrary application? What if the laws attempted to specify that only those guilty of the most outrageous, most heinous crimes might be subjected to death as punishment? Again, we have been assured that current laws do this. But there will always be inconsistency, and innocents will be put to death.

But capital punishment poses a more basic moral, spiritual, and ethical question: Is anyone fundamentally, intrinsically, irredeemably bad—so bad that his or her enforced exclusion from society would not suffice to protect the public; so bad that the safety of society can be insured only by ending his or her physical existence? I don't think so. I can understand why the bereaved loved ones of a murder victim might be unable to see the possibility of any good in a person convicted of murder, but I cannot understand how most people could accept such a despairing view of human nature. Americans seem to have lost their faith in humanity, forgotten the value of human life. The renewal of faith in human potential and the elevation of respect for human life should begin with the restoration of those values to our laws.

Who truly believes that God would create something totally wrong, without value or higher purpose? I no longer believe that anything living is absolutely evil. I don't think I ever really did. And I believe the American people would also reject such one dimensional moral blindness if they searched deeply within their own souls, or if they were allowed to observe all of America's condemned instead of the media's choice of sensational highlights.

Compare what has been accomplished in recent years in physics, engineering, and medicine with the current state of criminology, which is still stuck in the age of Hammurabi. I am convinced that when the genius of this nation is harnessed for the highest human good, the protection and nurture of all life, there will be no condemned, no death rows. I think this is not only possible but inevitable, a simple matter of progress, the first step being a renewed faith in one another and the placing of a higher value on life. I do not expect this to happen overnight. Nor do I expect everyone to share my views. I am convinced, nevertheless, that humanity will save itself.

Meanwhile, those of us condemned to America's death rows will continue to die, as will those destroyed by wars, those preempted by abortion clinics, and those fallen victim to numerous other senseless institutionalized cruelties. We have been repeating the lesson "Forgive them for they know not what they do" for more than 2,000 years. In this writer's view, we should be close to mastering it.

15

Joseph P. Payne, Sr.
Death Row, Virginia

I know what being under sentence of death for a crime you didn't commit is like. Although the number of innocent people on death row may be small compared to the number that are guilty, my heart goes out to the innocent and their families and friends. As well, it goes out to all death-row prisoners and their families and friends because many have become victims of murder whether they wanted to or not.

Death row is hard on anyone who is not actually so cold blooded and heartless that they don't have any care for human life. Since I've been on death row, I have seen people who did not care about the lives of others before, but with time for reflection and time away from drugs and the stresses they were under before, they changed. If given the chance, I don't think they would rob or kill again. It's hard to keep hope and stand strong, even though it is what we must do.

When a person says, "Wait, I'm innocent," the response is usually, "Sure you are, just like everyone else in prison is." The cry of innocence is rarely believed, especially after false or fabricated evidence has been used to convince a court of the person's guilt. Not only are innocent pleas unbelieved because so many who are guilty deny the guilt, but also because of people's hate, fear, and disgust with the crime, particularly the crime of murder. People care more about putting people in prison or in an execution chamber as a pay-back, or in the hope that the punishment will act as an example that will serve to deter crime, rather than actually finding out if a person is innocent or guilty.

99

It is my opinion that fear, hate, and lack of knowledge about what can be done to reduce crime block people from trying to eliminate the causes of criminal behavior.

One reason being under sentence of death is particularly hard on the innocent person is that the judicial system has several laws that can prevent the innocent from having facts and issues concerning their conviction heard in the appeal process. One such law is the contemporaneous objection rule. This is a rule of law which basically states that if a person's trial attorney does not make timely and proper objections during trial to preserve certain issues about the trial proceedings for appeals, the issues cannot be raised on appeal. I had several important issues that I wanted the appeals court (Virginia Supreme Court) to consider in my case and because my lawyer did not make objections during trial, the court refused to consider them under this rule. Many valid and pertinent issues are not heard simply because trial counsel did not make the proper and timely objections. This could mean the difference between life and death for an innocent person.

Another law which can mean the difference between life and death and which legally prevents the innocent from presenting issues on appeal is a law called "procedural default." Here again if a person or his attorney doesn't present an issue during trial or at certain stages of the appeals, but they try to do this later, the courts won't consider the issue unless there is newly discovered evidence which could not have been presented sooner to support the issue. Both procedural default and the contemporaneous objection rule leave no room for human error by the defendant or an overworked defense attorney. So a lawyer's accidental omission of something important could very well mean an innocent person will be put to death, simply because the law doesn't allow for human error.

Also, in many death cases, "future dangerousness" is being used as a legal ground to impose a sentence of death despite the fact that psychiatric research has shown that such a prediction is humanly impossible.

Two other rules of law that are supposed to protect the innocent but often fail to do so are used at the trial stage. One is the reasonable-doubt standard, and the other is the use of circumstantial evidence.

A defendant on trial for capital murder by law is supposed to be protected from conviction if there is a reasonable doubt that the defendant may be innocent. This reasonable-doubt standard is being ignored or simply not applied in many cases. When the evidence suggests there is reason to doubt whether a defendant committed the crime of murder, or that the defendant intentionally planned to murder the victim, this doubt is often outweighed by people's fear of crime, the desire to set an example as a deterrent, the desire to make sure someone pays for the crime, or the desire to achieve political career gain. The reasonable-doubt standard of law is thus made worthless.

If a person cannot prove his innocence in court or presents only enough proof that reasonable people can't be sure if the person is guilty or not, I believe that many times jurors consider the defendant's appearance, race, religion, or background rather than the fact that there exists reasonable doubt as to the guilt of this person. I also think if the defendant is rough looking or fits an undesirable or prejudicial stereotype, the fact that the police don't have anyone else to convict and make pay for the crime again prevents reasonable doubt from being considered.

Social deterrence and pay-back will outweigh the reasonable-doubt standard. Anyone who denies that this type of decision making is practiced by judges and jurors is foolishly assuming that judges or people sitting on a jury don't respond from human feelings and error.

The use of circumstantial evidence is the other part of a trial that I feel is unfair and does allow innocent persons to be convicted and imprisoned or executed. Circumstantial evidence is evidence that suggests but does not prove that a defendant may have or could have been the person to commit the crime. Circumstantial evidence does not show without a doubt that a particular person did an act. It only creates a possible theory of how and why a person might be guilty. Take a creative prosecutor and give him circumstantial evidence, and more than likely he can tell a story so convincingly that people will believe it even though there is no evidence directly linking the defendant to the crime.

Our judicial system has many weaknesses. Witnesses testify falsely, prosecutors convince jurors of a false set of events, police manufacture or misrepresent evidence against the innocent, and our appeal and trial process has laws such as those I've just mentioned that prevent the innocent from proving their innocence. What good is the law if it can't protect the innocent from false imprisonment?

This lack of protection of the law is almost always going to affect the people who can't afford to pay lawyers and investigators to help them prove their innocence, and those who have to depend on court-appointed attorneys who are overworked, underpaid, and inexperienced. But as long as people—financially well off or poverty stricken—allow these types of laws to exist, any innocent person set up by someone is at risk of being imprisoned or executed wrongfully.

Our judicial and law-enforcement system is failing the people. When an innocent person spends fourteen years on death row battling the system to prove his innocence, fighting laws that continuously block his ability to prove his innocence, the people have not been protected. The reason is that the person who committed the crime is probably still out in society hurting or destroying people's lives.

I'm sure there will be plenty of people who say, "Be serious. That sort of thing doesn't occur very often." These people need to be informed of cases where it has happened. An article called "Miscarriages of Justice in Potentially Capital Cases"* written by Hugo Bedau and Michael Radelet, which tells of approximately 352 such convictions that were discovered only through investigation, is a good starting point.

This investigation discovered that many of these people spent numerous years on death row or in prison. Some were within minutes of being executed before they were found to be innocent, and some were executed and buried before it was found out. Despite the many miscarriages of justice—and I'm sure there are many more that haven't been investigated properly—our judicial system is passing laws that make it harder and harder to prevent the innocent from being falsely convicted and executed.

Some examples:

- David Ronald Wilson was convicted of second-degree murder in Maimi in 1967. He was freed in 1971 when the state admitted that the eyewitness testimony against him had been perjured.

- In 1934 Louis Berrett and Clement Molway were identified by eight eyewitnesses as the men who killed a theater employee. Just prior to the final arguments at their trial, the actual killers confessed. The jury foreman was later quoted as saying, "This trial has taught me one thing. Before it I was a firm believer in capital punishment. I'm not now."

---

*Stanford Law Review 40:21–179.

- In 1961, Clark, Hall, and Kuykendall were convicted of murder and sentenced to life imprisonment. One year later, an important witness against them confessed that she had lied at the trial. In return for implicating these three defendants, the police guaranteed her lenient treatment for another crime.

- Larry Hicks was convicted in 1978 on two counts of murder and sentenced to death. Two weeks before the scheduled execution, a volunteer attorney became interested in the case. After Hicks passed lie-detector tests, the Playboy Foundation provided funds for a thorough reinvestigation. In 1980, the original judge ordered a new trial because Hicks (who had a below-normal IQ) had not understood the proceedings well enough to assist in his own defense. Later that year, at the new trial, evidence established Hicks's alibi and that eyewitness testimony against him in his original trial was perjured. He was acquitted and released: "The case of a young man with no family, friends, or funds who avoided the electric chair mainly by a stroke of extraordinary good luck."

- Isidore Zimmerman was convicted of first-degree murder for providing guns used to kill a police detective and was sentenced to death. Zimmerman was not at the scene of the crime. Zimmerman was two hours from execution when Governor Lehman commuted the sentence to life. After twenty-four years in prison, and after the rejection of several appeals, an attorney volunteered to reinvestigate the case. The conviction was reversed, a new trial was ordered, the indictment was dismissed, and Zimmerman was released. The New York Court of Claims agreed that the prosecutor knew Zimmerman was innocent, suppressed evidence, and intimidated witnesses into perjuring themselves. In 1983, he was awarded one million dollars by the state, but he died four months later.

As long as innocent lives are being forced to be incarcerated for many years, in prison or on death row, and innocent lives are being allowed by law and society to be executed, I can't keep from talking about it. And I feel that others should be speaking out as loudly and strongly as possible.

For me personally, speaking out and writing about it help me to endure the hell of facing the electric chair for a crime I didn't commit. I find it impossible just to sit here waiting for them to come and lead me to the seat without fighting as hard as I can. It's hard to watch them carry other human beings away to be executed, and I can't sit back, as so many in society do, and say, "Hey, that person is an animal and a murderer. They should be killed."

I know the families and friends of the condemned suffer. I know my wife suffers greatly and has had many nightmares, and I expect other families go through the same feelings. They have done nothing wrong and yet society enforces a law that affects and tortures people's lives just as badly as the criminal. I cannot accept the social belief that one type of murder is acceptable and another type is unacceptable or that the people on death row cannot be rehabilitated and forgiven for human failures. I see too many who have changed after being incarcerated into caring people.

The limbo my life has been put in since I was sentenced to die has been extremely tiring. At first I felt like committing suicide. I wondered if death would not be more peaceful than living in a world of such hate and disregard for human life. There are times that depression and insomnia overwhelm me and make it hard to look at anything positively, but some inner strength helps me to endure it and overcome it before it can destroy me.

I have been lucky in one way since I have been on death row. I met a beautiful and caring woman, and after corresponding, visiting, and many phone conversations, we were married. My wife gives so much of herself and her kindness in standing beside me; she gives me strength that she may not even be aware of.

I have written a booklet titled "The World You'll Regret Entering—Prison," which I am distributing and looking for help to distribute more widely. It's intended for juveniles and adults who want to know how people end up on death row, what it is like, and how they can prevent themselves or their children from following in the footsteps of so many others who through human failures and weaknesses have ended up in prison.

I believe the facts about the injustice in my trial and the wrongs committed against other innocent persons need to be shown to the people who will sit on juries in capital cases so they can make better judgments. As long as people tolerate bad laws and police and prosecutors who manipulate and fabricate evidence against innocent people, then they and their families and friends are at risk of being put into one of the worst nightmares of our society. That is to say, until people are aware of and speak out against the policies and practices that so easily allow the innocent to be convicted and executed because of the use of false, circumstantial, or officially manufactured evidence, people are simply allowing one more type of criminal behavior to take place.

Two Internal Affairs investigators and four prisoners fabricated a story against me and another prisoner. Internal Affairs had been trying to convict the other man of another, similar murder. It is possible that the prosecutor of the case was also aware—or should have been—of the falseness of the case presented against me. But rather than trying to protect the innocent, the prosecutor was more concerned with adding to his career.

The prosecutor even recommended a ten-year sentence reduction to the Board of Corrections as payment to these prisoners for their false testimony. One prisoner, who was allegedly an eyewitness against me, was paid the ten-year sentence reduction, and after my trial was also paid an additional five-year sentence reduction for services rendered. This additional five-year sentence reduction was conveniently paid to this prisoner after he had called the prosecutor's office and admitted that he had given perjured testimony. In a fourteen-page affidavit this so-called witness stated:

Within two or three days, Fairburn and Stokes showed up and informed me that if I persisted in stating I perjured myself I would get an additional twenty years for perjury, and I would not get an extra sentence reduction for testifying at Payne's trial. . . . On advice of Fairburn and Stokes I sent a letter to Commonwealth Attorney Lewis, stating that I did not perjure myself and that I only said that because I was under pressure. A few days after I sent the letter, I got an additional five year time cut. I received a sentence update sheet which indicated the cut was for services rendered. Shortly after I sent Lewis the letter concerning my perjury, I was sent to Utah (against my will). I believe I was sent to Utah because the Commonwealth was afraid I would admit to having perjured myself at both trials.

As of December 1987, I had this fourteen-page affidavit from this prisoner stating that he had lied about my being the one to commit the murder. Upon advice of the investigators he had rehearsed the other witnesses concerning what to say at my trial. As part of my defense, I have three eyewitnesses who have submitted affidavits on my behalf stating that I was not the one to commit the murder. I have other affidavits from people who were not allowed by my attorney to testify at my trial, who state facts concerning the time periods before and after the crime was committed, which implicate other people and show my innocence, as well as a conspiracy on the part of the prosecution witnesses to set me up. I have affidavits claiming that these investigators tried to bribe my witnesses with promises of a ten-year sentence reduction if they cooperated with them and testified for them instead of me.

By the beginning of 1988, this had all been presented to the District Court of Powhatan where I was convicted. It went before the same judge who said I received more than a fair trial despite my protest to him that my lawyer had refused to put on more witnesses. Yet, here I am still sitting on death row, unsure if the state will admit that they have convicted an innocent man, or whether my case will end up like Joseph Giarrantano's; in his case the courts refused to admit to the corrupt manner in which the death sentence and conviction were obtained. I sit here wondering whether I, like Joseph Giarrantano, and God knows how many others whose cases are filled with proof of innocence, or at the very least a reasonable doubt, will end up as another statistic of innocent persons murdered by the state.

I also wonder how people support such a barbaric and savage law which leaves to chance whether the innocent will be unjustly murdered. This lack of moral standards is exactly why the United States has such a high murder rate. People are so insensitive to the lives and feelings of others, that it's no wonder they are becoming more and more violent at a younger age. According to my moral standards, whether a person is guilty or innocent, human life is sacred and able to be improved. To destroy life intentionally is contradicting the laws that say murder is wrong.

16

Michael Sharp

Death Row, Texas

I want to tell you about how the Holy Bible has been used by a lot of Christians of all denominations to defend the death penalty. These Christians usually quote in their defense Genesis 9:6, where God tells Noah: "Whoever sheds the blood of man, by man shall his blood be shed"; Leviticus 24:17: "If anyone takes the life of a human being, he must be put to death"; and also Deuteronomy 19:21: "Show no pity; life for life, eye for eye, tooth for tooth, hand for hand, foot for foot."

When people quote such passages because of their belief in the death penalty, you can see the hardness of their heart and the evil gleam in their eyes as they throw their chest out and say, "Yeah, God said, 'eye for eye, tooth for tooth.'" Usually that's all of the verse they remember. They obviously don't remember the other various laws either, which are given in Exodus, Leviticus, and Deuteronomy. If they did, they wouldn't be spouting off about an eye for an eye, and they wouldn't be so quick to say, "I believe in the death penalty."

I have found twenty-seven offenses that prescribe the death penalty in three Bible books alone. All of these offenses are a part of the same Mosaic laws from which comes the eye-for-an-eye verse: Exodus 21:12—murder; Exodus 21:15—striking your parents; Exodus 21:16—kidnaping; Exodus 21:17—cursing your parents; Exodus 21:22,23—causing a woman to miscarry; Exodus 22:2—if a home owner kills a thief after sunrise. Other infractions that, according to the Bible, should be punished by death are working on the Sabbath, adultery, homosexuality, worshiping other gods, and giving false testimony against your brother.

Why don't you Christians, who demand the death penalty with Old Testament Bible verses, demand the death penalty for all of the proscribed offenses outlined by God? Why do you demand the death penalty to suit your personal purposes, and not God's? Is it because you might find yourself on death row awaiting execution along with millions of other Christians?

Every single one of us has broken one of these laws, even if it was so simple a thing as working on the Sabbath day or reading horoscopes. Everyone is guilty!

The point that most Christians don't understand is that the Mosaic laws were given to us by God so that we would know how to conduct ourselves until the seed of Christ came.

The laws were given to us to show us that we can't keep God's laws even when they are written down for us. A person cannot be saved by trying to keep Mosaic laws. When we realize this and see that we are helpless and that without God we are nothing, then it only leaves us one thing, and that's to receive the righteousness of God by faith in Jesus Christ.

Read Galatians, chapters 3, 4, 5, and 6. "All who rely on observing the law are under a curse, for it is written, cursed is everyone who does not continue to do everything in the book of law."

Now it doesn't take a high IQ to figure out that verse. Those of you who are claiming belief in the death penalty because of God's words —"Life for life, eye for an eye"—are under a curse unless you are continuing to do everything written in the book of the law. Are you living under a curse?

I believe I have made it plain to you with Scripture that the Mosaic law no longer exists for those of us who prefer to believe in Christ. Jesus Christ's blood is our new covenant and those of us who have accepted him have solemnly promised to emulate and imitate the manner of life he led in the flesh.

You Christians who believe in the death penalty should read John 8:3–11. What did Jesus say on the subject of the death penalty? A woman had been caught in the act of adultery and when she was brought before Jesus, and He was asked what should be done with her, He said, "If any one of you are without sin, cast the first stone." No one condemned her, neither did Jesus. Jesus stated in John 13:34, "Love one another as I have loved you."

Read Matthew 5:21, 22. Jesus said, "You have heard it was said of them of 'old time' thou shalt not kill, but I say, whosoever is angry with his brother is in danger of judgment." I believe if you read all of Matthew, chapter 5, you will not only see that the laws are in your mind and written on your hearts now, but you will also see that the new laws are more strict and demand more from the Christian. I also believe this shows it's impossible for a human to go through life without sinning. This is why we are judged by faith and not law. We are all sinners. That's why Jesus said in Matthew 7:1, "Judge not that thou be not judged."

In Romans 2:17, it states, "Do not repay evil for evil"; 2:19, "Do not take revenge"; 2:21, "Do not overcome with evil, but overcome evil with good." How many of us can look Jesus in the eye and say, "I'm doing just as you asked, Lord." Not many, would be my guess.

If we were a true Christian nation, as we claim to be, and loved our brothers and sisters, as Jesus commanded us to, then we wouldn't have all the problems we have in our society that cause men and women to overcrowd our prisons and fill our death rows.

We need to reconstruct our Christian attitudes and ethics; we need to heal our nation instead of prolonging its death. Every single one of you will have to admit our country is going to hell. It's high time we all stand up and be what we already call ourselves—Christians.

We can never fix all of society's ills and completely stop crime and murders, but by following the directions of Jesus we can turn our country around. It is our Christian duty to abolish the death penalty and empty our prisons. We do this by getting our Christian ethics in order and loving and caring for one another, as stated in Galatians, 5:14: "The entire law is summed up in a single command, love your neighbor as yourself."

For further information read your Bible. May the grace of Jesus Christ be with our nation's Christian spirit.

A sinner, a Christian, a death-row inmate,

Michael Sharp

17

Hugh Melson
Death Row, Tennessee

I have made a point all of my adult life never to argue politics or religion with anyone. Everyone has their own views concerning these two subjects, and it is next to impossible to change their minds. I never thought I'd be writing about death row and if anyone had ever told me ten years ago that I'd be sitting on death row, I would have thought they were crazy. It just goes to show that one never knows what life has in store for them; your life can be turned upside down in a matter of minutes.

I was convicted of the murder of a west Tennessee woman. In my opinion I was not a very likely candidate to wind up where I am. I was a family man and had a good job, never drank too much, and I never did get involved with any drugs at all. I never committed an armed robbery in my life and since I've been an adult, I've held a job all the time I was free.

I was involved in farming all my life and really enjoyed it. My parents were never divorced and I had a good, healthy, and happy childhood. I was never abused at all, and my parents and I got along real well, better than most I guess. My daddy always had a job and, while we were never rich, we always had plenty to eat and a place to live. Both of my parents worked, and I worked, too, even as a kid and got to keep the money I made.

I graduated from high school with pretty good grades. My parents wanted me to go to college, but the Korean war was going on then and I thought I'd get drafted, so I just joined the Navy.

I suppose the years in the Navy would be what I'd call uneventful, even though I went to Korea twice. I never had any trouble while in the service, and after my second tour, I came home.

I had not been out of the service long when I got into trouble. I was arrested for grand larceny, but the charge was later dropped to petty larceny. I was only twenty-one years old at the time and was sentenced to three years in prison. I served seventeen months. That was the last time I ever got into trouble until I was arrested twenty-five years later.

Those twenty-five years were uneventful and happy—just a normal, pleasant life. I worked for a while as a route salesman driving a wholesale delivery truck for a dairy. Things were going well with the job until the owner announced that he had sold out. The company was placed under new management, and several of the employees got laid off. I was one of the four to stay on the job, but when another man took over, I quit. I couldn't see eye to eye with this man.

Leaving the dairy started a new part of my life, one that would last for over twenty years. My daddy was foreman of a big, west Tennessee farming-and-cattle operation, so I went over and talked to him and the man who owned the place. I started work the very next day.

I had always gotten along with my father, so there was no problem in working with him every day. My wife and daughter moved to the farm and we were happy.

I had a lot to learn about cattle but it was fun learning. The years sort of slipped by, but they were happy years. I was doing well and was satisfied with my life at that time.

In the late spring of 1968, another big change took place for me. My father developed lung cancer, the fast-moving kind. He was just fifty-seven years old when he died.

The owner of the farm called me into his office and asked me if I wanted to be the foreman. It included more benefits and more money, so, of course, I said I would love the job. Life moved on for the next twelve years uneventfully.

One day the owner told me that he was going to be out of town for the day and asked me to look at a leak at his house. I had to go to town to get some parts to fix the leak, so I put ten gallons of gas in the farm pickup and went into town. When I got back to the owner's house, his wife accused me of putting the gas in my truck, and she and I got into a slight argument, which the maid happened to overhear. I thought I had it straight with her, but it turned out later that I didn't. I have never denied that I was in the house that morning or that she and I had a fight.

I got through there, went home, cut my yard, and had some lunch. My wife was going to the shopping center and asked me to go with her. I told her that I had a few things that I had to do, so I didn't go with her. I didn't know then that the next time I would see her would be in jail.

There was a tenant house on the farm that also had a leak in the roof, so I went out to see about that. I did the work, and the man who lived in the house and I sat down and drank one quart of beer each. About 3:30 P.M. the sheriff's deputies came to his house, talked to me for a few minutes, and then arrested me.

I found out that the owner's son had come home from school, found his mother dead, and called the police. The deputies asked how much I had drunk that day, and I told them the truth. They ordered my truck impounded and taken to town. I was later charged with first-degree murder in the case.

When I got to the jail, I asked to make a phone call, which I was entitled to. I called my wife. She had already seen a story about the murder on the TV news, so she knew before I called to tell her. She asked if I needed an attorney and I said that I didn't think so at that time. She insisted on getting one for me in the morning.

The next morning a young lawyer with a prominent firm came up to see me. He said the boss of the firm was out of town, but he would take my case. We talked and the first thing he asked me was whether the sheriff's deputies would find a gun in my truck when they searched it. I told him that there wasn't a gun in the truck.

I was kept in isolation and was not allowed to see anyone except the lawyer for the next few days. Then my attorney told me that he had to give the case up. I think pressure had been put on him not to take the case. My daughter had to go out and find another lawyer willing to take the case.

My family was not allowed to visit with me during this time, and I wasn't allowed to have a shave or shower. My lawyer finally got the sheriff to agree to a visit, and I was also allowed to shower.

My bail was set at $250,000, which, of course, we could not meet. Even the state supreme court agreed that the bail was excessive, but that was out of their jurisdiction. As a result, I had to stay in jail until my trial, a period of some eight months.

What can I say about a county jail that is good? It was crowded all of the time and dirty. The food was terrible and the noise was deafening. I received a visit twice a week and was taken for a psychological test to see if I was mentally sound. The examiners said I was mentally competent to stand trial.

My lawyers filed for a change of venue due to all of the adverse publicity. There was something in the paper and on the television almost every day, so I would not have had a fair trial in that town. A change of venue was denied and I had to stand trial in my home town anyway. To be honest, at that time, I thought that I would stand a better chance at home than I would anywhere else. How wrong I was again.

The DA admitted that all he had on me was circumstantial evidence, but he was going to make a case and was going to ask for the death penalty. The woman hadn't been shot, as thought at first, but had been beaten to death. They took a tool out of my tool box from the truck and said it was the murder weapon.

The victim's family hired an expert witness, and they hired a special prosecutor. Money was no problem to them like it was for my defense. The state admitted that no fingerprints were taken at the crime scene or off of the murder weapon. My truck sat for about seven hours unsecured till it was towed into town. I don't feel that I had a fair trial, and yet I was sentenced to death.

I have been on Tennessee's death row for eight years now. I remember how the guard laughed and mocked me for being there when I was first brought in. As I was taken to the cell, I thought how small it was. It takes a lot of adjustment to live in such a small place when you don't get out of the cell except for one hour a day. I wasn't allowed to bring my TV and I didn't have any money on me, so it wasn't very comfortable.

I found one man willing to give me coffee until I could get some money put in my account, and I will never forget him for that. He is still a good friend of mine today. My wife and daughter came to visit and left some money in my account. They brought me a TV, so I guess I was in as good a shape as I could be on death row.

I never knew that there was any place as bad as this place. I will never get used to it, and I don't think that I can ever adjust completely. I have honestly heard guards say that they wished the state would execute every one of us, like we were animals in cages.

I suppose I would have to say that what bothers me most is being away from my family and loved ones. That is a hard thing for anyone, and I guess some people adjust better than others do. To me, that will always be the hard part. I guess the confinement is hard too. All my life I have been active and worked outside, and now I live in a six-by-nine cell. The conditions have worsened over the past five years here on the row, as the rules change from day to day. We used to go to the yard and other places without cuffs with never any trouble. Now our hands are cuffed behind our backs all the time. We used to walk to the commissary and pick out what we wanted; now the guards bring it over once a week.

I do not know what my fate will be, but I know the love and support of my family and a few close friends mean more than anything in the world to me. If I quit and laid down, I would be letting them down, and that is something I won't do. I will hang in there and fight just as long as I can.

18

Steve West

Death Row, Tennessee

Today my heart and soul were so very pained, I felt as if I couldn't go on any longer. My wife came by for a special visit and carried with her the heart-rending news that my mother had died. I took the news very hard and thought that there was nothing left for me to go on for. As I sat here earlier this evening, listening to a Christian tape my mother had sent to me a short time ago, things started coming to me.

I must admit that I am still pained, but the loss is a bit easier to bear now. On the tape are several songs concerning a son and his mother. I believe she sent me the tape to give me strength when she passed on to the Lord's side. I sat there listening to the songs over and over, and reading her letters; with each one came the onslaught of tears to my eyes. I went from anger to disbelief to a form of mild shock.

But then it came to me. All of the songs dealt with love and trust in the Lord. Not only did they relate to a mother and son's love for each other, but to the mutual love they held for the Lord. In this I have found a great comfort. Yes, the tears are still present, and the pain in my heart is great. But one of the songs talks about a son who dies and goes to Heaven. There, the Lord greets the young man and tells him, "Shake Hands With Mother Again."

My mother wrote a final letter to the entire family and in it she said many things, some harsh, some encouraging, all loving. She told me that should she be dead when my life takes a turn for the better, she would still be there to share in that happiness and that she'll be proud of me no matter what. Today my life did take a turn for the better. Not because my mother is dead, but because of the things that her death has shown me.

If anything, my mother's death has reassured me of the reality and blessedness of Christ. I know that to live my life as Christianlike as is possible will please my mother and make her proud. Instead of allowing Satan to steal my joy and hinder me in my faith, my mother has renewed that faith and given me a deeper reason to continue on.

Mother, I miss you dearly. As Christmas comes upon us, you will be in my thoughts and prayers. I have two special praises when Christmas is here. One is for the birth of Christ, the other is for the new birth of you. You now have a perfect body with no ailments or pain, no more arthritis to hurt you, nothing but joy and happiness. It is hard, mother, but as each day goes by, I will remember you in prayer. I will remember your warm embrace, your gentle touch as you brushed childhood tears away, and the loving faith you've given me in Jesus Christ, Our Lord.

Words can't possibly explain what I am feeling, but I hope that you know of the love I have for you. I look forward to the day when I stand at the Lord's side and He tells me, "Shake Hands With Mother Again."

It's a difficult life, to say the least, brothers and sisters. Here we sit, society's rejects, the dirt swept under the rug awaiting that "Vacuum Cleaner" to suck us into another world.

It's painful to sit here day after day knowing that the state only wants to kill us. We're existing at their expense so they can pick the time they wish to kill us. They spend money to keep us alive, to spend money to kill us. Talk about a catch-22 situation!

But there's more torment than just the waiting. We have to go through the abandonment of family and friends; the social and institutional neglect; and on top of that, most of us have to go broke. We're locked away with no money, no way to earn money, and no one to send it to us. How many of us have heard that money is in the mail, only to find it never arriving? Yes, we're a penniless society of misfits, but I've found in Christ and my Christian friends a richness never before imagined. Many of my friends write and tell me that they are so blessed by knowing me. As a Christian I extend to them a smiling face and a happy heart. My problems are unimportant and not worth mentioning. Trust is given to God and He does provide for the things needed as long as we give Him the hand to do so.

We can all complain about our circumstances, but what good does it do? Complaints often lead to more friends leaving our lives. When we accept the things the Lord has placed in our lives, we can and do feel better. When we cease to complain to our friends, they begin to look at their own problems as being small. What greater witness of God's love is there than for a free person to hear from a death-row inmate who has no complaints. Many of my friends say that if I can live happily here, knowing the state wishes to kill me, then surely they can live happily out there where they have the ability to change things.

I am broke, but not broken. That can be taken in many different ways, but I prefer to think of it this way: materially, I am a very poor man, but in blessings I have to be in the Howard Hughes category. I have a wonderful wife and three beautiful daughters. That's more than most inmates have, so naturally I feel blessed. But there's more. I have Christ in my heart and soul. With Him I have found I can triumph over all things. When I was in the free world, things would upset me and I would complain. Now, I don't allow things to upset me. I merely accept them for what they are. If it's within my power to change them, then I will; if not, then they're accepted as part of the life I must live.

My friends are true friends. They aren't people who will be gone as soon as the going gets rough. They love and accept me for who I am and I accept them for who they are. We share the words of our Lord and are united in His fellowship. In these people we have great treasures.

When Christ is allowed into your life, you cannot help but look at the world and its people in a different light. You may still do things wrong, but you're affected by that. You feel genuinely sorry for that wrong and before you know it, you're before the Lord in prayer asking for forgiveness. You tend to do more and more good things, and you feel better for this. Sometimes you sit and think, Hey, that was kind of nice of me, and it really felt good. It's a matter of laying up your treasures in Heaven.

Broke? Yeah, we're all broke. But with Christ we begin to see the things that really count. Our sinful thoughts and our reasons for complaining begin to fade. Think about it—how rich are you? Are you a complainer making all around you miserable? If so, give Christ a chance. You've already touched the bottom; with Him you can only go up.

These words are kind of hard to understand from a man facing the death penalty, aren't they? After all, what can I gain by living the rest of my life behind bars and then walking those final steps? Ever think of what it's like?

A week prior to that walk they take you away from the people you've lived with for the last few years. Big deal, huh? After all, they're just a bunch of murderers anyhow. Then you notice even the faces of the guards are different. Maybe none of those who knew you over the past years has enough in his heart to watch them prepare you for execution. Maybe he even sees a little good in you.

Sitting in that small cell with limited items around you, an uncomfortable feeling comes. This is it, they're going to fry me. Each day brings something new. Your attorneys tell you, "The governor can still commute your sentence; there's hope yet." But you know it's all a bunch of bull. I guess they're trying to solace their own hearts. After all, they did represent you and brought you this far; why shouldn't you believe them?

But as they shave your head, you begin to really believe it's all over. The night before you're scheduled to take that long walk, you begin to look over the last few years of life. What was it all about? Was it spent any different from the life that got you here in the first place? Or was it led the same way, taking advantage of whoever you could and looking out for number one?

And then you think of God. Is the Big Guy for real? Is there a heaven and hell? Is life all over for me now? Will I rest and just know nothing or will I have to spend forever more suffering worse than even now? You search desperately through your memories, reaching for anything to show you're worthy of going to heaven. Have you done anything good at all? Now you wonder if works will get you in heaven or if it takes something else. Man, why couldn't I have listened to those Holy Rollers when they used to come back and see me?

You remember the times you sat there and thought of just giving up your appeals. It was a heck of a shock to learn you weren't alone. I guess all of us have given it a thought or two. And the times you thought of committing suicide. Either we don't have any family or friends to help us or care about us and life doesn't seem worth living, or we have good support and it doesn't seem fair to put them through the pains of waiting for you to be killed. Either way we figure taking our own life is the best for everyone involved. Then people can get on with their own lives and we can forget everything.

Why didn't I kill myself? It probably comes down to the same thing you're thinking now. Is there a heaven and hell, where I am going; what if I've been wrong all these years and this Christian stuff is real?

I should have killed myself. Even if I did get a break, I'd still spend the rest of my life in this place. That's no life to live. Yeah, but at least it's life.

You go over it in your mind. I guess I didn't give up because while I'm alive there's always hope. Once they hit the switch, it's all over and there's no turning back. Maybe life in this place wouldn't have been so bad. Maybe I could have met someone, got some friends, and made life bearable. Heck, maybe I could even have worked on my time and gotten out one day. There are a lot of possibilities when you're alive, aren't there? The last few years weren't so bad. You wrote some letters; made some calls; you figure you brought a little happiness to someone.

The guards take you out of the death cell to let you eat your last meal with some people who have come to see you. You walk into the room and find it's not full of people, but there are a few present. As you look at the meal you kind of laugh. "McDonald's. Always loved it on the street." The people dare a little chuckle as if the noise will somehow break more than the silence. You sit down and look around at the faces.

Looking into the eyes of people who know they'll be here tomorrow and you won't is pretty unnerving. Then you notice, those eyes have tears in them. They're crying because of you. All this time and you thought you were all alone. These people care; even if you don't know each one of them, they still care about you.

If you were free, maybe you could hook up with one of them and have a real friend, somebody you could get to know as family. There you go again, thinking of what could happen if you had any life left to live. But it's all over, you're eating your last meal, and in a few short hours you're a dead man.

Too soon the meal is over and you're back in the cell. The guards are asking you to put a rubber diaper on. You know it's for real now. There's no hope.

The door is just down the hallway. You want to walk out like a man, but your legs are so weak. The guards give you help in walking— got to be on time, remember the paperwork.

You're sitting down and they've strapped a belt around your waist and tied your arms down. Now they've pulled your left pants leg up and are placing some type of electrode against your skin. They place them over various parts of your body and put the dead man's hat on your head. The clock is ticking and you can hear each movement. The warden is talking, trying to break the spell of death in the air. Everyone is uncomfortable.

He steps forward with a hood to place over your head and asks, "Is there anything you'd like to say?" You think about it again. Heaven and hell, which is it going to be for you? You shake your head, and the light vanishes with the hood. In your heart you begin to cry, Dear God, I know I haven't tried to believe in You and to be honest I really don't even know if it's all real or not. If You're there, please forgive me for the things I've done. Forgive me for the doubt I've always had. Don't let me go to hell, God, please don't let me go there. The warden sounds, "One minute. . . ."

Time seems to stand still. You continue to plead to God for life. The clock keeps ticking; how loud it is. "Thirty seconds, all clear." Your heart races, it's almost over. In a few moments you'll know all about heaven and hell.

The phone rings; it is the governor and he has commuted your sentence to live.

You sit there in disbelief. Maybe God is giving me time to learn about Him. Maybe he read my heart and knows how much I wanted to see if it was real or not. Maybe now I can know for sure.

As they take the straps from your body, you again think of giving up, of suicide. Then you see those faces, the people you didn't even know who shed tears for you. It's different now; this time you're going to search those people out. This time you're going to have friends and maybe even an adopted family. This time it's not only your feelings which count, but the feelings of those who love you, those you never knew existed.

You shake as you walk from the room. You shake because you're still scared. You shake because you realize there is a life ahead of you and that no matter what comes, you'll face it because when there's life there's hope. You begin the walk back and you know things are going to be all right.

You may live the rest of your life in prison, but you're going to live a life. The people around you can see a radiant glow about you. Even they can see that there's no giving up in you now. The people who were at your last meal come up and hug you. Tears begin to form in your eyes. You remember your worst day in prison, and it was this day. You remember your best day in prison and it was this day. I was dead, but now I have a chance to live, a chance to really learn about people and God.

And that's all it takes to keep going, a chance, "Thirty seconds, all clear . . ."

Part Two
Victims

19

Coretta Scott King
Widow of Martin Luther King, Jr.

I believe that the death penalty is unchristian, un-American, and uncon-stitutional. There is overwhelming statistical evidence that the death penalty is racist in its application, but even if the death penalty was not racist I would be firmly opposed to it because the death penalty makes irrevocable any possible miscarriage of justice. . . .

I also oppose the death penalty because state-sponsored executions set dehumanizing examples of brutality that only encourage violence. Al-lowing the state to kill its own citizens diminishes our humanity and sets a dangerous and sadistic precedent which is unworthy of a civilized society.

Although my husband was assassinated and my mother-in-law was murdered, I refuse to accept the cynical judgment that their killers de-serve to be executed. To do so would perpetuate the tragic cycle of violence that feeds on itself. It would be a disservice to all that my husband and his mother lived for and believed.

The death penalty adds to the suffering of the surviving family members and loved ones of victims and offenders alike. For them, revenge and retribution can never produce genuine healing. It can only deprive them of the opportunity for forgiveness and reconciliation that is needed for the healing process.

We call on all Americans of good will to join us in our movement to put an end to the shameful spectacle of government murdering its own people and to help us create the kind of society in which we can all take pride.

20

Senator Edward Kennedy

In my view, the death penalty violates the Eighth Amendment's prohibition against cruel and unusual punishment. It is true that the Supreme Court has not yet concluded that capital punishment is unconstitutional. But I hope that someday, the Court will recognize that the death penalty is cruel and unusual. Government should not have the power to put a human to death. No matter how brutal the crime a person has committed, the infliction of death at the hands of government brutalizes our society.

I also oppose the death penalty because of the likelihood that innocent people will be executed. No system of justice, however wise or resourceful its judges and juries may be, can eliminate this possibility. That is a risk we can take when the punishment is imprisonment, because jailed defendants can always be set free when their innocence is proved. But that is a burden we cannot accept when the punishment is death.

Moreover, there is no convincing evidence that the death penalty deters crime. True, some statistical studies purport to show a marginal deterrent effect. But for every study claiming deterrence, there are other, more convincing, studies demonstrating that the death penalty is not a deterrent to violent crimes.

Some of the most convincing evidence is found in the experience of other western democracies. Not one of these countries has capital punishment for peacetime crimes, and yet every one of them has a murder rate less than half that of the United States.

Finally, our long experience with capital punishment demonstrates that it is applied in an arbitrary and discriminatory manner. For all of these reasons, I oppose the death penalty.

21

SueZann Bosler

Father Was Murdered

My father was a minister, and so we were used to people knocking on the door all the time. Some needed a place to sleep, others needed money for food. On December 22, 1986, we came home after Christmas shopping and unloaded the car. We were getting ready to go up north to visit family, and we were happy just knowing we would be seeing our relatives for the Christmas holidays. I was twenty-four years old and was living with my father at the time.

My father sat down in the living room to read. He loved reading and would do it every chance he got. I took a shower and was still in my robe and underwear putting on my makeup when I heard the doorbell ring. Suddenly, I heard my dad making these weird noises and I knew that something was wrong, so I ran out of the bathroom to see what had happened. As soon as my dad had opened the door, this black boy lunged forward and began stabbing him in the chest, over and over. He shoved my father inside, stepped into the living room, turned around, and locked the door behind him. When I ran out, I saw my dad holding himself up on the kitchen doorway. The boy ran to where he was and began stabbing him again. I must have screamed because he turned and looked at me.

Instinctively, I ran to protect my father instead of running away. Everything was happening so fast. As I approached, he tried to stab me in the chest, but I swerved to the left, and the knife stuck in my back. He kept on stabbing me in the back until he knocked me down on the kitchen floor. I could see my father was trying to get up on his knees to help me but the boy turned around and began stabbing my father in the back again. Over and over I saw the knive hit its mark in my father's body. I felt fear and wanted to scream but nothing came out of my mouth.

I finally made it up on my feet and tried to help my dad again, but by then he had collapsed. The guy backed me into the living room. We were in an eye lock. He had the knife up by his head, while I kept on looking into his eyes. I was in a state of shock wondering if this was really happening. Then, as if in slow motion, I saw the knife coming toward my face. He wanted to stab me in the face but I turned my head to the right and the knife went into the back of my head. He pulled it out and stuck it in again. I fell down on the floor because I had lost so much blood. I didn't lose consciousness but I was weak. I could feel him standing above me to see if I was alive, so unconsciously I held my breath to pretend I was dead. I don't even know why I did that, but it saved my life. He turned away and walked into the bedroom, and I could hear him searching. All this time he never said a word, just kind of mumbled now and then.

I was thinking that maybe I could run out and get help. But I was afraid that he might come back too soon and catch me trying to get out. He came back to the living room because he hadn't been able to find anything of value in my room and began to pace back and forth behind me. Next he ran into my sister's room. My dad had already sent her to college so there wasn't anything in there.

Then I heard him in the kitchen turning my purse upside down, and my keys falling to the floor. When he reentered the living room, he was so mad he threw a chair over my body. He then went into my dad's room to change his shirt. He had so much blood on his own shirt that he took one of my fathers. While he had been stabbing my father and me, he had cut his own hand. His finger prints were found all over the place and this helped in convicting him during the trial.

When he came back out he was still really upset. He must have seen me breathe because he came over to me, pulled down my underwear, and started hitting me. I was praying real hard. I knew I was going to go to heaven, but I told the Lord, "You know I'm not going to just lay here and let him rape me. I'm going to fight and he'll have to stab me until I die." I just kept praying to God.

Then as suddenly as it started, it stopped. He didn't do anything else to me, but just went out the front door. I could see my father lying on the floor in a pool of blood, and I watched his shoulders rise and fall and then collapse. I prayed for him not to be dead. As the boy opened the door, he jammed it against my father's body. This made me so mad; it was really upsetting to me to see the door hit my father's body. Finally, when I saw him lock the door and leave, I tried to get up. It took a little while because I had lost so much blood and was weak.

I went straight to the phone. I didn't go to my father because I wanted to get help for him. I dialed the operator and she connected me with 911. The dispatcher treated me like I was a prank phone caller. I told him my address five or six times and that I and my father had been stabbed. I finally hung up and dialed it again and got a different dispatcher. I was so upset by this time that I hardly knew what I was doing. This dispatcher sent the police and ambulance and kept me on the phone talking until help arrived. As soon as the police got there and I knew we were safe, I fell unconscious.

The police didn't think I was going to live, so they had a helicopter take me to Jacksonville hospital. A detective rode with me because they thought I was going to die on the way and they wanted to see if I could give them some information on who had committed the crime.

This all happened about two in the afternoon, in the middle of the day, but it wasn't until midnight that I was taken into surgery. When the knife went into my head, the tip of it went into my brain. They had to take pieces of flesh out that had been mangled in there. When I woke up, I asked everyone about my father. The doctors and nurses lied to me because they thought I would die if I knew my dad had been killed. For a week they didn't tell me the truth until I became a little stronger.

Finally a week later I was strong enough, and I then learned that my dad had died from the attack. I was in the hospital for a month before I came home. In the meantime the police brought in a bunch of pictures for me to look at to see if I could recognize any of them. I picked the boy out immediately who had killed my father and wounded me so badly.

He was caught a week later and held for trial. When I was in the courthouse, waiting to testify, I noticed a lady that I had gone to beauty school with. It turned out she was the boy's aunt. I thought, what a small world it is that this lady I had known would have a nephew who would one day murder my dad.

After I testified at the trial, I felt sorry for this boy, whose name is James Campbell. I was angry at what he had done, but still I felt sorry. At that time it was harder to deal with my anger, but as time went on it became easier. I do not hate this boy for what he did, but I haven't come to love him yet. I'm still dealing with those feelings. If I hated him and wanted him dead, it would destroy not only him, but also me.

In the sentencing part of the trial, I went before the jurors and asked them not to give him the death sentence. I looked right into James Campbell's eyes and said, "You're life is as valuable to God as anyone's." I was able to plead for his life, and as a result he didn't get the death sentence.

I feel stronger for doing that. I remembered that one time my father told me if anything bad were to happen to him, he didn't want anyone to get the death penalty for it. This conversation came back to me during the trial and I had to ask for James's life because this is what my father would have wanted me to do.

I feel that I made the right decision in what I did. I still have medical problems and I can't do the things I used to be able to do. I still have a lot of pain, but it's getting better as time goes on.

I feel the death penalty is wrong. I hear a lot of people talking about killing someone who has harmed someone in their families. I can't imagine how this would make that person happy. If they were to kill James Campbell, it wouldn't bring my father back. He is gone and nothing will bring him back in this life. People should think about that, because it's not going to do any good to kill someone for killing someone else, and I can't see how it would make them feel any better about it.

I have to look into the present and the future and go on with my life. I attend talk shows and speak out against the death penalty because I feel it's wrong. I don't ask people to believe as I do, but I ask that they give me the respect to listen to my views.

I feel in many ways this tragedy could have been prevented. James had been abused as a child, and he was raised in a society where he lived with people who did drugs. What else did he learn? To me these things have a lot to do with it. I want these people to stay in jail but I also want them to get the help they need: counseling, education, job training, so they'll have a trade if they ever get out of prison. I never felt the need for revenge and I believe it's my deep love and faith in Jesus that has carried me through this tragedy.

22

Camille Bell

Son Was the Fourth Child Killed
in the Atlanta Child Murders

I grew up in Pennsylvania and moved to Atlanta in 1967 with the Civil Rights movement. I met my husband through the Student Nonviolent Coordinating Committee (SNCC). They were the people who organized the original freedom rides, and we were both members. They dissolved in the '70s.

I married and we had four children, Maria, Johnnathan, Tonia, and Yusuf. I lived in the intercity neighborhood of Atlanta as it was close to everything. My husband and I broke up after ten years of marriage, and it was hard raising the four children.

The day my son disappeared was a normal day. Yusuf had been outside playing with the other kids, when he came running in and asked if he could go to the store for the lady who lived a couple of doors down. This wasn't unusual for him to do, to go to the store for one or the other of the neighbors. I gave my permission and he left for the store. He went to the store for her and after leaving to come home, it seems he just sort of disappeared off the face of the earth. The store clerk remembered him being there because she had kidded him about buying snuff.

When he hadn't gotten back in an hour, another neighbor and I walked back up to the store to look for him. We didn't see him and we asked a number of people if they remembered seeing him there.

They hadn't so we came back to the house.

I called the police because Yusuf was the type of boy who would go to the store and come right back. He was a very responsible type of kid who would do as he was told and not fool around. Had he wanted to go somewhere else, Yusuf would have come home and asked me.

Now if Johnnathan had gone to the store, I wouldn't have worried after an hour because Johnnathan never comes right back when he's sent on an errand. He's the kind of boy who would get sidetracked by friends, a football game, or anything else that might catch his fancy. So it would have taken a few hours of his being missing before I would have even thought to call the police.

The policeman who came to investigate the disappearance had seen Yusuf and he remembered him because it had been such a hot day. The temperature was in the nineties and the police department had to start wearing their winter uniforms that day. It was in October and usually it had cooled off by that time, but not this year. He noticed Yusuf walking down the street swinging a stick. He didn't have on shoes or a shirt and so the policeman had thought to himself that this little kid sure looked comfortable and cool. That's why he remembered seeing him.

The policeman took the report and told us that he'd keep watch as he was on patrol. He wasn't able to file the report until 24 hours after a disappearance of anyone over seven years of age. The thought behind this was that if the child had run away or wandered off, perhaps he would come back on his own and wouldn't get a juvenile record.

Unfortunately in this case and in many others, this rule was a problem because nobody would start to look for a missing child until he had been missing for 24 hours.

After several days, Yusuf had not come back, so we contacted different people because the police department didn't have the man power to search. I'm not saying the people in missing persons didn't do all they could do, but there were only four people on missing persons. They had to handle all the crimes against children in Atlanta along with the missing persons.

Because of the murders in Atlanta, and the various other murders around the country, the law on missing children was changed. From the efforts of the mothers of those killed, and John Walsh's efforts, things began to happen. They worked together with the federal government to get the Missing Children's Act passed.

The Missing Children's Act eliminates the waiting period across the country. It allows parents to add their children's names to a national computor system, and people begin to search for the child almost immediately.

I guess if you counted the children who were murdered during this time, Yusuf was probably the fourth. But he was the first to get enough publicity to make the general public aware that someone was missing. Two bodies of murdered children had been found but it only rated a couple of lines in the newspaper, way in the back. Then another child was found dead while Yusuf was missing. Besides the police, few people knew these kids were missing because there hadn't been any news coverage, and the missing children were black and also poor, so this made them not very important to the police.

I felt like my son was alive, that whoever had kidnapped him would bring him back to me. I promised them if they would just bring my son back I wouldn't press charges. All I wanted was my son safe and sound. I didn't hear from the kidnapper and time went on. It was a pretty rough time and we prayed that Yusuf would be found alive. But eighteen days after he disappeared, they found his body in an abandoned school that should have been boarded up but wasn't, about a mile from my house.

When the detective came and told me that Yusuf was dead, I went into shock. I couldn't believe that I wouldn't see my son again. My neighbor and friend was with me and she told me that I would have to make it through this thing and she would be there with me.

We got through the funeral and I found myself doing things automatically. I didn't realize that I was even doing them at the time as I was still in shock and didn't want to believe that my Yusuf would never put his arms around my neck and kiss me. I didn't want to believe that I would never see him again. I didn't want to face it but I had to. I don't know what I would have done without my friend Sarah. She was there for me during all this time.

A couple of months later, other children started disappearing in Atlanta, so I got together with a number of the parents. We tried to figure out what was going on, and we created a support group for all of us. We didn't get help from the police department or see any investigations being done. We had to go to the police department and tell them what was going on. We told them that we as parents felt the murders might be connected and we felt a task force should be put together. We never got any of that.

The police treated our children's murders as if they were misdemeanors because our children were poor, and we were black. They chose to ignore the murders of those people they didn't feel were important. The police department just didn't respond. Their attitude confused me because the powers that be were also black. I had to feel that the mayor of Atlanta cared about our children; after all, he was black too. But he didn't.

In a lot of ways I felt betrayed by the people that I had helped into office. But along the way I learned that power corrupts, no matter what color you are. Finally, there were many, many children missing and dead. People started asking why nothing was being done about these children being killed. Why weren't the police out there looking and having media coverage? The authorities are quick to impose the death penalty on poor blacks who commit crimes, but when the same poor blacks become victims, no one bothers to investigate. If my kid had been the one who went to the store and killed somebody, they'd have wanted to kill him, but because he was a victim snatched off the streets, they didn't even want to investigate.

The families of the children who had been murdered set up their own investigations. We couldn't depend on the police, so we hired our own investigators. And from that investigation, we have a number of names of people who are more logical suspects than Wayne Williams, whom the police arrested for the murders. In some cases, we practically know who the killers are and so do the police. It isn't Wayne Williams.

I believe that Wayne is young and dumb, and so he believed that he couldn't be convicted of the murders if he was innocent. When they started to come down on him, instead of doing what any normal person would do, like saying he wanted to see his lawyer, he called a press conference. He did a lot of dumb things and that convicted him.

I have always been against capital punishment in any form. I feel it is wrong in every case. None of us has the right to take the life of another human being, because if we're wrong, we can't give back the life we took. I don't necessarily think of killing someone as punishment. When a person is dead, you're no longer punishing him. You're punishing only the people who love the person you've sentenced to die. That being the case, why would I want to have any mother go through what was hurting me so much? So when I think of capital punishment, I have to think of the families of those you want to kill, because those are the people you punish when you kill. If a person ends up in prison and has to live each day just trying to survive, he will think of why he is there. That, in my opinion, is punishment.

I feel that the person who killed my son is still free today. I don't seek revenge in the way most people probably think I would. I don't want the person who murdered my child to be killed, but that doesn't mean I don't want him punished. If you can't give me back my child in life, don't kill in his name.

23

Marietta Jaeger
Daughter Was Murdered

When my seven-year-old daughter was kidnapped, raped, and murdered, I relied on my faith to get me through it. God continues to redeem Susie's suffering in a lot of ways and I'm grateful for that. When I hear other stories I think, "I couldn't get through that, but I guess God gives us the strength to go on in our own situation. I guess that's the best we can hope for."

Susie was abducted from her tent during the night while my family and I were on a camping vacation in Montana. We never heard anything unusual that night and it wasn't until morning that we realized she was gone.

In the beginning I felt hatred for whoever had taken my child. I ran the whole gamut of rage, heartbreak, and depression. I would have strangled this man with my bare hands with a big smile on my face. But my Christian upbringing had taught me that forgiveness wasn't an option, but a mandate. I really struggled with that and I had my wrestling match with God. But He had laid a good foundation in me, and I knew the principles I would be accountable for, so in the end I surrendered to Him.

A whole year went by without our knowing whether Susie was alive or dead. Then exactly a year later, on the anniversary of her abduction, the kidnapper called me. The effect of the sound of his voice in my ears was to fill me with concern and compassion for him, even though I was utterly desperate for word of where my child was. He called me in response to a newspaper article that had been printed that day. I had given an interview, in which I had said that I really felt concern for the kidnapper and would give anything for the chance to talk to him. I feared that I'd never get the opportunity. He was challenged by that. He had gone for a whole year and felt no one knew who he was, so in a very clever way, he managed to make a telephone call to me.

Evidently, it was important to him that he make the call to me one year later to the minute, right in the middle of the night, just at the time he had taken her out of the tent. But he wasn't counting on what my faith in God had done for me. He was taken aback by my attitude, and he began to calm down and ended up staying on the phone for over an hour. In that environment of concern and compassion, he inadvertently let down his guard and revealed a great deal about himself. In the end he broke down and cried.

I taped that whole conversation, again a sign that God was present. We had a tape recorder connected to the phone in the hope that he would call us. He had made calls to other people demanding ransom for her. I had made up my mind to believe that she was still alive until such a time that I would have to believe otherwise. When the FBI listened to the tape, they were able to identify him by means of what he had said.

I met him a couple of times before he was arrested for the crime. The FBI asked me if I would agree to come to Montana to talk to him in the hope that he would break down and admit to the killing of my daughter and other murders he was suspected of committing. He agreed to a meeting because he was so sure that no one was going to pin anything on him.

The FBI took me there and I talked to him three different times. He had good control over his emotions and didn't break down. The first time I saw him, I was struck by his eyes. They were jet black and appeared to have no bottom. I felt the presence of evil and mental illness in him although he spoke very lucidly, and was very polite to me. I could just tell by looking into his eyes that this boy was not normal. He was a very sick young man. It was hard for me to talk to him and I remember at one point I grabbed his hand and didn't want to let go until he told me where my little girl was. But in the end I had to just let go and give him to God.

A week after our conversations, he called me again. In that conversation, he completely incriminated himself. I taped that conversation also and it was concrete proof that the FBI could use in court, and that brought about his arrest.

Once incarcerated, his home was searched and they found evidence to prove him guilty. As part of his mental illness, he kept parts of his victims in the freezer. He was a very, very sick young man. He had maintained his innocence right along and had even passed a polygraph and the truth serum test.

Confronted by the evidence and reminded by the FBI who were in charge of the investigation that the death penalty would be sought if he didn't admit to the kidnapping, he admitted the crimes. At that time in Montana they used the death penalty and he was offered a chance of psychiatric help and a life sentence if he would confess to the murder. That had been my prayer for him, and I had asked the FBI to offer him that instead of the death penalty. He told police where other bodies of his murder victims were buried in that district. He would not admit to those in other areas where the death penalty was in effect. After giving his confession, he hanged himself in the jail cell.

When he was first arrested, everyone in his neighborhood was shocked to think that he was even suspected of being the murderer. He seemed like the average kid next door. There had been a few outbursts of violence in his youth, but no one could see that he needed psychiatric help.

Initially I had struggled with the desire for revenge, but by the time he was arrested, I was convinced that the only healthy response was for me to forgive him. I have to say that meeting other parents of victims only confirms my own experiences.

I see again and again how people perceive their kind of justice by seeing the offender executed. In the end when it's all over and done with, they are left empty, dissatisfied, and unhealed. Those who retain an attitude of vindictiveness are done in by their own lack of forgiveness. They become tormented, embittered, and very unhappy people, and the quality of their lives is greatly diminished.

I gave God permission to change my heart and I tried to do what I could to facilitate that change. For me that meant that, however I felt about this man, in God's eyes he was just as precious as my little girl was. Even though he wasn't behaving as such, he was indeed a son of God. And as such that meant he was worthy of dignity. Rather than use the very derogatory terms that came to mind when I thought of him, I had to speak of him with respect.

I prayed for him every day, which was not an easy thing to do in the beginning because I didn't want anything good to happen to this guy. I disciplined myself to do it and the more I did it, the easier it became. I continued to ask God to help me and give me guidance to change my heart.

I think the concept of capital punishment violates the mandate of forgiveness that we as people of God will be held accountable for. I think the capacity for compassion and forgiveness is what sets us apart from the rest of creation.

As an alternative, mandatory life in prison provides for the protection of society and yet it still does not deny the criminal the possibility of repentance and rehabilitation. Most importantly, it makes it impossible for the execution of an innocent person. People will say it's a matter of justice for the victim's family. I say that no amount of retaliatory deaths will compensate me for the value of my daughter's life, nor will they restore her to my arms. To say that the death of anyone is just retribution is to insult the worth of our loved ones. You can't put that kind of price on their lives.

I think the worst way I could have memorialized my little girl, whose life was a gift of joy and beauty and goodness, would have been to kill somebody in her name. That for me violates the beauty of her life. The best way is not to inflict death but to know that all life is sacred.

By the time Susie's killer was convicted, I had finally come to understand that God's idea of justice was not punishment but restoration. I am a Christian and Christians believe that Jesus is the word of God. If I look at the life of Jesus, I see that He did not come to destroy, punish, or put to death. He came to reconcile us and to restore to us the life that had been lost.

That was what I wanted for this young man who had taken my daughter and killed her, despite the fact that he admitted to the rape, strangulation death, and decapitation of my little girl, as well as to the murder of an eighteen-year-old girl and two young boys in separate instances. That was the miracle that God worked in me in that whole fifteen months.

Killing those on death row is just premeditated murder. When I started getting into the death-penalty issue, I was amazed to find out that innocent people have been murdered. I've known of cases where the man driving the car during a crime was given the death sentence but the one who committed the murder got life. I can't see how this can be a fair punishment. It's just so arbitrarily administered. That alone should demonstrate that it can't be a just resolution to a situation.

In the state of Montana, where my little girl was killed, the death penalty was in effect. This did not deter the man who killed my little girl in the least, and he had taken the lives of lots of other children also. Likewise, Ted Bundy committed most of his crimes in states that used the death penalty and it sure didn't deter him either.

Two years ago capital-punishment advocates tried to instate the death penalty in Michigan where we live. We've never had the death penalty since Michigan became a state, and there was a big campaign going on, so I got very involved. I went around and talked to people about it. Polls around the state found that 70 or 80 percent of the citizens wanted the death penalty. They thought it was going to make a difference in the crime rate. But then when you start trying to educate people, you realize they perceive it in a wholly different way. Their gut-level reaction is that the threat of death might deter them if they were ever tempted to kill someone. Therefore, they assume everyone would feel the same way.

The best tool we have is to educate people about the death penalty, to make them understand the facts about how it is administered. We also need to let them know that it's more expensive to execute someone than life in prison.

I don't know why God allows these things to happen. I don't think He makes them happen, and maybe He doesn't want to renege on His gift of choices that He gives to us. I don't understand. I just simply decided to believe that even though I can't see it, hear it, feel it, or understand it, God loves me, and that this is not God's perfect world. He will redeem all the suffering and death. That's what I hold on to.

24

Sam Sheppard, Jr.

Mother Was Murdered

I was seven years old when my mother was murdered and it was a pretty confusing time in my life. She was found beaten to death in her bedroom of our home in Bay Village, Ohio. My father was a doctor and was arrested for the murder. It was pretty unbelievable and I remember the house being full of strangers that day and flashbulbs going off as I sat on the steps.

I was sent to summer camp so I wasn't directly in the limelight for the summer months until I was brought back for questioning. I remember the authorities being abusive and they even took my fingerprints as if I had something to do with it. That was a horrible experience for me and I'll never forget that. The detectives weren't even tactful about the fact that I had just lost my mother nor did they use good judgment in questioning me.

When I went back to school, I remember the kids making fun of me and saying my dad was a murderer. He hadn't stood trial yet and already they were saying cruel things to me. I felt like an outcast, the way people treated me.

My father's trial went on through October, November, and December of 1954 and the prosecution asked for the death penalty. He was convicted of second-degree murder and was front-page news every day. In that quiet town, there was a lot of fascination with the murder of a pregnant woman of the local doctor. Every newspaper across the country ran the story, and there was so much publicity it's no wonder my father didn't get a fair trial. It was this publicity that caused the Supreme Court to overturn his sentence ten years later saying that the trial had been conducted in a carnival atmosphere. The lies that were told in the newspapers led to my father's conviction; it was a trial by press and the press was responsible for putting my father away and, frankly, killing him.

After the trial I was taken to live with my father's older brother, Dr. Stephen Sheppard and his wife, Betty. I was to stay with them for the next ten years of my life. Uncle Steve is a very strong person and I credit him with holding our family together.

Over the years I was always known as the son of a convicted murderer. I was the outsider all the time. For the first year my father wouldn't let my grandmother or me come to visit. He was so sure that they would find him innocent and release him. He just didn't want us to see him in that kind of atmosphere. Finally, we were allowed to visit the prison and once a month we would see my father. It was a hard time, our visits. We couldn't hug each other or anything. All we could do was shake hands and sit across from each other at a picnic table. It would hurt to see him in that kind of place and I longed to run to him and have him hug me like before. As we would visit, I remembered the days when dad lived home with me. We would play basketball together in the driveway of our home and had a lot of fun, but now we were forced to visit once a month in the prison.

My father had it rough in prison; his life was threatened more than once and it was hard to stay alive in there. You didn't know who your friends were, so you had no close friends, but dad was a hell of a man and made it through the years.

My parents may have had some problems but they loved each other. My dad never killed her. He was released in 1964 when the U.S. District Judge Carl A. Weinman ruled that prejudicial publicity had made the first trial a mockery of justice. Once he was out, he married a woman who he had been corresponding with for years, and I went to live with them.

For two more years the case went through the federal courts and I remember my father keeping a bag beside the front door waiting to go back to prison. Finally, the Supreme Court upheld Weinman in 1966 and ordered a new trial. My father got F. Lee Bailey to represent him and he was acquitted. After that time, he couldn't find any meaningful work and had a hard time getting along socially. He died four years later.

I couldn't even attend his funeral because of the press. They had their cameras going until they lowered him into the ground. After the funeral, I moved east.

I have had a difficult time during the years and I couldn't talk about the case as it was too painful a subject. I saw a video one time in a store near my home about my father called "Guilty Or Innocent: The Sam Sheppard Case."

I became interested in capital punishment about that time. My father could have received the death sentence and he was innocent of the crime. They wanted to execute him and if he'd received the death sentence in Ohio in 1954, he would have been executed in a year. I frankly don't think I could have survived that.

The first time I spoke publically about my father's case was at a rally on the steps of the statehouse in Albany, N.Y., in support of Governor Mario Cuomo's veto of a capital punishment bill. Kerry Kennedy, a daughter of Robert Kennedy, also spoke and a letter was read from Coretta Scott King, widow of Martin Luther King.

I felt it was time for me to speak out. It's been thirty-five years and this seems like something I should do. If there's anti-penalty work to be done, I will be there.

I am working on a book on my father and the whole case. I have a lot of unpublished letters including love letters from my father to my mother and a lot of letters from my father to Ariane, his second wife.

Recently a man has been arrested for the murder of an elderly woman and forging her will with the help of his long time-friend. Richard Eberling was a handyman at our home at the time my mother was killed. Police found his blood in our home. He said he had cut his hand on a screen window, and that he hadn't been the one to kill my mother. He said he knew the circumstances of her death but wasn't going to say anything more. I feel that he is a likely suspect in the case and we're trying to get the case reopened. At this point the authorities are still dragging their feet and do not want to open up the investigation again.

I'm going back to Ohio for the first time in eighteen years and will be doing TV and newspaper interviews. People do not perceive my father's trial as a mistrial, so we need to communicate that and also urge them to open the case if at all possible. The county prosecutor and others have made outrageous, wrongful statements about the case. I'm a member of an organization called Solace, made up of family members of crime victims who oppose the death penalty, and I'm active in Amnesty International and the National Coalition Against the Death Penalty. I write a little music and poetry, and I do volunteer work at the shelter for the homeless.

I'm around, I'm together, and I'm relatively happy. I have my own base in life and I have my own platform. I'm Samuel Reese Sheppard. I'm no longer just Sam Sheppard's kid.

25

Six Accounts of Wrongly Convicted Prisoners On Death Row

Shirley Dicks

Timothy Hennis

Timothy Hennis was sentenced in 1986 to die in the electric chair in North Carolina for the murder of a woman and two of her daughters. The bodies of the murder victims were found on May 12, 1985, with stab wounds and cut throats in their home. Hennis claimed he was innocent to the crime. He told investigators that he had met the slain woman when he answered an advertisement seeking a home for the family's pet English setter. The jury returned the death sentence after three hours of deliberation.

Assistant District Attorney William Van Story IV said he didn't believe legal errors had been committed during the trial that could lead to a reversal on appeal. He said it would be difficult to determine what factors in the circumstantial case led the jurors to think that Hennis was guilty. The jury obviously believed the witness Patrick Cone, who said he saw Hennis walking out of the driveway around 3:30 P.M. that day. The jurors were also persuaded by the testimony of Lucille Cook, who said Hennis "looks like" a man she saw using an automatic teller machine on May 11, when Mrs. Eastburn's (one of the victims) bank card was used to withdraw $150.

For three years Hennis sat on death row until the Supreme Court ordered a new trial because the state's use of the victim's photographs may have inflamed the jury.

Charlotte Kirby, a newspaper carrier, came forward to testify at the new trial. She had seen a man walking across the yard the day of the murder. She later saw this same man at a fast-food restaurant when she had finished delivering the papers. She said she saw a light-colored van near the Eastburn's driveway. She told the jury that the man she had seen was about 5′ 7″ with a medium build and was wearing a toboggan hat and carrying a green laundry bag over his shoulder.

When Hennis's picture was put in the paper after his arrest, it did not look like the man she had seen. A friend urged her to come forward and tell the truth about what she had seen. She said she didn't because about that time she began getting threatening calls. "I thought if I didn't say anything, Mr. Hennis would spend some time in jail, and the man would come forward," she said.

It took the jury two hours before declaring Hennis not guilty, and he walked out of the Hanover County Courthouse a free man. As the jury read the verdict, members of Hennis's family burst into tears and closed their eyes. Hennis said he planned to report to Fort Bragg and expects to have to go to Fort Knox, Kentucky to clear up his army status.

During the original trial, the jury deliberated in the case while attorneys held a hearing on a defense motion to dismiss the case based on a defense allegation that the prosecution withheld documents and witnesses that could have aided Hennis. That hearing was halted when the jury announced it had reached a verdict. Defense attorneys said prosecutors ignored trial rules by failing to tell the defense about witnesses and documents that could have aided his defense. The defense attorneys focused much of their argument on John Andrew Raupach, who was interviewed by a prosecutor and three investigators while Hennis was on trial.

Hennis's attorneys said eyewitnesses in the case could have mistaken Hennis for Raupach. They said that under rules of discovery, prosecutors should have told them about Raupach. Van Story, the assistant DA, testified that he was not obligated to tell the defense because Raupach was not considered a suspect.

After the second trial, jurors said that Raupach's presence in the Eastburn neighborhood caused them to doubt that Hennis was the man seen on the night of the slayings. The defense motion states prosecutors did not provide the defense with other information potentially helpful to Hennis in time for effective use, including: photographs of a shoeprint found in the investigation which could have determined the shoe size of the assailant; details of head and pubic hairs found in the Eastburn house which did not match those of Hennis or any of the Eastburn family; a Fort Bragg crime-prevention checklist that strongly supported the defendant's alibi; the name of Ilsa Peabody, one of Eastburn's neighbors who testified that she saw Hennis at the Eastburn house a day before the murders; details about another neighbor of the Eastburns rumored to have argued with Mrs. Eastburn in front of the Winn Dixie store.

Investigators testified that they interviewed Raupach, and he told them he often walked home from his job. Raupach also told them he frequently wore corduroy pants at work and a dark Members Only jacket and a beret, and carried a knapsack over his shoulder. He told officers he had a collection of knives and read survival books and the mercenary magazine *Soldier of Fortune.*

It was noted that bloody corduroylike impressions were found on bed clothes in Mrs. Eastburn's bedroom. Also, Hennis and Raupach looked alike in height, weight, and hair color. Van Story said Raupach offered nothing that offset evidence of Hennis's guilt or exonerated Hennis. He said Raupach had an alibi regarding his whereabouts at the times Mrs. Eastburn's stolen bank card was used.

Detective Watts testified that on the night before Van Story interviewed Raupach, the youth gave authorities his jacket and knapsack. Watts said he put them in the trunk of his car without testing them for a possible connection to the murders. He also said he made no report of having the items in his possession.

Jurors said reasonable doubt led them to acquit Timothy Baily Hennis on murder and rape charge. "I don't feel like he did it," said juror Joseph Corbett. "I think he got a fair trial, and he got what he deserved."

Mrs. McDowell, another juror, said, "We kept coming back to the idea that Hennis didn't have to prove his innocence; the state had to prove his guilt, and the state couldn't prove his guilt. They could never put him inside the Eastburn house on the night of the slayings."

The jurors all sympthized with Gary Eastburn, the husband and father of the victims. Mrs. McDowell said, "I cried with him, and hope to God the murderer is found and punished for what he did to the family. But I hope they get the right man, and I don't think Hennis is the right man."

Randall Dale Adams

On Thanksgiving weekend in 1976, a police officer was gunned down and a manhunt ensued. Randall Dale Adams was convicted of the murder and sent to death row. His ordeal began when sixteen-year-old David Harris offered him a ride after Randall's car broke down.

They spent the day together and Adams claims that Harris dropped him off at his motel room around 10 P.M. Harris testified that they left a drive-in around midnight with Adams driving the car. He said police officer Robert Wood pulled their car over and Adams pulled out a gun and fired five shots into the officer. (It was later learned that Harris had previously stolen the weapon.)

Police questioned Harris when friends of his said he had been talking about killing a police officer. Still the police believed him when he said Adams did the killing. It took only six months before Adams was tried and convicted of the murder and sentenced to die in Texas.

It wasn't until 1985 that Errol Morris stumbled upon Adams's story while researching a documentary film about psychiatrist Dr. James Grigson, who testifies in death-penalty cases. In its zeal to help Morris, the Dallas district attorney's office turned over the records from Adams's trial. What Morris found in the prosecutors files shocked him. The slain officer's partner had told police at first that it was too dark and the windows were too dirty to see who had committed the murder. Then she testified that the killer had bushy hair like Adams. The prosecution argued that the defense could not cross-examine her because she was traveling; she was in fact staying at a motel in Dallas. She finally revealed to Morris that she had failed to pick Adams out of a lineup.

Morris decided that instead of making Dr. James Grigson the subject of his documentary, he would tell Randall Adams's story. He called the film "The Thin Blue Line." It has won two major film awards and helped Adams to win his freedom.

All the evidence pointed to Harris. Both the car and the pistol had been stolen by Harris and he had been in trouble before. Still, the prosecution bought his story. Adams's attorney, Randy Schaffer, contends that Harris supplied two things the prosecution wanted: an eyewitness (Harris) and someone to execute (Adams). Harris was too young for the death penalty.

Adams got a major break when Schaffer took his case in 1982 for expenses only. Then Morris began filming in 1985. The investigating officers sat before him in their best suits, preening for the camera, as did two prosecution witnesses whose stories fell apart. Most chilling of all, Harris all but confessed, saying to Morris, "I'm the one who knows" Adams is innocent.

On March 1, an appellate court unanimously threw out Adams's conviction, finding that the state was guilty of suppressing evidence favorable to Adams, deceiving the trial court, and knowingly using perjured testimony.

Adams was released and flew home to Ohio where his mother and family and friends were gathered. The next day his sister threw a party. Adams, now 40, seems to have made his peace with his jailers, knowing that to pursue revenge could poison his future happiness. He has learned to think the worst and hope for the least.

Doug Mulder, the former Dallas prosecutor who wronged him, is shielded by law from suits by convicts. But cases like Adams's leave a residue of uneasiness; if the Supreme Court had not reversed the death sentence, and if a filmmaker had not stumbled onto suppressed evidence in locked and forgotten files, Adams would have been dead long ago.

James Richardson

For twenty-one years James Richardson was in prison. He had been convicted of killing his seven children in 1967. The six girls and one boy began convulsing not long after eating lunch at their home in Arcadia, Florida. By the next morning, all of them were dead, poisoned by a potent insecticide.

The prosecution contended that Richardson, an illiterate farm worker, had killed his family to collect insurance. Last year his lawyers petitioned the court to overturn the conviction by claiming that prosecutors knowingly used perjured testimony and withheld evidence. A special investigation followed and Governor Martinez appointed a judge to decide if Richardson should be released.

The documents that Richardson's attorneys relied on paint a damaging picture of the original proceedings. For one thing, an insurance agent had explained to investigators that the children were not insured. The prosecution had evidence that completely refuted an insurance motive, but the insurance agent's statements were never furnished to the defense.

Who did poison the children if Richardson did not? Some believe it was the babysitter who served the children lunch that day. Betsy Reese, who served time for shooting her husband, was believed to be angry at Richardson because he had introduced her husband to his cousin, and the two reportedly ran off together.

Last year affidavits from two nursing-home attendants were drafted. The women said that Reese had confessed to the crime when she was lucid. Reese, now 67, and in the advanced stages of Alzheimer's disease, is no longer competent to stand trial.

Richardson believes he has made good use of his time in prison. He was sentenced to die, but that sentence was eventually overturned to twenty-five years. He learned to read and later got a graduate equivalency degree. "It's a terrible feeling knowing I could have died for something I didn't do, but then I tell myself that if I die, I would be going home to my children."

John Henry Knapp

Knapp was convicted in two separate trials of the arson murder of his two children. Only after a federal court stayed Knapp's execution was new evidence discovered supporting Knapp's claim of innocence. Knapp sought a second round of review in state court and was given a new trial based on new scientific evidence, not available at the time of his original trials. The evidence showed that the fire was actually started by the children. The state dropped all charges and the case was dismissed in 1987.

Henry Drake

Both Drake and a codefendant, William Campbell, were convicted and sentenced to death for the murder of a barbershop owner in 1975. A volunteer lawyer who took Drake's appeal in 1979 discovered that

Campbell, the sole witness against Drake, had recanted his testimony and admitted that he alone committed the murder. But Campbell's lawyer was bound by lawyer-client confidentiality. In 1985 the Eleventh Circuit Court of Appeals reversed Drake's sentence because of trial procedural errors. He was given a life sentence.

It was only in 1987, when Campbell died of natural causes, that his lawyer came forward with the exonerating information. The Georgia Board of Pardons and Paroles released Drake on Christmas, 1987.

Shabaka Waglini

Shabaka Waglini was born Joseph Green Brown in Charleston, South Carolina. In 1973 he was convicted of the robbery, rape, and murder of a Tampa white woman. A juror at his trial sent an affidavit to Shabaka's minister, the Rev. Joe Ingle of the Nashville Southern Coalition on Jails and Prisons, asserting that a jury member had advocated the chair for Shabaka, a former Black Panther, because, "That nigger's been nothing but trouble since he came down here, and he'll be trouble until we get him off the streets."

Only fifteen hours before Shabaka's appointment with death, a three-judge panel of the federal circuit court of appeals in Atlanta stayed the execution on grounds that the case merited further examination. Shabaka returned to his cell and began to petition for a new trial.

In the years that followed, ugly details came to light. During the first trial, the prosecutor had concealed Federal Bureau of Investigation evidence showing that the fatal bullet could not have come from Shabaka's gun. The prosecutor had allowed a crucial witness to lie while also misleading the jury in his closing arguments. After spending fourteen years on death row, Shabaka Waglini was declared innocent and released. The following is his own account of the ordeal.

> I was born in Charleston, North Carolina, and in 1966 I went to Orlando, Florida, where I was to live for most of my life. I'm sure that my being charged with the murder and rape of Mrs. Barksdale was a deliberate and intentional thing, brought by the police department and the Hillsborough County State Attorney's Office simply to frame me. Since I was black and they needed someone, I was perfect for the part.

I had a court-appointed attorney because I didn't have the money to hire one. He was just three years out of law school and had only tried three previous cases before a jury, and none of them were capital cases.

After the trial, the main prosecution witness recanted his testimony and insisted on telling the truth in spite of threats of a life sentence from the judge and the prosecutor. After many years, the state finally administered a polygraph test. The results supported the witness's statement that he had lied during the trial.

I became friends with Deborah Fins of the Legal Defense Fund in New York and she found another attorney for me. He wouldn't have been my choice, if I had one. He had just resigned as the U.S. Attorney for the State of Connecticut and had never handled a capital case either. He also believed in the death penalty, but when he came to see me I liked him. I asked him one question: could he fight? He never did respond, just sort of smiled and there was something in that smile. The smile was not just on his face, but in his eyes and there was something about it that told me here was a man I could trust.

When he read the transcript of my trial, he was astounded by the injustices he saw. It was the first time he had a chance to see capital punishment up close. We stuck it out and worked very well together. I came down to fifteen hours before my execution when I got the stay. I think it was at this point that my attorney changed his mind on the death penalty.

When my death warrant was signed by Governor Graham in 1983, my mother suffered a heart attack and stroke. Today she is still paralyzed from that stroke. I had no way of assuring her that I was going to be all right and it was too much for her. I tried to tell her that these people would never kill me, and it was something that I had to believe.

My cell was located about thirty feet from the electric chair and you had to stay in that cell for an average of twenty-three days. There are only two ways to get out of that cell. One is to get a stay of execution, the other is to take that walk to the chair.

I guess most of my emotions were of anger. The day before the execution, the guards came in to measure me for a burial suit, and it was then that I blew my cool. They made it seem like a ritual, a mechanical process, like I was an inanimate object or something, not a living human being. I was determined at that point to let them know that I was not just a part of a ritual, but a human being. I was still alive and breathing, and I would demand respect. I lashed out physic-

ally, and they responded in like manner. I lost four teeth in that alter-
cation. I was full of anger—anger at being treated in such a manner,
anger at my mother's heart attack, anger at the world.

We got the stay but it was given very grudgingly. The ballistic reports from the FBI showed the bullet that was taken from the body
did not physically match the chamber of the gun that I had. We didn't
even have the original autopsy report. We had the report of the medical examiner first on the scene, and this report said that the assailants
had blood groups AB and B. I am type A. The state knew this and
also knew the time of death was fixed at between 5:30 and 8:00 in the
evening.

At the trial, the state maintained the crime took place around noon.
We also found out from inmates that the key witness who testified not
only didn't know about the crime but was taught and trained by the
police and prosecution. He was taken out of the jail every day and led
around the scene of the crime, shown pictures of where the body lay,
and everything. This evidence was found by us and I turned to Tom,
the local counsel, and said, "What I like about you white people is that
you always like to write things down! Yes, man, you always write things
down and they come back to haunt you."

Today I have anger, frustrations, bitterness, and hatred. Those feelings will always be there. I choose to let that show, and I choose to
let people know of my feelings. I have to in order to survive. I dictate
my own emotions. When I was released, I had nothing but seventy-five
cents in my pocket. I gave away all my law books to the others on
the row, and I only had the seventy-five cents with which to make a
phone call. I called Tom, my lawyer, who is based in St. Petersburg,
and asked him to come and pick me up. In Florida, like other states,
when an inmate is freed, he is given a suit and one hundred dollars
and a ticket back to his home town. Since I had been at the county
jail the last couple of months, I was given nothing.

When I stepped out of the jail, I was met by reporters and was
blinded by the lights from the TV-station cameras that had been waiting for me. I didn't feel free. I am no longer restrained by bars, but
that's as far as it goes. During one interview a reporter asked me to
smile. I told him I wasn't going to be cute, I wasn't going to smile for
the camera. The death penalty is too serious an issue, and that's what
I'm about. I say what I have to say even though there's a lot of people
who don't want to hear it. No one owns Shabaka. I'm not a paid public servant. I'm myself, and I'll always be myself. I'm going to say what

I believe in my heart and what I believe is right.

I have more respect for the Nazis than I do for Americans. At least the Nazis had the courage to say, "I'm going to kill you, you, and you because I don't like the color of your eyes, the color of your hair, or skin." They didn't give you a fair trial, the right to appeal, and all the mockery and trickery that we have. What makes us any different?

I've had people say to me, "Mr. Brown, we understand your situation and we sympathize with you." I say, "Don't sympathize with me." They say, "If someone kills your mother, shouldn't they answer for it with capital punishment?" And I always respond with, "What if it were your mother who killed my mother? Would you still be for capital punishment?" I get no response to this question. Capital punishment not only has hurt me, but it has hurt my family. I say you people have already killed a member of my family. You killed my brother as sure as if you took a gun and aimed and pulled the trigger.

In 1970 my brother Willie needed a kidney transplant. He lived in Georgia and the doctors contacted me and came to Florida's state prison. I was examined and our kidneys matched perfectly. State officials in Tallahassee said that I could not be transported because of security reasons. The doctors then said they would bring Willie up to Gainesville, Florida, which is located twenty-two miles from the prison. Again I was denied the right to go and give my kidney. Nine days later, Wilie died because he didn't have a kidney transplant. So, in a sense the state of Florida killed my brother. They killed him.

Every time I go and see my mother and see the condition she's in I feel hatred. I hurt when I see my family suffer and I take offense. I can deal with what they did to me, but when you touch the ones I love and care about, I take offense. The families are also victims because they are being ostracized by society, exiled, and that is sad.

There are victims all the way around. Society teaches that when something violent happens to us we should seek revenge, but I always ask the questions about who out there will volunteer themselves to be a sacrificial lamb for me, so I can release fourteen years of anger and frustrations? I get no volunteers. Society tells me I shouldn't act that way and I should suppress it. I have to suppress my outrage because, you see, they have no programs in society for people like myself.

I've got to live the rest of my life with the knowledge that I had a brother who's no longer with us because I was denied the right to give him one of my kidneys. I don't care what happens to me. I'm a survivor and always have been, but when you touch that which is precious to me, then you can say, Shabaka and you are enemies. I'm not through with Hillsborough County, Florida, not by a long shot. I'm going to bring them down.

Shabaka spends his free time discussing the death penalty. He has testified before the Connecticut legislature when they debated a new death-penalty bill, spoken to the press in numerous states, appeared on radio and talk shows, and addressed a benefit for the Southern Coalition on Jails and Prisons. He says that his major concern is for those men and women still on death row. He is doing all he can to work for the end to this ultimate punishment, a punishment that he knows came within fifteen hours of taking one innocent man's life.

Many apologists will say that Shabaka's release after fourteen years on death row shows the system works. The system failed. What worked was a dedicated group of death-penalty monitors and attorneys. Without committed volunteer attorneys, Shabaka would likely be dead today. Evidence of his innocence would not have been found, and people would have thought the system worked, because it had convicted, sentenced to death, and killed the guilty party, when in fact, it would have killed an innocent man.

As he sweated out those years, there were scores of convicts throughout America's prison system whose sentences were less severe, though their crimes were almost identical to the one for which Waglini had been convicted. Those who were truly dangerous among these criminals would, or should, never be released. Others, after serving long terms, would be released on parole, and scarcely a soul among them would be returned to prison for a subsequent crime.

Why hadn't Waglini been permitted to join this favored majority? Why had he and a small fraction of other felons been singled out to die while vastly larger numbers of criminals paying penance for misdeeds virtually the same as his were allowed to work out their destiny?

The absence of answers, which emphasizes the blind inequity of the death penalty, is another major reason why its use is immoral and unacceptable. But in Waglini's case, the questions were really academic because he was innocent.

The Shabaka Waglini case illuminates the most sordid defects of capital punishment. His blackness and poverty helped doom him. He was ruthlessly cheated, and it was never his privilege to be granted, even for a phantom crime, the incarceration that is meted out to others and that carries the possibility of redemption. He would not have died a criminal but a victim whose innocence would have been as surely entombed as his body in its burial suit.

Part Three
Expert Views

26

Hugo Bedau

Professor of Philosophy, Tufts University

Hugo Bedau is considered by many to be America's most knowledgeable expert on capital punishment. He is a member of the Philosophy Department at Tufts University in Medford, Massachusetts, and is the author or editor of four books on the death penalty: The Death Penalty In America *(considered the most comprehensive work ever compiled on capital punishment);* The Courts, the Constitution and Capital Punishment *and* Death Is Different. *With Michael Radelet, he co-authored a book-length law-review essay, "Miscarriages of Justice In Potentially Capital Cases" (*Stanford Law Review *40: 21–179).*

I oppose the death sentence for several reasons. I think that one of the most significant things I have learned from the study of capital punishment is the way in which the criminal law visits harsh penalties— the harshest of all being death—in an unfair way. History has shown that capital punishment has never been applied fairly.

It is extremely hard to draw up reasons why it is fair to kill the murderer who kills seven people, and not the person who kills just one person. You make one exception and you end up widening it. Exceptions, the more one thinks about them, begin to be arbitrary.

Some states have the death penalty for cop killers. I don't feel we should make exceptions in favor of the police. If the police get special treatment, why not firemen? Everyone's life is equally important. Why should the police get this kind of special vindication or revenge if they are killed on the job?

I see little proof that capital punishment is a successful deterrent, because it has been used throughout recorded history in one way or another, yet murders and other crimes continue to occur. It's true we don't know how many people have been deterred. We don't really have a perfect account of all the murders that have taken place. But it's also true that we don't know how many innocent people have been sentenced to death and executed.

Capital punishment is simply judicial murder. It is the dignified exercise of the state to extinguish the life of one of its members. When that's done by private individuals, it's murder, and it's a crime.

In the past sixty years in this country over half a million criminal homicides have been committed. By comparison, only about 4,000 executions were carried out, and all but fifty of those executed were men. If we could be assured that the 4,000 persons executed were the worst of the worst, repeat offenders without exception, the most dangerous murderers in captivity—the ones who had killed more than once and were likely to kill again, and the least likely to be confined in prison without imminent danger to other inmates and the staff—then one might accept half a million murders and a few thousand executions with a sense that rough justice had been done.

But the truth is otherwise. Persons are sentenced to death and executed not because they have been found to be uncontrollably violent, hopelessly poor parole and release risks. Instead, they are executed for entirely different reasons. They have a poor defense at trial; they have no funds to bring sympathetic witnesses to court; they are immigrants or strangers in the community where they were tried; the prosecuting attorney wants the publicity that goes with sending a killer to the chair; they have inexperienced or overworked counsel at trial; there are no funds for an appeal or for a transcript of the trial record; they are members of a despised racial minority. In short, the actual study of why particular persons have been sentenced to death and executed does not show any careful winnowing of the worst from the bad.

It shows instead that the executed were usually the unlucky victims of prejudice and discrimination, the losers in an arbitrary lottery that could just as well have spared them as killed them, the victims of the disadvantages that almost always go with poverty. A system like this does not enhance respect for human life; it cheapens and degrades

Citizens against the death penalty. **Left,** actor Mike Farrell with Joe Ingle, Nobel-prize nominee and founder of the Southern Coalition on Jails and Prisons; **center,** capital-punishment expert Hugo Bedau; **right,** Sam Sheppard, Jr.

Left, Jimmy Wingo on Louisiana's death row in 1985. His execution, which took place in 1987, was described by H. Edward Rowe (President, Christian Mandate for America) as: "The murder of a young man within a total vacuum of hard evidence that he had ever in his life been present in the home of the murder victims."

Right, Jimmy Wingo at the pardon board hearing in which his final appeals for reconsideration of his case were denied. H. Edward Rowe described the scene as "a futile clemency hearing before a morbid panel of professional deniers, whose role is to uphold the 'system' rather than be swayed by compelling evidence." **From left,** Minister James Allison, Jimmy's spiritual advisor; Warden Hilton Butler; Jimmy Wingo; and Robert Selcove, Jimmy's attorney.

Jeff Dicks has now been on death row for thirteen years. During that time, he has had to watch his daughter grow up from a distance.

Above left, a visit from his daughter Maria when she was four years old.

Above right, Jeff and Maria in 1990; she is now thirteen years old.
"The first time I say my daughter she was a year old. I can't tell you the feelings of love I experienced as I held her in my arms. She would put her arms around my neck and say, 'I love you, daddy.'"
—Jeff Dicks

Below, Jeff with his sister Laurie and niece Jessica.

"When people usually think of death row, they envision the likes of Charles Manson and other notorious mass murderers. They are taken aback to see that the men on . . . death row are not that much different from people you meet everyday. There is no crazed glint to their eyes. . . . They are sad and frightened. And they are human beings. The saddest thing about the death penalty is that innocent people are sometimes sentenced to die." —Shirley Dicks

Below, Shirley flanked by her son Jeff and husband Nelson inside the prison.

"The routine stays the same day after day. There are no activities whatsoever. You're always walking straight ahead without really seeing. There is always something missing. It's like a hole right through you. You can't figure out what it is, but you always have that empty feeling." —Jeff Dicks

Above, Shirley Dicks with her son Jeff on Tennessee's death row. During Jeff's first year on the row, the twenty-three-hour-a-day confinement in a ten-by-eight cell took its toll and he lost twenty pounds.

it. However heinous murder and other crimes are, the system of capital punishment does not compensate for or erase those crimes. It only tends to add new injuries of its own to the catalogue of our inhumanity to each other.

Michael Radelet and I found 350 cases in which defendants convicted of capital or potentially capital crimes in this century, and in many cases sentenced to death, have later been found to be innocent. Out of those 350 cases, twenty-three of them were executed. Our total of twenty-three wrongful executions is not an estimate, and it cannot serve as a basis for a reasonable estimate, of the total number of wrongful executions in the United States during this century. Estimating the extent of the problem of convicting the innocent in potentially capital cases by extrapolation from our data is not possible. The cases in our catalogue are only a nonrandom subset of an indeterminate number of the relevant cases. The full story of *all* cases disposed of by an execution must be examined before such an estimate would be possible. Of the seven thousand executions in this country since 1900, we examined only a hundred or so. Our findings prompt us to echo the words of an earlier investigator who noted that the catalogue of erroneous convictions "could be extended, but if what has already been presented fails to convince the reader of the fallibility of human judgement then nothing will."

In virtually every year in this century, in some jurisdiction or other, at least one person has been under death sentence who was later proved to be innocent. Based on this evidence, it is virtually certain that at least some of the nearly two thousand men and women currently under sentence of death in this country are innocent.

It is useful in the broad context to recognize that many such cases of incipient error do occur. No doubt the risk of executing the innocent grows as the risk of arresting, indicting, and trying the innocent also grows. The risk that really matters is the risk of erroneous conviction. It is also true that the risk of convicting the innocent is increased so long as due process errors are committed and uncorrected. But involuntary confessions, perjured testimony, planted circumstantial evidence, and other errors and mistakes are irrelevant for the purposes of our study except when they play a role in securing the conviction of an innocent defendant.

Miscarriages of justice are caused by a wide variety of factors. Some involve the decision by the police and prosecution to seek a conviction of the defendant despite lack of firm belief that he is guilty. Some are the result of negligence on the part of the authorities. Others are the product of well-intentioned error that anyone might make.

In a few instances, a convincing record indicates that the defendants were victims of what can only be described as a "frame-up." Some of the most notorious—such as the 1915 case of Joe Hill and the 1916 Mooney-Billings case—were part of the pitched battles fought by employers earlier in this century against union organizers. Mooney and Billings were eventually cleared and released, but Hill was executed. In two other famous cases—the Sacco-Vanzetti case and the Hauptmann case—the convictions, death sentence, and executions were achieved by a large cast of characters, probably never systematically orchestrated into a frame-up in quite the manner that was done in the Hill and Mooney-Billings cases. In other less-known cases, where error was knowingly perpetrated by the police or the prosecutors, or both working together, the magnitude of the corruption of justice may have been as great as in the Hill and Mooney-Billings cases.

Clear injustices perpetrated by the police compose nearly a quarter of the errors we have identified, and perhaps not surprisingly they were usually coerced confessions. In 49 percent of the cases, the confession was later shown to have been coerced.

In 1924, Hardy was convicted in Michigan largely on the basis of testimony against him that was later proved to have been provided by a witness who had tried to testify in his favor, only to be discouraged from doing so by police threats.

In 1961, also in Michigan, Clark, Hall, and Kuykendall were convicted of murder and sentenced to life imprisonment. A year later, the chief witness against them admitted she had lied at the trial because the police had promised her lenient treatment for another crime if she would implicate these three defendants. In twenty-two of our cases, this type of improper conduct by the police helped to bring about a wrongful conviction.

Overzealous prosecutorial tactics are not limited to suppression of exculpatory evidence. Sometimes the prosecutor will stoop to the introduction of fraudulent incriminating evidence, as in the 1933 Fisher case in New York. William Fisher was convicted and sentenced to prison largely on the basis of a gun offered in evidence—a gun the prosecutor knew had not been fired by the defendant. Other times the police and prosecutor may manage to discredit unfairly a witness who might otherwise have come to the aid of the defense.

There is no common or typical route by which an innocent defendant can be vindicated, and vindication, if it ever comes, will not necessarily come in time to benefit the defendant. The criminal justice system is not designed to scrutinize its own decisions for a wide range of factual errors once a conviction has been obtained. Our data show that it is rare for anyone within the system to play the decisive role in correcting error. Even when actors in the system do get involved, they often do so on their own time and without official support or encouragement. Far more commonly, the efforts of persons on the fringe of the system, or even wholly outside it, make the difference. The coincidences involved in exposing so many of the errors and the luck that is so often required suggest that only a fraction of the wrongly convicted are eventually able to clear their names.

Many innocent defendants have used the system, notably the appellate courts, to win their freedom. But in the bulk of the cases, the defendant has been vindicated not because of the system, but in spite of it. Most victims of miscarriage, like other felony defendants found guilty, have expended all their financial resources trying to avoid conviction. Once convicted and imprisoned, few have attorneys who are willing or able to continue to fight for them. In short, the lesson taught by our data is how lucky these few erroneously convicted defendants were to have been eventually cleared.

To think that these cases show that the system works is to ignore that, once a defendant is convicted, there is no system to which he can turn and on which he can rely to verify and rectify substantive error. The convicted defendant can initiate an appeal based on procedural error in his trial, or on newly discovered evidence, but not on his factual guilt or innocence. This leaves most erroneously convicted defendants with no place to turn for vindication.

Next to establishing that no crime occurred, perhaps the most convincing disclosure of error occurs in cases where the actual perpetrator intervenes. This happened in forty-seven of our cases. The true offender confessed. In a few others, a person already in prison for another crime, confessed his guilt to a previous crime for which the wrong man had been convicted, and this conviction was verified.

I must repeat that Radelet and I have not, nor has anyone else, examined all of the more than seven thousand executions during this century in light of all the available evidence. Until this is done, proposing trends in the execution of the innocent is idle speculation.

In Florida charges against Joseph Green Brown were dropped and he was released after spending nearly thirteen years on death row and once coming to within fifteen hours of being executed. The state had made a secret deal with its chief witness to testify at Brown's 1974 trial. Eight months after the trial this witness admitted that he lied, but it was not until 1986 that the Eleventh Circuit Court of Appeals voided the conviction, ruling that the prosecutor had knowingly allowed the witness to lie and mislead the jurors in his closing argument.

Earl Johnson was executed in Mississippi on May 20, 1987. Johnson was convicted of killing a police officer, who was in the position of investigating an assault. The victim of the assault initially said that Johnson was not the man who assaulted her, but Johnson confessed to the murder. He immediately claimed that the confession had been given only after the police had threatened him and his grandparents with physical violence. The assault victim then changed her story and implicated Johnson.

In Pennsylvania in 1947, David Almeida and his codefendant were engaged in the armed robbery of a supermarket. A police officer was killed while attempting to apprehend them. Later evidence proved that the fatal bullet was not fired by Almeida, or even by one of his codefendants, but by another police officer. Nevertheless, Almeida was convicted of murder and sentenced to death. On appeal his conviction was overturned.

In 1975, Jerry Banks of Georgia was convicted on two counts of murder and sentenced to death. The conviction was reversed on appeal on the grounds that the prosecution knowingly withheld evidence. In 1976, Banks was retried, reconvicted, and resentenced to death. Appellate courts refused to vacate this conviction. His attorney was later disbarred. In 1980, a third trial was ordered because of newly discovered evidence. Part of this evidence came from a previously silent witness, whose testimony revealed that the fatal shots could not have come from Banks's weapon. Banks was released later that year when all charges against him were dismissed by a circuit-court judge. Three months later, after he learned his wife wanted a divorce, Banks killed her and himself. In 1983, a suit against the county for mishandling the case was filed by Banks's children, and the county agreed to give them $150,000.

In 1983, Anthony Brown from Florida was convicted of first-degree murder and sentenced to death, despite a jury recommendation of life imprisonment. The only evidence against Brown was from the testimony of a codefendant, who was sentenced to life for his role in the crime. On appeal, the conviction was reversed and a new trial was ordered because Brown had not been notified before the state took a crucial deposition in the case and had thereby been deprived of his right to confront and cross-examine an adverse witness. At retrial in 1986, the codefendant admitted that his incrimination of Brown at the first trial had been perjured, and Brown was acquitted.

In 1982, Neil Ferber from Pennsylvania was convicted of first-degree murder and sentenced to death. In 1986, at the urging of the district attorney, the trial judge ordered a new trial. A polygraph test indicated that the state's star witness against Ferber, a former cellmate, had perjured himself at the trial, falsely claiming that Ferber had confessed to the crimes. An earlier polygraph test, administered before trial and with the same results, had not been revealed to the defense. A homicide detective and several other prosecutors were also convinced of Ferber's innocence, and an eyewitness to the crime was positive that Ferber was not the man she saw. Two months after the new trial was ordered, charges against Ferber were formally dropped.

In 1962, Gerald Anderson of Idaho confessed to the murders of two neighbors. Anderson was in jail for ten months, although his confession was the only evidence against him. It later became evident that the confession had been obtained by coercion. Meanwhile, another man confessed and was tried and convicted of the crimes.

In 1942, William Wellman of North Carolina, a black man convicted of raping a white woman, was sentenced to death. He was spared when the governor became convinced that Wellman's alibi claim was really true. After Wellman's conviction, evidence was obtained that proved he was hundreds of miles away from the scene of the crime and that the conviction was based on mistaken identity.

Paul Dwyer, whose home was in Maine, was arrested in New Jersey in 1937, after a routine search of his car revealed the bodies of two murder victims. He was held incommunicado, pleaded guilty, and was convicted. In prison Dwyer protested his innocence, claiming that a deputy sheriff in Maine had threatened to murder his mother unless he secretly disposed of the two bodies. A year later, after investigation of Dwyer's charges, the sheriff was indicted, convicted, and sentenced to prison. Dwyer, although cleared, was not released from prison until 1959.

Two recent decisions by the Supreme Court indicate that it does not judge the risk of wrongful conviction to be so great as to warrant certain minor modifications in the imposition of the death penalty. Requiring a unanimous jury vote to impose a death sentence is one procedure that would reduce the probability of wrongful execution, but in 1984, the Court, in upholding the constitutionality of Florida's jury-override provision, rejected an effort to require a simple majority vote, and it is unlikely to demand a unanimous jury verdict to impose a death sentence. Also, several studies have found that the exclusion from capital juries of citizens who stand opposed to the death penalty makes such juries more conviction prone and sympathetic to the prosecution. Nevertheless, in 1986 the Court refused to prohibit the exclusion of such jurors.

Evaluating the argument against the death penalty based on the fact that innocent defendants have been and will be executed requires some care. As it is certain that there are and will be such cases, death-penalty proponents cannot evade the problem. Ernest van den Haag, one of this country's most vocal death-penalty proponents, agrees, but then argues that the benefits of capital punishment outweigh this liability.

Van den Haag's defense of the death penalty despite his concession that some innocent defendants will be executed can be criticized on grounds other than the impossibility of performing the calculations his argument requires. One could accept his cost-benefit logic for the sake of the argument, and still point to at least three objections.

First, there is little or no empirical evidence on behalf of any of the alleged benefits of the death penalty that make it superior to long-term imprisonment.

Second, van den Haag's comparison of the death penalty with other activities that cause the death of the innocent (building houses, driving a car, playing golf or football) is misleading for two reasons. Those who participate in the latter voluntarily consent to their exposure to risk, whereas there is no reason to believe that the innocent defendant has consented to the risk of being executed. Furthermore, the intention of capital punishment is to kill the convicted, whereas this is not the intention of the practices to which van den Haag draws a parallel.

Third, and most importantly, we need to consider basic issues of individual rights in a democratic society. We suspect that those who reason as van den Haag does might see the issue differently were they the innocent defendants facing the executioner.

Capital punishment is cruel and unusual. It is a relic of the earliest days of penology, when slavery, branding, and other corporal punishments were commonplace. Like those other barbaric practices, it has no place in a civilized society.

There is an alternative to capital punishment: long-term imprisonment. Such a punishment is retributive and can be made appropriately severe to reflect the gravity of the crime for which it is the punishment. It gives adequate (though hardly perfect) protection to the public. It is free of the worst defect to which the death penalty is liable: execution of the innocent. It tacitly acknowledges that there is no way for a criminal, alive or dead, to make amends for murder or for other grave crimes against the person. Finally, it has symbolic significance. The death penalty, more than any other kind of killing, is done in the name of society and on its behalf. Each of us has a hand in such a killing. Thus, abolishing the death penalty represents extending the hand of life even to those who by their crimes have "forfeited" any right to live. It is tacit admission that we must abandon the folly and pretense of attempting to secure perfect justice in an imperfect world.

Searching for an epigram suitable for our times in which governments have launched vast campaigns of war and suppression of internal dissent by means of methods that can only be described as savage and criminal, Albert Camus was prompted to admonish: "Let us be neither victims nor executioners." Perhaps better than any other, this exhortation points the way between forbidden extremes.

27

Michael Radelet

Professor of Sociology, University of Florida

The Death Penalty As a Human Rights Issue

POLONIUS: My Lord, I will use them according to their desert.

HAMLET: Use every man after his desert and who shall 'scape whipping? Use them after your own honor and dignity. The less they deserve, the more merit is in your bounty.

—*Hamlet,* Act II, Scene I

During the last decade, the popular and political arguments supporting America's use of the death penalty have been undergoing gradual and significant changes. First, now that most formal religious organizations have endorsed statements in favor of abolition, no longer are the arguments that God is a retentionist widely heard. Second, since it is now clear that executions cost many times more than an alternative sentence of life without parole (Garey, 1985), responsible retentionists no longer claim that hiring the executioner will save more tax money than feeding and housing death-row maggots. Third, the argument that executions will deter future murderers is endorsed by virtually no contemporary criminologists, and retentionists are left to speculate that this lack of deterrent effect results from the infrequency of the death penalty's use. Fourth, those who once argued that the death penalty is necessary to prevent convicted murderers from killing again or walking the

streets after a short confinement have been silenced by research showing the probability of repeat homicide is miniscule (Marquart, 1989)
and the widespread availability of long-term or life imprisonment without parole (Wright, 1990).

Fifth, death-penalty retentionists have conceded the inevitability of
executing the innocent, although they argue this risk is small and outweighed by the death penalty's "moral benefits and the usefulness of
doing justice" (van den Haag, 1986:1665). And, finally, retentionists are
also troubled by the clear findings that the race of the victim correlates
with sentencing outcomes, other factors being equal. The retentionists'
response is simply that those who murder blacks should be sentenced
more harshly.

Consequently, by admission of retentionists and even the Supreme
Court, today's support for the death penalty is increasingly centered
on one issue—retribution. Because of the immense suffering caused by
murderers, we kill them because we despise them and want them to
suffer in return. Imprisonment for lengthy terms or even life is simply
insufficient to give these animals their just deserts.

These changes in the nature of death-penalty debates should be
welcomed by abolitionists. After all, most abolitionists would be opposed to capital punishment even if it was cheap or even if it showed
modest deterrent effects. They are just as opposed to the death penalty
for black offenders, juveniles, the mentally ill, and the obviously guilty
as they are opposed to its use on other prisoners. The abolitionist position argues it is no more possible to say certain categories of offenders
are more deserving of execution than it is to say that some are more
deserving of prolonged physical torture. The focus of the argument on
retribution is in no small part a consequence of abolitionists having
won the debates on the other issues that have heretofore distracted the
discussion. Long before retentionists, abolitionists have been arguing
that retribution was the guts of the issue.

In this paper, I would like to explore one aspect of human-rights
issues involved in retributive justifications for the death penalty (cf. Grahl-
Madsen, 1987). I will discuss the families of death-row inmates. My
data are experiential. Over the last decade I have testified in thirty death-
penalty cases and worked in one way or another, sometimes as a paralegal,
on a hundred others. To varying degrees, I knew each of the last twenty
men executed in Florida, and have inherited property, arranged funerals,

sprinkled ashes, and passed the eve of execution with several. I have also spent a few thousand hours housing and working with their families, and in five cases was with the mother or closest relative while their loved one was being killed.

My argument is:

1. An inclusive view of the "human rights" affected by capital punishment includes both the rights of the prisoner and the rights of the family. Specifically, the human right of relevance for families is that innocent people have a right to be spared terrible and avoidable agonies.

2. Experiencing the pains of the condemnation and execution of a loved one is a terrible and avoidable agony. Imprisonment, too, hurts the family, but this pain is unavoidable and can be legitimated by society's right to protection (i.e., deterrence and incapacitation).

3. Even if just desert may, for the sake of argument, legitimate the pains the death penalty imposes on the guilty defendant, it does not justify the pains imposed on the defendant's innocent family members.

In a 1978 paper, Gibbs reviewed the difficulties of precisely defining retribution, but concluded that its essential ingredient is that retribution justifies punishment "solely for the reason that those on whom it is inflicted deserve it" (1978:294). It's just that simple: they deserve it. If one argued that retribution might justify torturing murderers, retentionists conventionally respond with the idea of *lex talionis*, a response that is not compelling because of its selective use (e.g., *lex talionis* would justify executing all murderers or raping all rapists). Further, *lex talionis* might justify torturing mass murderers or heinous murderers, an idea that most retentionists would reject.

Parenthetically, I note that the same reasons that make most reject corporal punishment on amorphous human-rights grounds could also be used to reject the death penalty. Along these lines, in 1989, a Delaware legislator introduced a bill authorizing flogging for certain offenders, pointing out that if we can kill prisoners, "then I don't know why beating them is any worse" (*San Antonio Express-News*, Jan. 29,

1989). I agree completely, as the retributive doctrine draws no lines and would justify both. If retribution permits the state to kill its citizens, there is no clear reason why the doctrine would not allow the state to slice off the prisoner's legs.

Let us now take a closer look at the incremental suffering imposed by the death penalty that those who argue for retribution claim is deserved. As do life-term prisoners, death-row inmates face loss of liberty and all sorts of related pains. Confinement is quantitatively more painful for condemned prisoners than it is for other prisoners, in that various states may restrict death-row inmates to their cells, cut off access to prison jobs, phones, classes, gyms, religious services, libraries, outside gifts, etc. But there are qualitative differences as well (Bedau, 1980: 162–64). Those serving life imprisonment do not have to cope with the anticipation of a preordained death, the uncertainty of appeals, the agony of losing best friends to the executioner, and the legally imposed label of not being worth living (Johnson, 1981). Compared to these, the issue of whether the death is by injection, electricity, or burning at the stake is trivial. I believe that these pains, in themselves, should be considered human-rights abuses, but that is not my point today.

In my work with death-row inmates, I have often found that the above pains are secondary to the anguish they feel when seeing what their death sentences put their families through. We often get a glimpse of this through the last words of executed prisoners, when families are regularly acknowledged and comforted. The primary component of the suffering caused by the death penalty over long imprisonment, as perceived by the inmate, is its impact on his family.

Death-row inmates have good reasons to suffer because of what their predicament does to their moms and dads and kids, as the suffering of these family members is real and immense (Radelet et al., 1983; Vandiver, 1989). While I do not underestimate the tremendous suffering experienced by families of homicide victims, I also recognize the suffering of the families of the condemned. Perhaps one ought not to compare the anguish of families of murder victims with that of the families of death-row inmates. Pain is pain, anguish is anguish, and each person's suffering reaches to immeasurable proportions. But whereas the one suffers from the unpredictable behavior of individuals, the other suffers from the premeditated arm of the state.

Several incidents come to mind that justify this assertion. On April

18, the governor of Florida signed a death warrant on Marjorie Adams's son, her only child. Two days later, her husband, the condemned man's father, dropped dead. A fortnight thereafter, Mrs. Adams was back at the funeral home, this time to bury her son.

In January I had the duty to call Louise Bundy to tell her that her son was dead. Ted Bundy never saw the 700 celebrants outside Florida's execution chamber, but his parents did, and the spectacle added to their anguish. Two weeks later I had to call her again to tell her that postautopsy pictures of her son were about to appear in a supermarket tabloid.

Kay Tafero, while in Washington to bury her husband with military honors at Arlington Cemetery, learned that a death warrant had been signed on her only son. The next week, while visiting him in prison with a glass wall between them, Mrs. Tafero fainted when the prison's lights went out, as the auxiliary generator was being tested for its anticipated use in fueling the electric chair.

A couple of years ago, Willie Darden's fiancée broke into a hysterical screaming fit in my front yard as she left for what she thought was to be her last visit.

I remember driving six members of the Bartow family to their home a few hours after their loved one was executed. The next morning the inmate's teenaged daughter, Regina Thomas, was hospitalized for what was described as a mental breakdown. I hope never to see a better example of powerlessness than that felt by a family member while their loved one is being executed.

In large part, the death penalty is worse than life imprisonment because it terminates the opportunity to experience social relations (Bedau, 1980:163). But social relations are a two-way street; if you die, my opportunity to interact with you is just as destroyed as your opportunity to interact with me. In this, capital punishment hurts those with close relationships with the inmate as much as it hurts the prisoner himself. While the inmate receives support from attorneys and ever present comrades in neighboring cells, the family is left to anticipate the execution with overwhelming helplessness, powerlessness, often in ignorance of criminal process, and always in isolation. Much more than life imprisonment, death creates an "ever widening circle of tragedy" (Turnbull, 1978:54), claiming its victims with shotgun inaccuracy.

It should be noted that the actual punishment of death cannot be experienced by the prisoner. He can dread it, but because death extinguishes consciousness it cannot itself be experienced. So, capital punishment loses its object at the moment of its infliction. The family, however, remains to feel and absorb the loss. John Spenkelink has now been dead for twelve years, but I saw his mother recently and can assure you that her suffering is not over.

Few would deny that to kill the innocent is to violate their fundamental right to life. But many would agree that even worse than being killed ourselves would be to stand by helplessly as a loved one was being killed. Death-row families are often bonded by the same unconditional love that bonds other families. They are no different. Having your child killed after a decade of design is an experience that can be worse than death itself. As Camus wrote, "The relatives of the executed man thereby experience a misery that punishes them beyond the bonds of all justice." (1959:30)

Returning to the death penalty's retributive goal, I suggested earlier that we be guided by the definition of retribution constructed by Gibbs: we use the death penalty because its victims deserve it. Problems of executing the innocent aside (Bedau and Radelet, 1987), the primary increase in suffering caused by the death penalty over life imprisonment is its vicariousness: it affects innocent family members as much as the guilty prisoner. A death penalty promoted on the basis of just desert cannot be just when it destroys the innocent as much as it punishes the guilty.

What remains is to discuss how the retributive justifications and consequences of the death penalty, in its effects on the innocent, can be viewed as a human-rights issue. The concept of "human rights" is not the concept of a moral absolute; it is a social construction. Consequently, how social groups differ in time and place in their definition of such rights (see Bedau, 1982) is a more useful topic for discussion than specification of what a human right "is" or "is not." Various governmental and international bodies have made several attempts to specify basic human rights (Amnesty International, 1987:3, 221–26; 1989: 82–85, 241–58). No matter how defined, these rights have meaning only when governments recognize and protect them. Indeed, the question of human rights can be viewed inversely as the question of what rights governments retain for themselves or what rights the people give to their governments.

In the United States, we have given our government far broader rights to kill the sons and daughters of our fellow citizens than the government actually exercises. After all, if our current death-penalty statutes were used to their limits, far more people would be condemned and executed than is presently the case. Framing the issue in terms of governmental rights, rather than in terms of the human rights of killers or their victims, exposes the heart of the question. The question becomes what kind of society do we want to be.

I advance this thesis because I believe it may be useful in our death-penalty debates of the 1990s. I believe the argument that the death penalty violates basic human rights of the prisoner, though correct, is not convincing to the public. After all, the unconditional love that a mother has for her son is not likely to be widely shared if her son turns out to be a heinous murderer. Those of us who work with death-row inmates do not have a very likeable clientele, and it is difficult to generate much sympathy for them. But parents ought to be able to recognize the anguish of another parent. When the death warrant was signed for Dennis Adams, it was signed for Marjorie Adams's son. Coretta Scott King perhaps has said it best. Her husband was assassinated and her mother-in-law was murdered. Precisely because she knows the horror experienced when an innocent family is deprived of a loved one, she does not want that horror to be experienced by any other innocent family. ". . . I could not support execution of their killers because it would be a disservice to all that Martin and his mother had lived for and believed." (King, 1986). What kind of society do we want to be?

Amnesty International. 1987. *United States of America: The Death Penalty.* New York: Amnesty International.

Amnesty International. 1989. *When the State Kills.* New York: Amnesty International.

Bedau, Hugo Adam. 1980. "Capital Punishment." Pp. 148–82 in *Matters of Life and Death: New Introductory Essays in Moral Philosophy,* edited by Tom Regan. New York: Random House.

———. 1982. "International Human Rights." Pp. 287–308 in *And Justice For All: New Introductory Essays in Ethics and Public Policy*, edited by Tom Regan and Donald VanDeVeer. Totowa, N.J.: Rowan and Littlefield.

Bedau, Hugo Adam, and Michael L. Radelet. 1987. "Miscarriages of Justice in Potentially Capital Cases." *Stanford Law Review* 40: 21–179.

Camus, Albert. 1959. *Reflections on the Guillotine.* Michigan City, Ind.: Fridtjof-Karla Publications.

Garey, Margot. 1985. "The Cost of Taking a Life: Dollars and Sense of the Death Penalty." *University of California-Davis Law Review* 18: 1221–73.

Gibbs, Jack P. 1978. "The Death Penalty, Retribution and Penal Policy." *Journal of Criminal Law and Criminology* 69: 291–99.

Grahl-Madsen, A. 1987. "The Death Penalty. The Moral, Ethical, and Human Rights Dimensions: The Human Rights Perspective." *Revue Internationale de Droit Penal* 58: 567–81.

Johnson, Robert. 1981. *Condemned to Die: Life Under a Sentence of Death.* New York: Elsevier.

King, Coretta Scott. 1986. "Michigan and the Death Penalty." *Indianapolis Star,* June 18.

Marquart, James W., and Jonathan R. Sorensen. 1989. "From Death Row to Prison to Society: A National Study of Furman-Commuted Inmates." Forthcoming, *Loyola Law Review.*

Radelet, Michael L., Margaret Vandiver, and Felix M. Berardo. 1983. "Families, Prisons, and Men with Death Sentences: The Human Impact of Structured Uncertainty." *Journal of Family Issues* 4: 593–612.

Turnbull, Colin. 1978. "Death By Decree." *Natural History* 87: 51–66.

van den Haag, Ernest. 1986. "The Ultimate Punishment: A Defense." *Harvard Law Review* 99: 1662–69.

Vandiver, Margaret. 1989. "Coping with Death: Families of the Terminally Ill, Homicide Victims, and Condemned Prisoners." Pp. 123–38 in *Facing the Death Penalty: Essays on a Cruel and Unusual Punishment,* edited by Michael L. Radelet. Philadelphia: Temple University Press.

Wright, Julian. 1990. "Life-Without-Parole: An Alternative to Death or Not Much of a Life At All?" Forthcoming, *Vanderbilt Law Review.*

28

Joe Ingle

Southern Coalition on Jails and Prisons

For more than fifteen years, Joe Ingle, founder and executive director of the Southern Coalition on Jails and Prisons (SCJP), has tirelessly campaigned for abolition of the death penalty in America.

Nominated for the Nobel Peace Prize in 1988 and 1989 for his work, Mr. Ingle has carried the abolitionist fight throughout the United States. His efforts have been the subject of hundreds of newspaper and magazine articles, and he has appeared on scores of network and cable broadcasts including "The Today Show," "20/20," "West 57th Street," and National Public Radio.

Because of Mr. Ingle's inspiring dedication and leadership, thousands of citizens have been guided to a new understanding of the death penalty and have made a commitment to support the work of SCJP, validating the organization as the foremost abolitionist group in America today.

Although his activities have opened the eyes of many people and changed public opinion, no one knows better than Mr. Ingle that his ministry is unpopular with many people. His crusade is often a lonely one, depending in large part on inner strength. Perhaps this latest recognition by the Nobel Prize committee will renew his resolve and his hope. The nomination is a most deserved honor.

Joe Ingle wrote the following piece on capital punishment in response to public reaction to the execution of Ted Bundy.

The state of Florida's killing of Ted Bundy gave us a glimpse of the collective soul of our country and what I saw leaves me sickened. Execution parties—"Fry Ted" parties—were held throughout Florida including Florida State University. The bloodthirsty gathered outside of the Florida State Prison the morning of the electrocution with ghoulish banners and full-throated cries sounding more like a pack of wild dogs than human beings. The brave souls who protested the execution outside of the prison were verbally abused. The presence of police kept the protestors safe from the celebrators.

Stepping back from the feeding frenzy of the mobs, which was exacerbated by the media coverage, one wonders what is going on here. How can a nation that proudly claims itself the leader of the western world engage in such a barbaric activity? Since we seem to have lost the ability to survey ourselves with even a modicum of perspective, it is helpful to remember that Canada, England, and our European allies have discarded the death penalty as an uncivilized relic of a more primitive era. We alone of our western allies kill our citizens and even engage in a morbid fascination manifested in the behavior of cheering for executions. Indeed we are keeping company with Iran, South Africa, China, and the Soviet Union by killing our citizens. We have truly lost our moral compass on the death penalty and are simply killing for the joy of killing. Collectively, we are manifesting the traits of a mass murderer as the execution toll rises to 106 with Ted Bundy's killing.

Those of us against the death penalty must educate people concerning why we don't want so-called "serial killers" killed by the state. If those of us who have experience with death-row prisoners are gullible enough to believe what Ted Bundy says he did, then I must acknowledge I see why repealing the death penalty is so difficult. Just because a person is handsome and glib doesn't mean he is mentally competent. The mere fact that Ted Bundy was on death row reveals he was seriously deranged because, of all people, Ted Bundy should have taken the life sentence offered by the state of Florida rather than glamorize himself by getting the death sentence. But you don't get books and movies made about you for serving out a life sentence in prison. Ted Bundy knew that and the tragedy is that he was so sick he couldn't do what was best to preserve his own life and the lives of his victims, not to mention the pain he inflicted on the people who loved him. It is my fervent hope we will learn from the madness of electrocuting Ted Bundy. George Santayana put it best: "If we do not learn the lessons of history, we are doomed to repeat them."

Interview with Joe Ingle

I began my interview with Mr. Ingle by asking him how he first became interested in the plight of prisoners:

> My personal interest in prisons began when I was in seminary in New York. I was just a white boy up from North Carolina and I didn't know anything about prisons when I heard about the uprising in Attica. I was reading in the *New York Times* about these guys who were angry about the conditions they were in and had control of the prison. I could see where all this was heading, for Governor Rockefeller was taking a very hard line. Sure enough he sent in the highway patrol and over forty people were killed. And interestingly enough, when you look at who was killed and who did the killing, prisoners and guards were killed, but they were all killed by the troops who were sent in.
>
> Prisoners didn't kill any of the hostages and it seems to me they conducted themselves rationally. They were very angry over the conditions that they were living in, and they were very responsible in regard to what they were talking about, but the governor just exterminated them and took the prison.
>
> I started to visit the Bronx House of Detention, which is a big jail for the Bronx. I went up there for the first time and I'll never forget it. The guard took me to the cell block and opened the door. He slammed the door behind me. The first thought I had was, oh my God, he's locked me in here with all these animals. I started talking to them and I learned a lot. I learned that we are all socialized to regard people in prison as animals. I had been taught to feel that way. That's the way our society regards prisoners, unless they actually do what I did and go in and meet the inmates.

Joe decided to go back south and went to Nashville, Tennessee. He, along with three others, started the Southern Coalition on Jails and Prisons in the spring of 1974 in six southern states. Over the years it has expanded to eight states. In the beginning the Coalition was not even thinking about the death penalty, for it had been struck down.

Joe is an ordained minister of the United Church of Christ. His church is death row, the "congregation of the condemned" as he calls it. Most of his time is spent with the death-row inmates and comforting the family members. He lobbies governors, congressmen, members of the press, and whomever else it takes to get sentences commuted and to rid the judicial system of the death penalty.

> We got the whole organization involved in death row in the spring of 1976 as we felt that the Supreme Court was going to reinstate the death penalty. It got more intense as time went on. We've done everything from visiting governors to finding lawyers trying to keep people alive no matter what it takes. There's been almost a hundred people executed since we started. We're just involved in a whole range of activities about the death penalty.
>
> When you sit and try to figure out why people support the death penalty, it all boils down to only one thing—revenge. I am a Christian and what can a Christian say? I can't be a vengeful person, and I can't make the state into the instrument of my revenge. The ability to think critically led me to reach this important conclusion in my life.

The Coalition, which has about twenty employees at offices in all of the southern states, attempts to build opinion against the death penalty and gives moral and financial support to individuals who have been sentenced to death. An important part of this work is to find attorneys to volunteer their services to those who cannot afford an attorney. Public legal assistance is terminated when a case has passed the lower court. Most have court-appointed attorneys.

There was a riot in 1975 in a Tennessee state prison and Joe Ingle was called in to negotiate on behalf of the prisoners. He and the prisoners negotiated with the administration all night long.

> Once again the prisoners operated in good faith, and we worked out a compromise with the administration. But while we were doing so, they ordered in the cops and highway patrol and they came in and overpowered the inmates. They beat them, and put dogs on them. We didn't know what was going on for we were in the basement of the administration building and you are kind of sealed off there.
>
> The next morning when I found out what had happened, I went to the prison hospital. I'll never forget this one kid. His parents had come down from east Tennessee when they had heard he was seriously injured. He was sitting up in his bed. He had been literally beaten black and blue. Someone had taken a billy club and just clobbered this kid. We filed suit for the people who had been hurt by the police. We won a few thousand dollars for six different people.

We also filed a state-wide condition suit and that led to what we know now as the Grubb suit. In 1980 the judge said the whole prison was unconstitutional. Since then the state has been forced to comply with the court orders in terms of how many inmates you can have in the prison system, and if you can double-cell them.

Since then there has been some progress. Tennessee has single cells in the main prison now. In 1975 when the suit was started they had people packed in worse than sardines. Tennessee had one of the highest murder rates of any prison in the United States. Today that is not true. It's the result of the lessening of overcrowding.

After an inmate has been sentenced to die, his appeals automatically start. They go through the state courts and then the Supreme Courts. This whole process takes from eight to twelve years to finish and unless someone drops their appeal, they will not die immediately.

In 1984 Ron Harries dropped his appeals and Bill Groseclose, another death-row inmate and friend, went into court and said that Harries wasn't competent to make that decision. He wasn't competent for several reasons. The coalition felt that the conditions on death row had really affected his judgment, and we alleged and proved that Ron Harries had suffered extreme impairments over the years. He had a history of being institutionalized. It's really sad. We got all the documents, and judge Nixon ruled that Harries was not competent.

As a result of that, the momentum of executions in Tennessee has been slowed down. The judge will have to rule on the condition suit, and unless someone drops his appeals I don't think we will have executions in this state this year and probably not next year either. People are being executed left and right in other stat s. We are very lucky here to have been able to put the brakes on that process through the courts.

I've got little doubt that Jesus Christ would not have sat still for executions. Jesus said that if you are my disciples, you respond with love, with forgiveness, and reconciliation. Jesus knew that you don't stop murder by becoming a murderer. You stop the process by refusing to murder.

When asked if he was ever sorry that he had chosen this life rather than a community church Joe's reply is quick.

My church is the folks on death row—the congregation of the condemned, it's been called. I am sorry, not about not having a nice little church, but I feel like Isaiah did. "How long, O Lord, how long?" How many people are we going to kill? How long will this madness go on? When I sit there with someone's child weeping and trying to understand why daddy is being exterminated by the state, I wonder, My God, how long?

Over the years Joe has visited all the death rows in the south. He has corresponded with over 400 of the 1200 persons sentenced to die. He has become friends with those who do not have relatives or whose families do not want to have contact with them. He is with the inmates at the last. Because of his efforts many sentences have been commuted to life.

I feel that I am called to do this type of work. I feel like this is what the Lord wants me to do. I do not go into prison and lay a guilt trip on someone for not being a Christian because it's been my experience that the way you relate to an inmate is the way you relate to anyone else. When you are nice to them, they will return the respect. That's the way I operate. As a result, I've got a lot of good friends on death row. Unfortunately, eighteen of them have been killed by the state.

That's been hard to deal with, to get close to someone and then they get killed no matter how hard you work for them. I'm able to maintain a balance because I can come home to Tennessee into a situation where we don't have an immediate threat of an execution. Now, if I had to go to Florida and all the other states for an execution and then come home to one, I'd probably be ready for a looney bin.

Joe is married and just adopted a baby girl. He and his family live on a twenty-two-acre farm just outside of Ashland City highway. When I asked if this job interferes with his personal life, Joe replied:

I guess it does. Willie Darden is a good example. He was executed last month. People have committed murder since Cain and Abel. Just because someone commits the act doesn't mean they are non-human. They're still a child of God, just like you and I. Willie had asked me to be at his execution, but since he heard we had just adopted a little girl he told me to stay home with my family. But I'd known him since 1977 and there was no way I could not go down. I didn't want to be in that hell hole in Florida State Prison but the fact of the matter is I needed to be there for Willie and me. Sure it interferes with your personal life but Becca and I talk about that and really deal with it.

I don't know when we will stop murdering people, whether randomly on the streets or systematically in our death chambers. The only way to prevent continuation of the suffering and grief murder occasions is to prevent murder. I don't know how to stop the 20,000 murders we inflict on each other a year. However, I do know that we can prevent additional grief and pain to the families of the condemned by simply halting executions. Murder has enough victims in our society without the state creating a whole new class of murder victims' families—the families of the executed.

Joe Ingle is a firm believer in alternative sentencing:

We have people in prison that do not belong there. In Tennessee we have 61 percent of people in prison for nonviolent crimes. We ought to have them in restitution programs where they are paying back the people they committed the crimes on. Even more we need for the victim and the perpetrator to sit down and work out a restitution. If the courts did that instead of paying $18,000 a year to lock him up, they'd be doing the taxpayers a favor. The chances of that person committing another crime are virtually nill once they know the person they've committed the crime against. It's a whole lot cheaper to do that. We would like to see some alternatives to incarceration in this state.

On death row I think the solution is to have a mandatory twenty-year sentence on anyone committing first-degree murder. Then they are up for parole. That's our substitute for the death penalty. Because our belief is if someone is innocent when they are executed, they are gone. You can't say "I'm sorry." That person's family is grieving and that person is dead. But if you have someone serving time, you can always rectify that mistake. If you can prove that they are indeed innocent, you can get them back in society. If they are dead you cannot do that. We stress life as an alternative.

The Georgia office of the Coalition recently succeeded in getting an amendment to the death penalty that says you cannot execute the retarded. This has been a long struggle which started in 1985. That will help us to set a precedent in Tennessee, for Georgia is not a liberal state. It has executed more people than any other state in the United States.

Last year, the coalition was also successful in not allowing juveniles to be executed for their crimes. In Tennessee we had that written in the law in 1980 so that is not a possibility here.

I think what is most important to me is the personal relationships with some of the death-row inmates. When you get to know someone on death row and care about them, you will do anything you can to stop the execution. They are friends just like on the outside.

Medical care for inmates is another major concern of Mr. Ingle.

Medical care for those on death row is just not there. One example is James Adams, a death-row inmate in Florida whom I knew for years. He was a rock man, which means he worked on the walkway cleaning. The guards put Draino in his food. He got violently sick and they had to take him to the hospital and treat him. It's a sad comment that the state of Florida was able to get away with that. Frankly, we were trying so hard to keep James alive that we didn't get a chance to file charges as soon as we could. To think of guards actually doing that just lets you know that to talk about medical care in a prison is like a joke. In Louisiana the doctors say that the guys are on death row; why do they need care? How do you deal with an attitude like that?

I think this work has destroyed a lot of people. I know some who have had breakdowns just having to deal with the onslaught of executions. When you see what happens to the families of the condemned, it's enough to make you cry, and I do. I was with Willie Darden's wife right after he was executed. What can you say? You can just be there and hold her and let her know that someone cares about her, that the good Lord loves her, and you hope that somehow she feels the strength to maintain. There's a lot of heartbreaking work in all of this.

We have studies to show that executing a person is more expensive than keeping him in prison. Who are we to put a price on a man's life? To say to you that your life is worth $100,000 but not $105,000 is ridiculous. Human life is sacred and we should be protecting it. We shouldn't be talking about how much it costs to exterminate somebody.

A 1982 study in New York, for example, calculated the cost of reinstating the death penalty there and concluded that the average capital trial and first stage of appeals would cost the taxpayer about $1.8 million. That's more than twice what it costs to keep a person in prison for life. A capital trial normally takes much longer than one in which the death penalty is not involved, and lengthy appeals follow. Trial and appeal costs, including the time of judges, prosecutors, public defenders, and court reporters, and the high costs of briefs are all borne by the taxpayers. *Time* magazine reported that the commutation of the death sentences of fifteen Arkansas prisoners saved the state an estimated $1.5 million, considering the many appeals that would have been argued.

For those who quote the Bible in saying they believe in the death sentence Joe has a ready answer.

In the Old Testament there are 26 references for the death penalty, but you look in the New Testament and there isn't even one. There is no indication in Matthew, Mark, Luke, or John that Jesus would be interested in killing anybody. No one is going to tell me that today anyone would advocate executing people for talking back to their parents, or for adultery, which they did in the Old Testament. And if you advocate that you're a Christian and are for the death penalty, basically you are saying that you believe Jesus tolerates the death penalty. If you look in the eighth chapter of John, not only did he speak out against the killing of one woman, but he raised the whole question of us judging people. When Christ was executed, he said about his enemies with his dying words: "Father, forgive them."

When I talk to someone who is for the death penalty, I try to find out where they are coming from. People have all different feelings about it. I try to find out why they are for it. They are usually for it because they feel it is a deterrent, and there is no information to support that. In *The Case Against The Death Penalty* (New York: 1977) Hugo Bedau says about deterrence:

> Persons who commit murders do not expect to get caught so the threat of dying in the electric chair has no deterrent effect on them. The vast majority of capital crimes is committed during moments of great emotional stress, in fear, or under the influence of drugs or alcohol. In the cases where the crime is premeditated, the criminal expects to escape detection. Evidence shows that the death penalty is no more effective than imprisonment in deterring crime. Where the death penalty is used there is no decrease in the rate of criminal homicide. In Philadelphia, there were as many murders after well-publicized executions as before. Death-penalty states as a group do not have lower rates of criminal homicide than non-death-penalty states. States that abolish the death penalty do not show an increased rate of criminal homicide after abolition. In addition, cases have been clinically documented where the death penalty actually incited the capital crimes that it was supposed to deter. After reviewing studies in 1976, the United States Supreme Court found no conclusive evidence that the death penalty deters violent crime. The United Nations came to a similar conclusion.

I think the only honest response to anyone who says they are for the death penalty is to help them to see that what they are out for is revenge. That's the only legitimate reason for the death penalty. I don't agree with that and I feel that if you are a Christian and go around talking about revenge you have a problem.

I can understand that though. If you lose someone in your family and you want the person who committed the murder killed, at least that's an honest feeling. A clear indication of revenge is a woman here in town named Anna LeVin-Aaron. Her husband was murdered. Andy Barefoot was arrested and executed for this crime. I told Anna that I do not believe the killing of Barefoot has accomplished anything beyond creating more suffering and grief. In this case, the mourners are the Barefoot family. Anna said that when he was executed she could finally finish grieving. She had felt that as long as Andy lived it was as if her husband's life wasn't important.

I knew Andy's sister, Susan Barefoot. She was upset when her brother was about to be killed. She wept, she hurt, and she felt all the despair and grief Anna had expressed. As she sat crying, she said to me, "Joe, I'm a victim. My family is a victim, too. When will it ever stop?" There is enough pain from murder in this society without the state sanctioning it and creating even more pain for people like Susan Barefoot. Surely, society does not want to perpetuate the suffering of Anna by transferring it to Susan.

Joe feels that one day we will look upon the death penalty as we now look upon witch burning. This country is the only one among western nations that kills its citizens. It's just a matter of time before pressure against the death penalty is felt in this country and people realize that this is barbaric and is something that must be stopped.

In Amnesty International's *United States of America: The Death Penalty* (Amnesty International Publications, 1987), the arbitrariness of death sentencing is discussed:

> Killer lives, accomplice executed. In one case there was doubtful evidence of intent on the part of the executed prisoner that a killing should occur. In the other the actual killer received a lesser sentence owing to chance circumstances.
>
> Texas prisoner Doyle Skillern and an accomplice were both found guilty of the 1974 murder of an undercover police agent. The accomplice fired six shots into the victim and was sentenced to life imprisonment.

Doyle Skillern, who had been sitting in a nearby car, was sentenced to death and was executed in January 1985—just before the accomplice became eligible for parole.

Roosevelt Green was reported to have been somewhere else when the killing in his case occurred. He had gone for gas when a co-defendant raped and murdered the victim. The trial judge said that Roosevelt was only an accomplice in a murder committed by another person and his participation in the homicidal act was relatively minor. However, the Georgia Supreme Court upheld his conviction saying that he should not have left the victim alone with a man he knew to be dangerous. He was executed in March 1985.

As a result of Joe's efforts, several prisoners have had sentences commuted. In March 1987, one man, Joseph Green Brown, was released after fourteen years on death row in Florida (see chapter 25). He had been within fifteen hours of being executed on one occasion. The Southern Coalition assisted in proving that Joseph Brown was innocent.

People do not understand that execution is a painful form of death. The law is written in each state that the person is conscious of what is going on. He understands that he is being killed. That's why the Supreme Court ruled that they could not kill the insane, because they did not know they were being killed. It's hard to believe what happened in the case of Louie Fransis in Louisiana. They strapped him in the electric chair and ran the electricity through him. It didn't kill him; the chair malfunctioned. They pulled him out and his attorney said, "You cannot put him back in that chair; it's cruel and unusual punishment." It went all the way to the Supreme Court and they said that he could be executed. Sure enough, they took Louie and put him back in the chair and killed him. That's how barbaric this thing is.

Amnesty International says in the *United States of America: The Death Penalty* that it is inhumane to execute inmates.

In a 1983 electrocution in Alabama, it took three charges of 1,000 volts over a period of 14 minutes to kill the prisoner. After the second charge smoke and flame erupted from his left temple.

In a 1984 electrocution, witnesses saw the condemned prisoner struggle to breathe for eight minutes after the first two-minute charge of electricity had failed to kill him.

In another execution by lethal gas in Mississippi, the prisoner is reported to have had convulsions for eight minutes and to have struck his head repeatedly on the pole behind him. Some witnesses claimed that he was not yet dead when deputies asked them to leave the witness room.

In yet another execution by lethal injection in Texas, the prisoner took at least ten minutes to die. A year later technicians in Texas were reported to have spent 40 minutes searching a condemned prisoner's limbs for a suitable vein in which to insert the needle.

In spite of all the tragedies Joe Ingle has witnessed, he remains optimistic that his cause will prevail:

I think we just have to remember that we will live to see the end of the death penalty in this country. It's just a firm conviction that I have. Basically, I don't think the good Lord is going to sit still for this. We've got to educate the American people about the death penalty. They do not understand how it's working. They do not understand that nine out of ten people on death row had court-appointed lawyers because they are all poor.

A defendant's poverty, lack of firm social roots in the community, inadequate legal representation at trial or on appeal—all are common factors among death-row inmates. Clinton Duffy, long-time warden of San Quentin and witness to over 150 executions, has testified that in his experience capital punishment is a "a privilege of the poor." Justice William O. Douglas noted in *Furman*, "One searches in vain for the execution of any member of the affluent strata of this society."

There is evidence that many defendants are assigned inexperienced counsel, ill equipped to handle such cases. A recent study found that capital defendants in Texas with court-appointed attorneys were more than twice as likely to receive a death sentence than those with retained counsel.

They do not understand that another thing that sends you to death row is the race of the victim. If you are convicted of killing a white person, you are a whole lot more likely to get the death sentence than if you killed a black person.

Different parts of states give the death penalty more often than other parts. A study of criminal homicide cases in Georgia found that just 15 percent of Georgia's 159 counties were responsible for 85 percent of death sentences imposed in the state from 1973 to 1978. It also found that death sentences were six times more likely to be imposed in the more rural central region of Georgia than in the north, and seven to eight times more likely than in Fulton County. A US Department of Justice report on capital punishment noted that nearly 63 percent of those under the sentence of death in 1984 were held by states in the south.

I have worked with eighteen people who have been executed and five of those I'm convinced were innocent: Willie Dardon, Tim Baldwin in Louisiana, James Adams, Bob Sullivan, and Edward Johnson. People are innocent who get the death penalty; it happens all the time.

In the Bedau-Radelet report on the "Miscarriages of Justice in Potentially Capital Cases,"* it was reported that nine cases involving death sentences imposed in the last fifteen years were released in the first six months of 1987 because of evidence raising doubts about their guilt. We now know of 24 defendants sentenced to death since the Furman decision, of whom 23 were later freed because of doubts about their guilt and one executed despite such doubts.

In Florida, two black men, Freddie Pitts and Wilbert Lee, were released from prison after twelve years awaiting execution for a murder they never committed. Had the execution taken place, two more innocent men would have died.

In 1984, Earl Charles won a suit for damages against a Savannah, Georgia, police officer for framing him on a murder charge. After nearly four years on death row, he was released when the district attorney's own reinvestigation of the case convinced him that Charles was innocent.

*Stanford Law Review 40: 21–179.

29

Victor Streib

Professor of Law, Cleveland State University

From an Interview with Victor Streib

I started working on the juvenile question in the mid '70s. I wrote a book called *Death Penalty for Juveniles* (Bloomington: Indiana University Press, 1987) on that topic, and since its publication, I've tried to keep my research up to date. Most of my present research and the book I'm writing now are on women on death row. I'm also an attorney and represent children and women on death row.

The number of persons currently under juvenile death sentences has dropped to the lowest point since 1983, when I first began recording the data. As of February 1989, twenty-seven persons were on death row for crimes committed while under the age of eighteen, the most typical age cutoff for juvenile court. These twenty-seven condemned juveniles constitute only 1.2 percent of the total number of persons on death row.

Most of these kids have had a difficult background. Dorothy Lewis has researched this subject and found that almost all of those on death row came from very abusive homes.* But there are some who did not come from such a background and whose homelife was generally good. I think the problem is not that they come from single-parent families, or that they're poor, but that they've seen violence in their families.

---

*See Dorothy O. Lewis, *Vulnerabilities to Delinquency* (New York: Luce, 1981), and Dorothy O. Lewis and David A. Balla, *Delinquency and Psychopathology* (New York: Grune, 1976).

They get the message very clearly that violence is the way to solve problems. Then when they are confronted by their own problems, they resort to violence.

Almost all of the juveniles on death row have had court-appointed attorneys. They had public defenders at trial, and when they are put on death row, they have to get an attorney to handle the appeals. In most of the states, the public defender cannot take the case beyond the trial level. They have to get a new attorney for the state appeal, and after the state appeal is through, and they're getting ready to go on into federal courts, then the state public defender can't work for them any longer. The state-paid public defenders are not allowed to represent anyone in anything other than a state action. Trying to find lawyers to represent them in federal action is very hard to do. So they are often left without any lawyer at all.

I think all of the twenty-seven kids now on death row have a lawyer. But a good number of the two thousand adults on death row do not have an attorney and could go all the way to execution without one.

The most serious problem is at the trial when they are appointed public defenders. The public defender, while he usually is a very competent attorney, has a big case load and not much experience in death-penalty cases. I think they often don't do as good a job as one would hope they would do at the trial level. By the time they get to the appeal level, if the trial hasn't been conducted in all the right ways, then it's hard to get relief.

There is an enormous amount of pressure on these attorneys. They have a huge case load, so they don't have as much time to devote to public-defender cases as they ought to, and there is a lot of political pressure in these cases. If an attorney takes a murder case in his home town and is representing somebody whom the press is hounding every day, and the politicians are making speeches about, it is pretty tough to practice law in that community. He's going to hurt his law practice and is going to make all his present clients angry; even his kids are going to get shouted at at school.

There's an enormous amount of difficulty for local attorneys to take local cases because they're sensationalized by the press and they make the attorney out to be some kind of monster, and it's just very difficult to deal with. It's easier for someone from out of state to come in and do the job. He's not going to care if anyone in the town likes him or not. He can leave and go home and nobody knows what he's been doing or who he's been defending.

The political pressures are really enormous for these attorneys and I really feel for them. They have to make a living and they have to live in their communities; so, while I criticize the general level of representation these kids are getting, I have to understand the difficulties these attorneys are facing.

We have fourteen states that have juveniles on death row at the present time. Only three of them have been executed since the death penalty has been reinstated. One was in South Carolina and the other two were in Texas. These were all seventeen-year-olds and they were executed in 1985 and 1986.

Charles Rumbaugh was born on June 23, 1957, one of several children in the west-Texas, white, Catholic family of Harvey and Rebecca Rumbaugh. Raised in a constantly moving family with a violent, alcoholic father, Rumbaugh committed his first serious offense when he broke into a schoolhouse at age six. ·At seven he was wild and uncontrollable. At thirteen he was placed in reform school. He spent the next four years there, fulfilling his ambition to learn how to commit more and better crimes. In Rumbaugh's own words, the Texas juvenile justice system "took a 13-year-old boy and turned out a hardened criminal."

Once released he began his life of crime in earnest. Soon he was in a mental hospital for treatment of manic depression. He escaped from the hospital early in 1975 and continued his life of crime. He decided to commit his next robbery at a small jewelry store. He pointed the gun at the jeweler and demanded money, but the jeweler resisted and reached for his own gun. They struggled and Rumbaugh got the better of him. He shot twice and killed him.

Police questioned Rumbaugh and he provided them with a written confession. He was tried and found guilty of murder and robbery, and was sentenced to death.

Rumbaugh seemed resigned to his death sentence. In a letter he wrote:

> If they were to come to my cell and tell me I was going to be executed tomorrow, I would feel relieved, in a way. The waiting would be over. I would know what to expect. To me, the dying part is easy; it's the

waiting and not knowing that's hard. I feel like I have been traveling down a long and winding tunnel for the past nine years, the length of time I have been on death row, and now I can see no end to the tunnel, no light at the end of it, just more long years of the same. I have reached the point where I no longer really care. . . . I'm so damn tired and disgusted with sitting here and watching my friends take that final trip to the execution chamber, one after the other, while I continue to wait and speculate about when my time will come. They're killing me a little bit each day.

The day before his execution Rumbaugh was visited by friends he had corresponded with over the years, and by three sisters and a brother-in-law. His mother went to the prison but at the last minute decided not to see him. Shortly after midnight, Rumbaugh faced his execution calmly. He refused communion and requested that no religious persons be with him at his death. He gave a last statement to the witnesses at his execution. "About all I can say is goodbye. For the rest of you, even though you don't forgive me my transgressions, I forgive you for yours against me. That's all I wish to say. I'm ready to begin my journey."

He was the first person to be put to death for a crime committed while under age eighteen in the post-Furman era of capital punishment. Was he deterred by the death penalty? "I was seventeen years old when I committed the offense for which I am about to die, and I didn't even start thinking and caring about my life until I was at least twenty."

Juveniles generally don't get treated as harshly as adults regardless of what they do. That's the reason we have juvenile courts, to take care of that. There is a principle in our law that assumes juveniles can't commit horrible acts and do serious harm to people. They are not held fully accountable for what they do. I think it's surprising that some actually do get the death sentence; they're the cases that slipped through the cracks, so to speak, or were treated strangely. I think it's fair to say that these are exceptional cases, and they are hard to explain because they are so very rare. They aren't the worst killers by any means, they aren't the worst kids, and they aren't necessarily in the same towns or the same states.

The death penalty for juveniles is gradually disappearing in most states, as it did in Tennessee. Most states are passing minimum-age laws for the death penalty, which stipulate that, no matter what the crime, if you're under a certain age, you can't get the death penalty. That's been going on since 1980. Even the states that want the death penalty don't want to see it applied to juveniles. Moreover, in the states that have no minimum-age provision in their death-penalty laws, the judges and juries have been reluctant to give the death sentence to a juvenile. It used to be that fifteen or twenty juveniles were sentenced to death a year, and now it's only two or three.

For the worst offenses by children, legal processes have been followed for more than a century that are markedly less harsh and punitive than those for similar offenses by adults. Attempts are made to protect children during legal proceedings and to impose nonpunitive, treatment-oriented sanctions on them for their offenses. Retribution and deterrence, the age-old justifications for adult criminal sanctions, have only recently made minor inroads into the practice of juvenile corrections. Even though juveniles, just like adults, sometimes commit horrible offenses and sometimes suffer horrible abuses, juvenile offenders and victims are legally, socially, and politically different.

In this century, the youngest person to be executed was fourteen, in South Carolina. His case has gotten a lot of attention because he was so very young. He was really just a little kid and was so small he didn't fit in the electric chair. They had to adjust the straps to make him fit and his feet still dangled.

From *Death Penalty for Juveniles*

Leaders in the legal, criminological, and social-policy fields almost universally oppose the death sentence for juveniles. The prestigious American Law Institute excluded the death penalty for crimes committed while under age eighteen from its influential Model Penal Code, concluding that "civilized societies will not tolerate the spectacle of execution of children." This position was also adopted by the National Commission on Reform of Criminal Law.

In August of 1983, the American Bar Association adopted as its formal policy a resolution stating that the association "opposes in principle, the imposition of capital punishment upon any person for any offense committed while under the age of eighteen." That was the first time in the history of the organization that it took a formal position on any aspect of capital punishment. The *Washington Post* endorsed the ABA's policy and urged it as a minimum requirement for jurisdictions having capital punishment.

All European countries forbid the death penalty for crimes committed while under age eighteen. More than three-fourths of the nations of the world have set eighteen as the minimum age for the death penalty. The United Nations endorsed this position in 1976. Another indication of the present global attitude is the condemnation of the death penalty by Pope John Paul II, the first such position by any Pope in history. Even in time of war, the Geneva Convention prohibits execution of civilians under age eighteen at the time of offense.

If the number of juveniles selected for death sentencing and possible execution is only a tiny portion of the number of juveniles who commit capital crimes, how are they selected? In an analysis of the cases of the eleven adults selected for execution from 1977 through 1983, the conclusion was that they were not unique and no rational basis could be discerned for their resulting in execution. Justice Brennan concluded that these adult executions were not "selected on a basis that is neither arbitrary nor capricious, under any meaningful definition of those terms." Extrapolating from these conclusions about adult executions, the inference seems much stronger in the matter of juvenile death sentences and executions. Their even rarer and more random pattern of occurrence leaves no alternative to the conclusion that they are most freakishly imposed. No rational selection process can be determined, and one is left to conclude that the basis of selection is arbitrary and capricious.

Does the Eighth Amendment prohibit the death penalty for crimes committed while under age eighteen? The Supreme Court has avoided giving a direct answer to this question but has provided a general analytical framework from which answers may be derived. The foregoing analysis suggests that the most persuasive answer, given this general analytical framework, is yes—the death penalty for juveniles is cruel and unusual under the Eighth Amendment. This answer follows from a step-by-step consideration of the supporting arguments for the death penalty as they apply to adolescents. In this application, the force of these supporting arguments either disappears or in some cases suggests that the threat of the death penalty may become an attraction to death-defying adolescents. The line should be drawn at age eighteen, since that is by far the most common age for similar restrictions and limitations. This line should emanate from the Eighth Amendment and should be imposed by the Supreme Court.

Indications of a trend seem to be appearing. More and more state legislatures, trial courts, and appellate courts are excluding juveniles from the death penalty. Specific provisions are appearing in statutes recently amended by legislatures. Trial courts, even when they are authorized to sentence juveniles to death, are very rarely doing so. Appellate courts are finding a variety of reasons to reduce the death penalties of juveniles without imposing a blanket prohibition on all such sentences. State laws seem to be moving, however gradually, away from the death penalty for juveniles.

While some persons have been executed for crimes committed as young as age ten, most of the juvenile offenders were age sixteen or seventeen when they committed their crimes; the average age was just over sixteen years. The younger offenders, particularly those under age fourteen, were executed in greatest numbers before 1900. That is also true of the nine female juveniles executed. The last juvenile executed was in 1912.

In line with the historical pattern for all executions in this country, the southern states predominate in juvenile executions, with 65 percent of the total. Georgia is the leader, with forty-one juvenile executions. Other leading states are North Carolina, Ohio, New York, Texas, and Virginia. Thirty-five states and the federal government have executed juveniles for their crimes.

This summary of the characteristics of these executed children and their crimes raises more questions than it answers. But perhaps it will at least serve to refute the commonly held belief that the death penalty has always been reserved for our most hardened criminals, and middle-aged three-time losers. While they are often the ones executed, offenders of more tender years, down even to prepubescence, also have been killed lawfully, hanging from our gallows, restrained in our gas chambers, sitting in our electric chairs, and lying on our hospital gurneys.

If we discard the death sentence for juveniles, what can be done about violent juvenile crime? Many persons support the death penalty for juveniles from fear of and outrage over violent juvenile crime. This fear and outrage are shared by all reasonable persons, whether they are for or against the death penalty. Two answers to this problem suggest themselves. The temporary solution is to impose long-term prison sentences on such violent juveniles. That would ensure that they were reasonably mature adults and had been subjected to whatever rehabilitative programs were available before they were set free again. Life imprisonment without possibility of parole seems an unwise choice, like any personal or business decision that we vow never to reconsider regardless of future events. Few of the violent juveniles would be good candidates for parole in less than ten or twenty years, but that option should be left open for them to work toward.

Unfortunately, no one yet has the cure for violent juvenile crime. It seems clear, however, that the death penalty for juveniles has been given a long trial period and has been found wanting. It's societal costs are enormous, and it delays our search for a rational and acceptable means of reducing violent juvenile crime.

30

Marie Deans

Death Penalty Legal Defense Coordinator in Virginia

The following is a speech given by Marie Deans at the August 1987 meeting of the American Corrections Congress in New Orleans, Louisiana:

First I want to tell you where I'm coming from—mainly because too many corrections officials make easy and inaccurate assumptions about people who do the work I do.

I am the death penalty legal defense coordinator in Virginia. Under grants from law schools and the Virginia Law Foundation, I track all death cases, assist and resource appointed attorneys, whether private or public defenders. Through other grants and donations, I recruit volunteer attorneys to represent those under sentence of death and serve as coordinator of the cases. In that capacity, I have constant contact with the attorneys, the men on the row (we have no women at this time), their families, corrections personnel, and chaplains who work with death-row inmates.

In the last five executions in Virginia, I have been in the death house with the men until a few minutes before they were killed. During the time they were in the death house—at least fifteen days in Virginia —I also worked with them, their families, and their attorneys on a daily basis. Occasionally, I also worked with the victim's family. Before I came to Virginia, I worked for a number of years in South Carolina and was with two men killed there. So I've been in the death house with seven men just before they were killed, and I've also been with several who received last-minute stays.

I am also a member of a murder victim's family. My mother-in-law, Penny, was murdered by an escaped convict in 1972, and I am the founder of a national organization of murder victims' families that opposes the death penalty in every case.

One of the reasons we oppose it is that studies from all over the world, including contiguous states with and without the death penalty in this country, show that if the death penalty has any effect on the homicide rate, it is to increase it.

It is clear to us that support for the death penalty is based on assumption rather than on fact. The facts all go the other way. It is also clear that the death penalty is a very expensive bogus "solution" in that it likely causes the deaths of additional innocent victims; depletes the resources of the states, the courts, the criminal justice system, and the corrections system; and serves as a red herring that keeps us from seeking effective solutions to homicide.

On the other hand, it is the cheapest ticket any politician can punch to further his career. There are over 100 families in our organization, most of whom do work similar to mine or work in states with no death penalty to be sure those states remain abolitionist. We do this work because we have been there. We know what murder leaves behind, and we deeply resent cheap, emotional, unknowing support of the death penalty, which likely creates additional families like ours and blocks efforts to find effective solutions, and we resent our pain being exploited to support this red herring.

Because we are exploited and used as pawns in what we call the politics of death, we recognize others who are exploited, victimized, and used as pawns. Although there are many people who have no sympathy for you, and many in our organization who have difficulty forgiving you, most of us see you as pawns, as exploited, and as being victimized. The problem for us comes because you are apparently willing pawns, while victims' families have no choice. Another problem is that we identify very strongly with the families of men and women on death row. While you may rationalize a difference between state killing and individual killing—calling one murder and one execution—we know that the impact on both families is the same. If there is a difference, it is that for the families of those who are killed by the state, it is worse, for they have to watch and wait helplessly as their loved one faces a predetermined death date. They live for years anticipating a killing and then live through it and then live with the aftermath. God knows what all the aftermath will entail. In Virginia alone there are seven children whose fathers were killed in Virginia's death chamber.

No matter what the circumstances of a particular victimization, the common wound is the psychic one of being treated like an object rather than as a human being. In this case, it begins with the murder of an innocent human being whom the murderer treated like an object. That act is not only dehumanizing to the victim, it is also dehumanizing for the murderer.

The death penalty consistently fails to do anything to rectify that act in any way. In fact, prisons, as they are today, fail as well. Neither do anything to hold the murderer responsible for his or her act of murder. So long as the murderer does not acknowledge his responsibility by seeing his or her victim as a human being and recognizing the humanity of his or her victim, society's punishment is a useless act of vengeance. That is not to say that some murderers do not come to recognize their victims' humanity and accept responsibility for what they have done. Some do, but they do it in spite of the death penalty and prison.

The dehumanization goes on. The victim's family is treated like objects by law enforcement and the courts, as sensational objects by the press and community, as political fodder by politicians. Certainly, turning a human being into a conductor of electricity is dehumanizing, but the dehumanization begins with law enforcement and the courts and goes on once that person reaches death row. Dehumanizing the convicted murderer also dehumanizes the family, because they are too often viewed as mere extensions of the "inmate." Their perception is that corrections people view them as murderers as well.

The people, including the governors, treat you as objects, and you are very helpful in that process, because you treat one another as objects. Your treatment of the people on the row and their families ends up dehumanizing you as well. I'm not saying you are being intentionally cruel. What I am saying is that you don't realize that you are being cruel; you are following procedures.

The mother of one of our clients drove all the way from Michigan to see her son and was strip-searched for a noncontact visit. When she was told she was going to be strip-searched and she objected, she was told she could leave without seeing her son. The ACLU investigated this incident and found out that the only reason they could find for the strip-search was the guard thought the man was a pain. The woman was in poor health and had never caused the prison one bit of trouble. That is diffuse punishment, and it is dehumanizing to everyone involved.

The psychologist Theodor Teik said about war:

> To kill one's enemies, bomb their cities, destroy their women and children and property in cold blood, emotionally indifferent, would be monstrous. Imagine yourself a soldier attacking Nazis. Is it possible to drive a bayonet through a human body in a mood of benevolent detachment? How abominable it would be to kill because of some well considered reason. It would be atrocious to wipe out lives without passion, hate, or vindictiveness, simply because it is a useful thing to do.

But with the exception of bombing, this is exactly what society is now demanding from corrections officials. How do you go on doing their filthy dirty work and acting like nothing happened? You do it by justifying the death penalty, by rationalizing your roles, by dehumanizing yourselves, by getting very involved in the details and the ritual. You try to turn yourselves into efficient technicians of death.

The problem is that killing is not an academic matter. It is a human matter. And just as murder is dehumanizing for the murderer, state killing is a dehumanizing act for those who kill by decree.

You can, of course, deny that. You can tell me that I've misunderstood all the guards, execution-squad members, counselors, assistant wardens, wardens, directors, and commissioners who have talked with me privately. You can agree with the private citizen in the audiences I speak to when I tell them they have no right to demand that you carry out their filthy, dirty work, and they respond, "Hey, they knew when they took the job. They made the choice to get involved in executions. If they don't like pulling the switch, they can leave. Plenty more where they come from." They think you are as expendable as the people on death row.

I've learned a lot while working in prisons, and one thing I've learned is that machismo isn't restricted to one side of the bars, so you can tell me I'm wrong about correctional officials being victimized by the death penalty, but I'll tell you what I hear if you do. I hear denial. Murder victims' families go through denial, too, and denial is an amazingly strong human defense. It isn't strong enough, though.

Now and then I run across corrections officials who genuinely don't care, who really are efficient technicians of death. I'm a lot more afraid of those people than I am of the people on death row.

I'll tell you something else I hear in the rhetoric. I hear fear—fear of losing your jobs, fear of going over the edge, fear of retribution.

Those are legitimate fears, but you do have choices. One is to go on carrying out state killings. Another is to leave individually and quietly. Many have made that choice. Another is to leave, but say why. There is another choice, and that is to take a professional stand together. The truth is you don't have to be death technicians. The truth is you are responsible for your actions, too. Whatever you do, I hope you won't lie to yourselves and others and say you have no other choice.

In my opinion, corrections will never be a true profession until you claim it as a profession. Until then, it will be a political pawn subject to whatever crackpot wind blows out of the latest party caucus or politician's ambition, including killing Velma Barfield* for a Senate seat.

There are almost 2,000 people on death row in this country, and they are adding about 200 a year. Eighty-six of those have been killed. You have thousands to go, and believe me the courts are cranking open the floodgates. But they are still going to let the people on death row sit for years waiting, and you are in charge of holding them for years and then killing them as long as you decide that is your job.

---

*Velma Barfield was the first woman executed since the reinstatement of the death penalty in 1977.

31

Watt Espy
Expert on the History of the
Death Penalty in the United States

Watt Espy has researched and documented 16,885 executions in the United States since the first recorded one in 1608 in Virginia. His research has convinced him that the death penalty fails in the objective of deterrence and has changed him from a proponent to an active opponent of state-run executions.

Citizens of the United States rightfully take great pride in the fact that one of our most sacred traditions, constitutionally guaranteed, is the freedom of the press to publish the news and to keep the public educated on and aware of the great issues of the day. This is a right that is not enjoyed by all of the people of this planet. In fact, no totalitarian government can allow its people open access to all of the facts on any given subject.

Neither can a totalitarian form of government exist without the death penalty. The power to permanently eliminate from society any of its citizens who deviate from the state government line or policy is an absolute necessity for the survival of every repressive form of government known to man.

In this article, I'd like to discuss the relationship of the former, an absolute necessity for a free society, to the latter, the very life blood of tyranny.

In demanding that our people be enlightened by an unfettered press, we can stand with honor in the company of such friends and fellow bastions of freedom as Canada, Great Britain, and our other allies. In our retention and use of the outdated, cruel, and barbaric practice of capital punishment, we not only come to a parting of the ways with other liberty-loving peoples, but we actually join hands with their worst enemies, such governments as Iran, the Republic of South Africa, the various communist regimes, and other dictatorships around the world.

Our views on the subject of state-sanctioned death are, to a great extent, hypocritical and it does not become us to refuse to accept this fact. We pride ourselves on being outspoken champions of human rights for all of the people of the world, and yet, according to the death-row census of 1988, there were 2,048 inmates on death row.

In our history, the journalistic coverage of crime has, generally speaking, been fairly thorough, though not always accurate, while that of executions has varied in treatment from time to time, depending on other nonrelated events which are, supposedly, more newsworthy, such as elections, wars, and various international and domestic crises.

There was a period when the press, in reporting the execution of some poor individual, would resort to headlines in the poorest taste imaginable, often bordering on the blasphemous or obscene. For instance, when Willie Bell, a fourteen-year-old black youth, was hanged at Macon, Georgia, on November 29, 1892, the *Macon Telegraph* headlined the event the next morning as follows: "Gone to Glory—Willie Bell Hanged Yesterday at 12 O'clock—Said He was Gwine to Glory . . ." Other headlines used by various newspapers in heralding executions were: "Jerked to Jesus," "Stretched Hemp," "Danced in the Air," "Swung into Eternity," and "Burned to a Crisp." In few of the written accounts were the condemned persons treated as human beings. More often they were referred to as animals, beasts, fiends, and unnatural creatures.

However, language moderated considerably with the advent of the twentieth century, and when executions reached their peak during the 1930s, except in such previously well publicized cases as that of Bruno Hauptmann, the Lindburg baby kidnapper, most were, if mentioned at all, noted in terse, one-sentence paragraphs hidden in an obscure section of the paper. Even though the media appeared to consider executions less newsworthy as they became more commonplace, they, nonetheless, fully met the challenge on reporting of criminal activity before the trial.

Journalistic coverage of such famous cases as those of Leo Frank in Georgia, Charles Becker in New York, and Sacco and Vanzetti in Massachusetts, to name only three, led to the inflammation of public opinion, which had the end result of what are generally considered today to have been miscarriages of justice.

I join with the rest of the news-reading public in saluting the *New York Times* for the general accuracy and fairness of its coverage on all topics. Yet, even this accepted and respected model for the journalistic community, ". . . committed 75 separate and independent contempts in the Hauptmann case, judged by common law standards, between the period of September 21, 1934, and December 31, 1934, before the trial commenced . . . ," charges Harold W. Sullivan in his book *Contempts by Publication: The Law of Trial by Newspaper* (Littleton, Colo.: Rothman, 1980).

One of the greatest fears that those of us who oppose the death penalty share is that, as executions again become more commonplace, they will also become less newsworthy and that, consequently, a blood bath may occur in this country without the people generally being made aware. Of course, as always, certain executions will always be considered great media events, and when certain of those on death row whose cases have received widespread attention are executed, such as Theodore Bundy, John Wayne Gacey, and the incredible Henry Lee Lucas, it will always be a journalistic field day. However, since the resumption of executions in the United States after the moratorium, we have seen the coverage lessen with each succeeding application of the supreme penalty.

The state-sanctioned death of an American citizen is now rarely mentioned on the television news reports with the exception of the 24-hour-news channel and those local channels serving the state in which it took place. It no longer draws front page coverage in most newspapers, but is relegated to an obscure section where it is likely to be overlooked except by those who read the paper page by page and line by line.

The media in general, and certainly the press, has not only the right but also an obligation to report the news on both the commission of crime and the subsequent final outcome of the issue, but it should be done in as fair and as factual a manner as is possible.

Since the resumption of the active use of the death penalty with the execution of Gary Gilmore on January 17, 1977, which, being the first such occurrence in ten years, received front-page coverage with large headlines not only in this country but all over the world, our news media has covered, with varying degrees of depth and accuracy, the other executions that have taken place in our country. Those of the more spectacular variety, such as Charlie Brooks (the first to die by lethal injection), Ronald Clark O'Bryant (the Halloween candy man), and Velma Barfield (the first woman) were covered as outstanding media events. Others, where the condemned and their victims were not so well known, were treated far less prominently.

My purpose is not to complain about this difference in the amount of media interest focused on different individuals, but rather about the way in which some of the cases, both before or at the time of the trial and at the time of the executions, were covered.

When Jimmy Lee Gray was asphyxiated in Mississippi on September 2, 1983, for the rape and murder of a three-year-old girl, the wire services and press made much of the fact that he had been paroled from the Arizona State Penitentiary after serving a portion of a sentence for "a similar crime." In truth, there was little similarity, other than that the crime was murder, between the two offenses. The Arizona crime had been committed when Gray, then seventeen years old, killed his high-school girlfriend during a trivial quarrel. This was hardly similar to the rape and murder of a three-year-old child, and, by not giving the actual circumstances of his prior conviction, the media, perhaps unintentionally, made it appear that Mr. Gray was some kind of pedophilic monster who had made a life's profession of molesting and murdering small children—a crime that provokes the wrath of even the most hardened of ordinary criminals, not to mention the law-abiding citizens who read the newspapers and rely on them for their information.

Until shortly before John Young's execution in Georgia on March 20, 1985, the public did not become aware of the fact that, when he was but a child of five, his mother was shot and killed by her lover as she lay sleeping in the same bed with him and a younger sibling. This fact had not been brought out by his trial attorney or the press until after he was sentenced to die. We can only imagine the trauma that a sensitive youngster at such an impressionable age must have experienced and the emotional scars that, without proper treatment and counseling, would have warped his mind to the extent that, fifteen years later, he would erupt in a maniacal fury and senselessly bludgeon to death three elderly people.

The wire services and newspapers reported that Morriss Odell Mason, executed in Virginia, was mildly retarded and a paranoid schizophrenic. However, they did not report that Mason, who was also a chronic alcoholic, had in vain begged his parole officer to assist him in entering a halfway house because he could not cope with his alcoholic and other problems. Surely this failure to assist by a man whose duty it was to aid Mason might be considered as partially responsible for the murders that he committed, the first of which occurred only a few days after the denial of his request.

On at least two occasions where lethal injection has been the means of killing a man, I feel that the press has failed to adequately portray the real horrors of this means of execution. When James David Autry was scheduled to die—after midnight, but before sunrise—on October 5, 1983, so anxious and determined were the responsible officials of the State of Texas that they would not be cheated of their victim, that they had Autry strapped onto the gurney of death, the catheters intravenously inserted, and held him in that uncomfortable position from shortly after 11 o'clock on the night of the fourth, in a state of preparation to inject the chemicals of death as quickly as the clock tolled twelve. Even when a stay was received from U.S. Supreme Court Justice White, Autry was obliged to remain ready to die for an additional fifteen minutes in order that the stay might be verified and the officials convinced that they were not being hoaxed.

After having undergone this terrible ordeal, the press made little mention of the previous mental and physical torture to which he had been subjected, when, only five months later, Autry kept his next appointment with death on March 14, 1984.

One of the reasons for having a free and uninhibited press is that, by presenting in an accurate and unbiased manner all of the facts on any given matter, national debates, soul searchings, and reappraisals of policy are encouraged among an enlightened people.

On March 15, 1986, Steven Morin was executed in Texas by lethal injection. The wire services and the press only casually mentioned the fact that, after he had been strapped to his gurney, Steven Morin's body was prodded by needles for over forty minutes before a vein large enough to take the catheter was located. Can you imagine the outrage that would be expressed by the media of this country if, in Russia, for example, the executioner spent forty minutes sticking needles into a man's body before executing him?

I can truthfully say that, after researching, documenting, and collecting all of the information that I could find on over 16,885 legal executions in the United States, I have found but few instances where, in my opinion, a serious effort was made by any more than a few individuals, to really understand the person about to die or the factors beyond his control that had motivated him to the actions for which the state declared his life forfeit.

Second only to the protection afforded them by the courts, those accused of crime are dependent on the media and the information that it imparts to the public for receiving a fair hearing before the bar of justice. Therefore, I hope that the future coverage of capital cases by the media, from the time when a suspect is first identified, will seek to more adequately present the accused as a human being rather than a monster in human form, and will attempt to establish for those who follow the accounts mitigating as well as aggravating circumstances. Only by such unbiased treatment of these sordid events and the perpetrators can the public be made aware of the reasons why people really commit these rash acts for which they may be condemned to die. Only by knowing the reasons why crimes occur can we seek to find ways of preventing them by attacking their actual causes, and, thus, make society a better and safer place for all of us.

32

Jerome D. Gorman, M.D.
General Practitioner in Richmond, Virginia

In the past decade, the Virginia legislature has examined lethal injection more than once as an alternative to the electric chair. Meanwhile, several other states have adopted lethal injection as their means of executing condemned criminals. With the state prison, which houses the electric chair, now scheduled to move, lethal injection is likely to come up again in Virginia during the next session of the General Assembly. Why this interest in replacing the electric chair or other traditional means of execution with an intravenous injection?

Proponents argue that intravenous injection is less painful, less stressful, and therefore more humane than electrocution. Similarly, electrocution may leave burn marks on the lifeless body, something which lethal injection would obviate. Efficacy has also been argued; circulatory arrest sometimes requires more than one shock, a most uncomfortable scene for witnesses. Expense may also be an issue; Pentothal, needles, intravenous (i.v.) tubing, and electrolyte solutions, all commercially available from any medical supply house, might be cheaper than a specially wired custom-built oak chair.

On close scrutiny, these arguments are less than compelling. That injection is more humane than electrocution may be true for witnesses, but not for the prisoner, whose cortical neurons are depolarized by the first surge of electricity producing instant unconsciousness. Regarding an unscarred corpse, who benefits? Certainly not the prisoner. As for efficacy, intravenous injection is not likely to be more swift and

sure than electricity, especially if venous access in a less than coopera-
tive prisoner proves difficult, as it inevitably will on occasion. And any
potential savings are insignificant compared to the huge costs of due
process and detention typical of capital punishment.

Yet the very persistence of the issue is evidence for a compelling
argument that won't go away. Quite simply, the compelling argument
is that capital punishment is hard on those in the system who admini-
ster it. It is distressing for one person to participate in the destruction
of another. Even when one accepts society's right to employ capital punishment, even when one is not personally the executioner, participation
is still distressing for most. Legislators, judges, lawyers, prison workers,
and others in the system are seeking to ease their own discomfort by
proposing lethal injection as a less aversive alternative to electrocution.

Lethal injection looks more like therapy than punishment. It involves a traditional and familiar therapeutic modality, intravenous general anesthesia typically with Pentothal and a muscle relaxant. The only
difference is that the patient, once put to sleep, is not recovered. By
wrapping punishment in a therapeutic cloak, the whole process leading
to that final moment feels less aversive to those who are required to
participate and is therefore more bearable. Direct physician involvement
(which isn't needed and probably won't be required) is not an issue here.
The issue is the use of a therapeutic model for capital punishment.

This use of a well known medical tool, general anesthesia, for execution blurs the distinctions between healing and killing, between illness and guilt. That is why it would be effective in easing the distress
of those involved. That is also precisely why physicians should oppose
it. Those distinctions between illness and guilt, between therapy and
punishment, are important to a just society. Once before in the twentieth century, physicians (in Nazi Germany) allowed themselves to play
a role in blurring these distinctions, with disastrous consequences.

It is to maintain these important distinctions that physicians, even
physicians who support the death penalty, are ethically constrained not
to play an active role in capital punishment. Lethal injection, because
it blurs these distinctions, is as much a perversion of medicine as is
using doctors to perform executions. The integrity of society is much
better protected with traditional means of executing, such as the electric
chair, the gas chamber, or the firing squad. They leave no doubt that
the act is one of punishment, not of healing, and that the subject is

a convict, not a patient.

Many physicians oppose the death penalty itself; others support it. Regardless of one's position on capital punishment, however, every physician can find good reason to oppose the use of medical tools in its execution. Every health-care provider should insist that the therapeutic model be used only for providing care which is meant to enrich and extend life, not to punish or eliminate it.

I am an opponent of the death penalty for a lot of reasons. Primarily it is the deliberate killing of another human being. It is not like killing in self-defense. As a physician I have personal objections to the taking of a life of a mature person. Actually, that would be against the hippocratic oath for me, an oath a few thousand years old.

I think it is clear that the death penalty is not a deterrent; in other words, it is not necessary to have the death penalty to protect the public. Perhaps in very primitive times, when people had no way of protecting themselves, it might have been necessary to execute. But that's no longer true in our society and hasn't been for a long time. The Supreme Court and many people admit now that capital punishment does not deter future violent crimes.

I have not witnessed an actual killing in the death chamber, but I was present outside of the prison here in Richmond during a pro-death-penalty rally. Just seeing the brutal sentiments stirred up outside by those who proposed the death penalty, the lust for death, for killing, for vengeance, I don't think it adds anything to the good order of society.

Actually, lethal injection is not a more humane way of killing. From the time you strap the prisoner down it takes longer than other methods. It is a hideous perversion and subversion of anesthesiology, a branch of medicine. In the name of "humane execution"—an oxymoron—several states have adopted lethal injection as the method for killing prisoners.

Lethal injection is humane only to witnesses, not to the condemned. While conscious, the prisoner is strapped down and immobilized on a stretcher. Then a large, hollow, bore needle connected to an intravenous solution is inserted by puncturing an arm vein. Some prisoners have required multiple painful probings and punctures before the needle could be inserted correctly.

Sometimes prisoners have been strapped down with nonlethal fluid dripping in for a prolonged conscious period while court deliberations on a stay of execution were continuing. Recently, a court granted a stay, but the lethal drugs already had been given, so the prisoner died. In another case, a prisoner had nonlethal fluid dripping in for an hour before a stay was granted. Several months later, the man was killed by lethal injection.

To kill a prisoner, a fast-acting barbituate drug is infused to produce unconsciousness; it is accompanied by a curanelike drug to paralyze all breathing muscles and a high dose of potassium to stop the heart.

In the medical practice of anesthesiology, when this sequence of drugs is used, drugs to restore heart action and breathing are administered at the end of surgery. At some level, the condemned prisoner still may be aware of a sense of suffocation and the painful effect of potassium coursing through his vein and into the heart.

From the moment a prisoner is strapped down, lethal injection is both more cruelly painful and longer than electrocution. In one case it took forty minutes of multiple punctures to probe around and find a vein big enough. There have been times when i.v.'s have been started and leaked, and they had to restart it. It's hard enough for an expert to get the needle in quickly, when treating the voluntary patient in the hospital but to do the same thing to a prisoner who has lousy veins and who may be resisting can be a daunting task.

Electrocution is quicker for the condemned because the higher consciousness center of the brain is rendered instantly inactive at the first electric shock, even though additional shock may be needed to stop the heart and breathing, which are involuntary processes.

There is no "humane" way to destroy another human. Execution is the most premeditated form of killing and is a necrophilic sado-ritual catering to attitudes of vengeance and retribution, attitudes which are destructive to a just and merciful society.

33

David Gottleib

Professor of Law, University of Kansas

A few years ago when Kansas was considering the death penalty, I was asked to find out what capital punishment would cost the state. I did not attempt to measure the cost versus life in prison; I simply had to find out how much more the state would pay if it did have capital punishment.

My original estimate was that it would be seven or eight million dollars extra. The legislative-research service did their own study and their findings were higher than mine. They figured that it would cost the state of Kansas about twelve million dollars to have capital punishment.

While on the surface it might seem reasonable to assume that it is less expensive to execute a person than to imprison him for life, that assumption is wrong. As Supreme Court Justice Thurgood Marshall explained in *Furman* v. *Georgia* in 1972:

As for the argument that it is cheaper to execute a capital offender than to imprison him for life . . . it is simply incorrect. A disproportionate amount of money spent on prisons is attributable to death row. Condemned men are not productive members of the prison community, although they could be, and executions are expensive. Appeals are often automatic, and courts admittedly spend more time with death cases.

At trial, the selection of jurors is likely to become a costly, time-consuming problem in a capital case, and defense counsel will reasonably exhaust every possible means to save his client from execution, no matter how long the trial takes.

During the period between conviction and execution, there are an inordinate number of collateral attacks on the conviction and attempts to obtain executive clemency, all of which exhaust the time, money and effort of the state. . . .

When all is said and done, there can be no doubt that it costs more to execute a man than to keep him in prison for life.

Every study that has been done since Justice Marshall's writing supports his assertion. Capital cases are very expensive. There are at least four reasons why this is so.

First, capital cases take far more time to litigate. Because the stakes are life and death, guilty pleas are a rarity. Virtually every case is taken to trial. For similar reasons, the defense contests every potential issue. Preparation for trial of a death-penalty case is generally far more extensive, with two to five times as many pretrial motions. Jury selection takes longer, since the jury must be qualified not only to rule on the question of guilt, but also to decide on the death penalty. The trial itself takes up to three times as long as an ordinary first-degree-murder case, with far more extensive use of experts and investigators.

Second, death-penalty cases require a second, separate trial on penalty if the jury returns a guilty verdict. There is no equivalent to this procedure in a regular murder case. The jury must sit for days, in some cases weeks, to hear evidence concerning whether the defendant should live or die. A host of expert witnesses may be required for this determination. As a result of this second phase, the time taken for a death-penalty trial is further expanded. While a non-capital trial lasting even a week is fairly typical, a typical death-penalty case may last from three to eight weeks.

Third, if the jury imposes a death sentence, a long appeal process will begin. The process includes a direct appeal to the state supreme court, a petition for *certiorari** to the U.S. Supreme Court, post-conviction applications in state courts, appeals of those applications, post-conviction applications in federal courts, appeals of those applications in a U.S. Circuit Court of Appeals, second and sometimes third appeals to the U.S. Supreme Court, and finally a petition for state clemency.

---

*A writ directed against an inferior court to bring the record of a cause into a superior court for re-examination and review.

The process can take more than ten years. The cost may be ten times the ordinary murder-conviction appeal. Obviously, a defense attorney will be obliged to pursue every possible legal means to avoid execution; unlike the normal case, there is no place for an attorney to recommend to his clients that he not take further appeals.

Fourth, during the time of these appeals, the defendant is housed on death row. Death row costs money to build and is more expensive to staff than an ordinary prison facility. The defendant is housed in a single cell and is unable to contribute to the prison by working in a prison industry.

The Kansas public defender's office estimated that the trial costs of defense services in capital cases could reach $31,000 per case, more than six times the current defense costs of that state's first-degree-murder cases. Their estimate was based on the assumption that the defense of a death-penalty case would require 800 hours of attorney time for an average bill of $26,000. They estimated expert services would cost $3,000 per trial and investigative services $2,000. They predicted 80 first-degree-murder cases per year for a total bill for trial-level defense services at $2,480,000.

The Kansas projections were well below actual figures being spent in many other states. Just as the defense must file more pretrial motions in a capital case, the prosecution must answer them. The prosecutor, as well as the defense attorney, must be present for *voir dire** of the jury, for the expanded trial, and for the additional sentencing proceeding. Capital cases will take four times as long for prosecutors if they take four times as long for defense attorneys. Moreover, if the defense presents experts and uses investigators, there is no doubt the prosecutor will utilize such resources as well.

In most states, far more money already is spent on prosecution than is spent on defense. States have estimated the disparity between prosecution and defense resources as anywhere from two to one as high as ten to one. The most conservative estimate is from a recent study in Maryland, which found that prosecution and defense costs there were virtually identical. Taking the Maryland figure, Kansas estimated prosecution costs in that state would be $2,500,000 per year.

---

*A preliminary examination and oath to determine whether a witness or prospective juror is competent.

There are at least three kinds of judicial costs in a trial: jury costs, security costs, and the costs of the judges and court personnel.

The Kansas public defenders' office estimated a substantial increase in juror costs for capital trials. Figuring 80 first-degree-murder cases per year and three weeks longer per trial than in ordinary cases, they projected additional juror costs of $168,000 per year. If the *voir dire* panel is 150 instead of 100 persons and *voir dire* lasts two days instead of one, the additional cost would be $160,000. The total increase in jury costs would be $328,000 per year.

Kansas did not develop figures for increased security costs of capital trials, but projected that such additional costs certainly would occur.

The increase in trial time required increases the judicial resources needed. In states where the judiciary chooses not to ask for new judges, the costs are borne at the outset by all those litigants who do not have capital cases. These litigants can expect less time devoted to their cases and increased backlogs. But as backlogs mount, state legislatures eventually are forced to supply additional judges. It costs approximately $150,000 to staff a courtroom full-time. If five additional judges are added in a state because of backlogs created by capital trials, the additional cost to the state would be $575,000 per year.

The Kansas public defenders' office estimated increases in appellate-defense cost (for the projected eighty cases) of $135,000 per year in attorney fees and $120,000 per year in additional transcript fees. Their estimate was based on a projection that of the eighty cases only sixteen would actually result in death sentences and that one attorney could handle four death-penalty direct appeals a year. The cost for four additional defense attorneys and one secretary was estimated at $135,000.

In other states, the cost of each direct appeal has been estimated as an additional $20,000 in Kentucky and California and up to $50,000 in New Jersey. Moreover, the estimated amount of time reported in other states was up to six months of attorney time for each appeal.

As with trial-level costs, the increase in prosecution costs for appeals is similar to the increase for the defense. Thus, Kansas estimated an increase of at least $135,000 a year in prosecution costs based on sixteen death-penalty appeals in any one year.

After completion of state direct appeals, a series of collateral appeals follows. Post-conviction applications are made in state courts and those applications are appealed; post-conviction applications are made in federal courts and those applications are appealed; final appeals are made to the U.S. Supreme Court and a final petition for state clemency follows. Additional defense and prosecution staff and time are required for these.

The state of Florida, which provides state funding for post-conviction appeals, is spending more than $1,000,000 per year for post-conviction defense alone.

Finally, a state with a death row is required to spend millions on housing those convicted of capital crimes. A death row capable of housing 100 inmates in maximum security confinement costs more than $7,500,000. According to former Kansas Secretary of Corrections Michael Barbana, construction costs for maximum security are greater than for medium security and run from $75,000 to $100,000 per bed. At that rate, a 100-person death row costs from $7,500,000 to $10,000,000. The state of Alaska predicted capital expenses of more than $2,000,000 to construct a 20-person death-row facility, a cost of more than $100,000 per bed.

In addition to the costs of construction, a Department of Correction is forced to incur additional staffing expenses. Studies have concluded that it costs far more to house an inmate in death-row confinement than in the prison's general population. The costs reflect the need to house each inmate in an individual cell, to separate the inmate from the general population, to provide separate recreation, and to increase security. According to representatives of the Florida Clearinghouse on Criminal Justice, during the eight to ten years involved in post-conviction review, an extra $15,000 per inmate probably will be required.

Part Four

Organizations Against the Death Penalty

34

National Coalition to Abolish the Death Penalty

The National Coalition to Abolish the Death Penalty (NCADP) is a resource, coordination, and support center for efforts to end capital punishment throughout the United States. It links individuals and organizations at the national, regional, state, and local levels for information sharing, mutual assistance, and campaign development. The NCADP promotes and facilitates public education and advocacy, aids groups seeking funding, coordinates press contacts, and monitors and responds to legal and legislative developments.

In 1972 the U.S. Supreme Court struck down the death-penalty laws of every state, declaring that the imposition of the death penalty at that time was arbitrary, "freakish," and "racist."

However, after a four-year moratorium, the Court, in *Gregg* v. *Georgia,* ruled that newly drafted death-penalty laws met constitutional standards. The first execution under these laws took place in 1977, when Gary Gilmore was put to death in Utah by firing squad.

The National Coalition to Abolish the Death Penalty was founded in 1976 in response to the resumption of executions in the United States. The NCADP was originally based in New York City as part of the American Civil Liberties Union. The NCADP moved to Philadelphia and incorporated separately from the ACLU in 1982, and in 1987, it moved its national office to Washington, D.C. The NCADP also has a field office in Indiana.

The NCADP is a coalition of over 120 national, state, and local organizations. Each affiliate holds one seat on the NCADP Board of Directors, which meets yearly to approve an annual budget, elect officers, and determine general direction for the organization.

The NCADP Executive Committee includes elected officers, fifteen at-large members, and chairpersons of standing committees. The Executive Committee meets quarterly and oversees the administrative and programmatic operation of the Coalition.

The NCADP is a non-profit organization under the Internal Revenue Service codes section and is tax exempt. Contributions to the NCADP are tax deductible under the regulation of the IRS. The NCADP receives no government funding.

There are many efforts currently underway to abolish the death penalty in the United States. Attacks on this form of punishment are being waged by lawyers, writers, and scholars; by a wide spectrum of religious bodies; by international and national human and civil rights groups; and by abolitionist organizations in each state.

These efforts each bring unique contributions to the abolition movement. It is through this combination of public education, legal challenges, moral suasion, international pressure, and direct organizing that the death penalty will finally be laid to rest.

As a facilitator and catalyst, the National Coalition to Abolish the Death Penalty is building a national movement which will abolish the use of death as punishment in the United States.

For more information, please contact: NCADP, 1325 G. Street N.W., Lower Level B, Washington, D.C. 20005.

35

Amnesty International

**From an Interview with David Hinkley,
Western U.S. Regional Director**

Amnesty International was started in London, in 1961, by a British lawyer. The focus of the organization has always been in three areas of human-rights work. For prisoners, we work for the release of those whom we call prisoners of conscience, i.e., those who don't believe in violence. The second area of our mandate is to work with all political prisoners, and the third is to work for the abolition of all forms of torture and cruel, inhumane, and degrading treatment, including executions, which we regard as the ultimate form of cruel and inhumane treatment, and a violation of life.

We've always been opposed to the death penalty but the work began to take on a much higher priority in 1977 when there was an international gathering in Stockholm which produced the Stockholm declaration plan to fight the death penalty worldwide by means of a campaign rather than simply by writing letters on behalf of individuals faced with execution. We also decided to confront legislation that kept the death penalty on the books and to do our best to create a public constituency against the death penalty.

In 1977, we began extensive research and action on the death penalty, and it has remained one of the organization's top priorities ever since then. In the past twelve years, we have particularly focused on those countries that use the death penalty most often. About a hundred countries still have the death penalty on the books, but some of them don't actually carry it out. In the 80s, for example, seven countries were responsible for over 80 percent of all the executions in the world. Unfortunately, the United States is one of those countries, along with the Soviet Union, Nigeria, South Africa, China, Iraq, and Pakistan.

We also work for repeal of the death penalty in legislation. We have an international network. There are Amnesty International members in 160 countries. We have grown very dramatically over the years numbering over 700,000 members. We don't get involved in prisoners of conscience or political prisoners in the United States. That's to protect our impartiality. We do work in our own country on the death penalty, which is vital for Amnesty USA because we don't want to be in the position of throwing stones at glass houses and from our own glass house. So we work extensively here in the United States for abolition of the death penalty. In the past several years, as large numbers of prisoners reach the end of their appeals, the United States has begun to execute in large numbers.

I became involved in Amnesty in 1973. I was a volunteer for nine years and I've been on staff for seven years. I was involved in the death-penalty issue long before I was with Amnesty. Since I've been on staff here in California, I've been working to develop state abolition teams all over the western United States. It's taken seven years but we now have state teams in all thirteen western states. As for the rest of the country, we have teams in almost every state whether or not they have the death penalty to make sure that the state doesn't reintroduce the death penalty and that the public is informed of our position on it. In the west our main interest is on California, where we have over 250 people on death row. Nationwide, the interest is on the south where most of the people are being executed.

We do most of our work through letter writing, and we sometimes demonstate and conduct vigils. For example, we had a march, in October 1989, from Sacramento to San Quentin. It was a ten-day march and Amnesty International played a leading role in organizing it. I was Amnesty's spokesperson. The march was made in concert with other abolitionist groups such as the American Civil Liberties Union, the NAACP, The Legal Defense Fund, the Catholic Church of Sacramento, and others.

Official Statement on Capital Punishment

The right to life and the right not to be subjected to cruel, inhuman, or degrading treatment or punishment are enshrined in the Universal Declaration of Human Rights and other international human-rights documents. The death penalty is a denial of those rights and its use in the USA has resulted in violations of human rights throughout that country. Amnesty International is calling on the USA to join the growing number of nations all over the world who have abolished the death penalty or are working toward abolition. In its report on the death penalty in the USA, the organization included the following recommendations:

- All governments in death-penalty states should abolish the penalty for all offenses in law.

- The death penalty should be abolished under the federal Uniform Code of Military Justice and the federal government should refrain from enacting the death penalty under federal civilian law.

- Pending the abolition of the death penalty in law, state laws and practice should conform to minimum international standards that preclude the imposition of the death penalty on juveniles or the mentally ill.

- Until the death penalty is abolished or a moratorium on death sentences is introduced, state governors and boards of pardons and paroles should broaden their criteria for granting clemency in capital cases.

- Amnesty International believes that the evidence of racial discrimination in the application of the death penalty is a matter of urgent concern and recommends that the executive or legislative branch of the federal government commission a thorough, impartial inquiry into the question.

Countless men and women have been executed for the stated purpose of preventing crime, especially the crime of murder. Yet, as documented, study after study in diverse countries has failed to find convincing evidence that the death penalty has any unique capacity to deter others from committing particular crimes. The most recent survey of research findings on the relation between the death penalty and homicide rates, conducted for the UN in 1988, has concluded: "This research has failed to provide scientific proof that executions have a greater deterrent effect than life imprisonment. Such proof is unlikely to be forthcoming. The evidence as a whole still gives no positive support to the deterrent hypothesis."

Undeniably the death penalty, by permanently "incapacitating" a prisoner, prevents the person from repeating the crime. But there is no way to be sure that the prisoner would indeed have repeated his crime if allowed to live, nor is there any need to violate the prisoner's right to life for the purpose of incapacitation; dangerous offenders can be kept safely away from the public without resorting to execution, as shown by the experiences of many abolitionist countries.

If today's penal systems do not sanction the burning of an arsonist's home, the rape of a rapist, or the torture of a torturer, it is not because they tolerate the crimes. Instead, it is because societies understand that they must be built on a different set of values from those they condemn.

An execution cannot be used to condemn killing; it is killing. Such an act by the state is the mirror image of the criminal's willingness to use physical violence against a victim.

Related to the argument that some people deserve to die is the proposition that the state is incapable of determining exactly who they are. Whatever one's view of the retribution argument may be, the practice of the death penalty reveals that no criminal justice system is, or conceivably could be, capable of deciding fairly, consistently, and infallibly who should live and who should die.

It is the irrevocable nature of the death penalty, the fact that the prisoner is eliminated forever, that makes the penalty so tempting to some states as a tool of repression. Thousands have been put to death under one government only to be recognized as innocent victims when another set of authorities comes to power. Only abolition can ensure that such political abuse of the death penalty will never occur.

There is no convincing argument that society cannot find ways other than killing to express its condemnation of crime. Indeed, the publicity surrounding an execution may divert attention from the crime to the person who committed it. Far from being condemned for his or her deeds, the criminal may actually become a focus of sympathy.

As has been found in countries where the death penalty has been abolished, a sufficiently severe punishment which is compatible with international human-rights standards can adequately demonstrate society's condemnation of the crime in question. Unlike the death penalty, non-lethal punishments can reflect the values of society rather than the values of the killer.

36

NAACP Legal Defense Fund

The administration of capital punishment in this country is rife with racism and discrimination against the poor. The purported "protection" afforded by this sanction is provided almost exclusively to white people. Prosecutors who contend—falsely—that the death penalty deters violent crime almost never use it to fight crime in minority communities. In state after state, studies show that the killers of whites are far more likely to be sentenced to death than the killers of blacks. Furthermore, America's death-row inmates are disproportionately black and overwhelmingly poor.

For more than two decades, the NAACP Legal Defense Fund (LDF) has fought against the death penalty and protected the constitutional rights of death-row inmates in the federal courts. In recent years, however, federal courts have been increasingly unwilling to grant relief to persons unconstitutionally sentenced to death. There is also inadequate information available to the African American community about race discrimination and the death penalty.

In response to the growing crisis in capital litigation, in 1990–1991, the Capital Punishment Program began to shift its focus from one devoted almost exclusively to federal appeals to one that also included community outreach, litigation at the trial level, public education, and legislative consulting.

Community Outreach

Last year, LDF reached out to African American communities where local prosecutors had abused their power by singling out people of color for the death penalty. We used information about the way "Jim Crow" criminal justice was being perpetuated to mount legal challenges to three capital sentences.

In *Fairchild* v. *Lockhart,* we staved off the execution of Barry Lee Fairchild, who claimed that he had been beaten and forced to confess falsely to a 1983 capital crime by deputy sheriffs in Little Rock, Arkansas. Hours before his scheduled execution, we submitted evidence that three other African American men had been beaten and coerced in the same 1983 murder investigation. After an appellate court granted an eleventh hour stay of execution, we learned that at least *fifteen* African American men had been beaten and told to confess to the same capital crime.

As this systematic brutality was uncovered, we worked with the state and local branches of the NAACP, the Little Rock Black Ministerial Alliance, and other groups to galvanize interest in Mr. Fairchild's case among people of color. As a result, there were numerous black people of all ages and walks of life at Mr. Fairchild's evidentiary hearing in federal court.

This community interest created an atmostphere of support in which the black men who had been beaten were less fearful about testifying. While Mr. Fairchild still sits on death row, we are hopeful that the appellate court will grant relief in his case, based on both the pattern of coercion and substantial new evidence that raises doubt about his guilt.

In *Brooks* v. *State of Georgia,* we represented William Brooks in the retrial of his murder case in Georgia state court. We worked with the black community in Columbus to demonstrate the ugly role of racism in death-penalty prosecutions in Muscogee County, Georgia—Mr. Brooks is black, while the victim was a white woman.

By reaching out to local NAACP branches, the Southern Christian Leadership conference, and other black organizations, we were able to meet with families of black murder victims and learn from them how the local District Attorney's office selected and handled capital cases. We discovered, for example, that the local prosecutor never called these black families and asked whether they wanted to seek the death penalty for the killers of their loved ones. By contrast, the prosecutor gave great weight to the desires of the families of white victims. At a pre-trial hearing, we used the testimony of these victims' relatives, statistics about race discrimination in the selection of death-penalty cases, and other evidence to show the racism inherent in capital prosecutions.

In addition, the organizations that we contacted took an active interest in addressing this racism, and mobilized vociferous opposition to race discrimination in death sentencing. In that atmosphere a jury unanimously voted to sentence Mr. Brooks to life in January 1991.

We launched a similar effort in Panama City, Florida, moving to bar the State from seeking the death penalty at the retrial of Kenneth Foster because it had previously been sought in a racially biased manner. Although the trial court refused to grant our motion and Mr. Foster is on death row, his case has stirred the black community to begin demanding the dismantling of two systems of criminal justice—one for blacks and one for whites. We are confident that the prosecutor's office in Panama City will now think much more carefully about seeking the death penalty, given the African American community's increased knowledge about the racism inherent in this ultimate sanction.

Battling Procedural Barriers

We provided direct representation in two Supreme Court cases in 1990, both involving a chilling trend: the rigid adherence of federal judges to procedural rules that prevent them from hearing important constitutional claims in death-penalty appeals.

Many of these restrictive rules are being applied to death-row inmates who file more than one "petition for a writ of *habeas corpus*" (the process in which unconstitutional practices in state criminal proceedings are presented to federal courts).

Serious constitutional violations and other injustices are frequently not presented in death-row inmates' first *habeas* petitions. There are two primary reasons for this: (1) the incompetence or inadvertence of the inexperienced, underpaid court-appointed attorneys who represent many death-row inmates; and/or (2) the concealment of crucial evidence by the State. Therefore, when evidence of constitutional violations becomes available *after* a first *habeas* petition, many death-row inmates file second or subsequent petitions.

Yet more and more federal judges are refusing even to *consider* blatant violations of the Bill of Rights, if evidence of those violations wasn't presented in an inmate's initial *habeas* petition.

This issue surfaced in the tragic case of Warren McCleskey. In the summer of 1987, when he was about to be executed, the federal district court found that Atlanta police had secretly arranged to place an informant in the jail cell next to him and to interrogate him unconstitutionally about his crime. The court ordered a new trial. Yet no trial was forthcoming, because in Novemeber 1989, an appellate court held that the issue of the informant *should* have been raised during the first round of McCleskey's appeals in 1981—even though the State had concealed its involvement with the informant from Mr. McCleskey's original lawyer! We argued the case before the Supreme Court in November 1990.

In April 1991, the Court ruled against Mr. McCleskey and set a new, rather horrifying standard that will force lower federal courts to dismiss almost all claims that were not raised in first *habeas* petitions. This ruling sharply curtails the ability of death-row inmates to file potentially life-saving challenges to egregious violations of the Bill of Rights.

Another case was an outgrowth of our ongoing challenge to the Texas death-penalty statute. In 1988, we had petitioned the Court for review in *Selvage* v. *Lynaugh,* arguing that the Texas statute, as applied, precluded full consideration of mitigating evidence by juries. The Court accepted this argument in a subsequent case, *Penry* v. *Lynaugh,* but nevertheless agreed to review crucial procedural issues in Mr. Selvage's case. The state contended that Mr. Selvage's constitutional claims should not be considered by appeals courts because they should have been raised earlier (before the *Penry* ruling).

Fearful that the Court could use Mr. Selvage's case as a way to create further procedural barriers to death-row petitioners, we persuaded the Court to return the case to state court.

In addition to this direct representation, LDF also continued to serve in an advisory capacity in all significant Supreme Court death-row cases.

Notable Successes in Other Cases

Last year, we were also active in the litigation of numerous cases in state and lower federal courts. In one notable example, we convinced the Supreme Court of Georgia that Eddie Lee Ross was denied effective assistance of counsel when he was represented by James R. Venable, a former Imperial Wizard of the Ku Klux Klan.

LDF provided critical assistance in preventing the first execution in California since 1967. Working on behalf of David Alton Harris, we brought to the attention of the federal courts an important organic brain disorder—fetal alcohol syndrome—heretofore not recognized by them as contributing to violent behavior. Based on evidence that Mr. Harris suffered from this disorder, his execution was stayed by a federal appellate court.

Looking Beyond the Judiciary for Relief

In 1990–1991, we were successful in getting executive bodies with vested clemency and pardoning powers to look beyond the procedural barriers erected by the judicial branch of government, and get to the substantive issues which merited that justice be done.

One case that drew nationwide attention was that of Joe Giarratano, who pleaded guilty in 1979 to a rape and double murder in Norfolk, Virginia, and was sentenced to death. His years in prison transformed him from a drug addict and alcoholic with suicidal tendencies to a self-taught litigator who wanted to live, learn, study, and be productive.

LDF submitted his clemency petition to Governor L. Douglas Wilder. We focused not only on Mr. Giarratano's metamorphosis, but also on new evidence uncovered since his trial that raised very substantial doubts about his guilt. This evidence was ignored by the courts in the course of Mr. Giarratano's appeals, because Virginia law imposed a one-year time limit on the introduction of new evidence to challenge a conviction.

However, the governor cut through the procedural knot erected by the judicial branch and examined critically the evidence before him. Based upon that review, bolstered by a tremendous outpouring of public support, Governor Wilder granted Mr. Giarratano a conditional pardon with the opportunity to be paroled after serving twenty-five years.

LDF also submitted a successful petition for commutation of sentence to the Georgia Board of Pardons and Paroles on behalf of our client Billy Moore in July 1990. Mr. Moore had been convicted and sentenced to death for murder in 1974, and had transformed himself into a deeply religious man. Twice the state and federal courts heard arguments that critical mitigating evidence in his case had not been considered by the sentencing court, and twice they erected procedural barriers to any form of relief.

In August 1990, the Board of Pardon and Paroles, like Governor Wilder, cut through the red tape and commuted Mr. Moore's death sentence to life imprisonment.

Legislative Consulting

Legislation offers some hope for addressing the racism and unjust procedural obstacles faced by far too many capital defendants.

In 1990, LDF was asked to advise Congress about the Racial Justice Act (RJA), a statute that would have allowed a defendant to challenge a death sentence with statistical proof of racially disparate capital sentencing patterns. The RJA was a response to the Supreme Court's rejection of the use of such statistical proof in 1987, in LDF's *McCleskey* v. *Kemp* case. We also consulted with Congress on reforms of the *habeas* review process that would address barriers erected recently by the Supreme Court that prevent adequate review of death-row appeals.

Fortunately, the RJA passed in the House as part of an Omnibus Crime Bill. Unfortunately, the *habeas* reforms we supported were defeated, and that same Crime Bill also included provisions that would have put new, draconian restrictions on *habeas* review.

The ultimate result was that none of the statutes were enacted. The Bush administration's aversion to the Racial Justice Act was so strong that it agreed to strip away the parts of the Crime Bill that it most wanted—including the restrictions on *habeas* appeals—as the price for allowing racial discrimination in the death penalty to continue.

Public Education

In 1990–1991, LDF produced a much needed visual presentation on race discrimination and capital punishment. The videotape brings home the message that the death penalty has historical roots in lynching, and that capital punishment must be viewed as a civil rights issue. We will use this videotape as a teaching instrument with schools, churches, and community groups. We have also broadened our educational efforts to include appearing on television and radio programs, writing articles in black newspapers and magazines, speaking at various community organizations, and drawing the attention of the national media to some of our cases.

For more information, contact the NAACP Legal Defense Fund, 99 Hudson Street, 16th Floor, New York, NY 10013.

37

Centurion Ministries
Seeking Justice for the Innocent in Prison

Our beneficiaries receive that which is most precious to all of us: life, liberty, and the pursuit of happiness.

Centurion Ministries, Inc. was founded in 1980 by James McCloskey. Mr. McCloskey is a 1964 graduate of Bucknell University and a former Naval officer, who was awarded the Bronze Star with the combat "V" for his Vietnam War service as an advisor to the South Vietnamese Navy in the Mekong Delta. He spent thirteen years in business, primarily as an executive for two different international management consulting firms, one in Tokyo where he lived and worked for five years, and another, The Hay Group, in Philadelphia, Pa. He left the business world for the ministry in 1979. Subsequent to earning a Master of Divinity degree from Princeton Theological Seminary, he began Centurion Ministries.

The primary mission of Centurion Ministries (CM) is to free from prison and to vindicate those who are completely innocent of the crimes for which they have been wrongly convicted and imprisoned for life. We also assist our clients, once they are freed, to reintegrate back into society on a self-reliant basis.

In addition to being innocent lifers, our beneficiaries have no help or resources other than Centurion Ministries. They are penniless and hopeless. Since each has lost his legal appeal, his freedom can only be secured by developing new evidence sufficient to earn a retrial.

We visit and listen to them in prison. We study the entire record (trial transcripts). A detailed autobiography is required. Thus, over varying periods of time, we develop an extensive knowledge of the inmate and his case. And once we are satisfied of their innocence, then we work to secure the truth.

In addition to working on individual cases, Centurion Ministries is a national advocate and center for the innocent in prison. To our knowledge there is no other agency (or person), private or public, anywhere in the United States that works exclusively and full time for the incarcerated innocent; we thereby fill a long neglected niche in America's criminal justice system. Thus, what we do strengthens the fabric of the criminal justice system rather than weakens it.

In achieving the objectives of our work, we at Centurion Ministries perform the following functions:

- conduct a thorough investigation in order to develop the new evidence required.

- retain and work with a suitable attorney in seeking judicial relief for our beneficiaries.

- raise and disburse whatever funds are required to meet all legal, investigative, and administrative costs necessary for the successful completion of our work.

- serve as ministers of hope and help to sustain prisoners throughout their long ordeal.

Since 1980 when CM began its work of seeking justice for the innocent in prison, we have freed and exonerated three innocent "lifers."

George De Los Santos. After spending almost nine years in prison for a 1975 Newark, N.J., murder, which someone else committed, a federal judge ordered his immediate release in July 1983. Ruling that the prosecutor's office knew that its star witness gave testimony against Mr. De Los Santos that "reeked of perjury," the court concluded that "had the jury known that this witness had for years told the prosecutor what he wanted to hear in exchange for his life and a license to commit crime, De Los Santos would have been acquitted."

Rene Santana. In February 1986, the murder charges against Mr. Santana were dismissed by the same judge, who presided over his 1976 trial. Mr. Santana spent ten years in prison for a 1974 homicide committed by another man. The primary state witness was coerced by the prosecutor's office into falsely identifying Mr. Santana as the man he saw flee the scene of the crime.

Shortly before Mr. Santana's freedom this witness visited him at prison and expressed his sorrow for what he had done.

Nate Walker. In May 1976, Nate was sentenced to life in prison for a 1974 Elizabeth, N.J., kidnapping and rape. Ten years later Nate's trial prosecutor agreed that Nate Walker was an innocent man. A twelve-year-old semen specimen was located and analyzed. It proved that Nate had a different blood type from the real rapist. Nate was then officially cleared and freed by the county's presiding judge. His release won national attention for Centurion Ministries and its work.

38

Southern Coalition on Jails and Prisons

On the subject of the death penalty, the basic sense of fairness and compassion shared by most Americans is thwarted by false assumptions and misinformation.

The Southern Coalition on Jails and Prisons (SCJP) recognizes that understanding alone will not end the death penalty in America. Merely helping citizens understand that the death penalty is not even-handed, does not deter crime, does not save money, and does not protect against executing the innocent will not put an end to the death penalty. But helping citizens understand does raise discomfort to a level which invites them to consider alternatives. SCJP offers the following: a freeze on all executions, with life sentences as an alternative to executions, and a twenty-year minimum penalty without an intervening possibility of parole.

SCJP believes these alternatives are both humane and just. Moreover, a recent Gallup poll proves that when Americans understand the facts about the death penalty, and are offered a responsible alternative, support for the death penalty becomes a minority opinion and therefore subject to political defeat.

SCJP believes that total victory against the death penalty is possible, because concerned citizens have been moving America ever closer toward abolition over the past four decades.

In the 1940s, death was mandatory for many crimes in many states. In addition to murder, death sentences were routinely given for burglary, armed robbery, kidnaping, and rape, and two or three executions were carried out every week. Today, the death penalty is strictly limited to first-degree murder and is no longer mandatory for any crime.

Over the past few years, under the determined, committed leadership of Joe Ingle, concerned citizens have rallied around SCJP to help build a proud record of accomplishments. For example, in North Carolina, SCJP's lobbying and testimony before the state legislature helped pass a historic bill to prohibit execution for crimes committed by children younger than seventeen. Also, in Georgia, SCJP played a major role leading to passage of a law forbidding execution of the mentally retarded.

Now SCJP is determined to expand these crucial precedents to states all across America and to send a loud message to Capitol Hill where actions by the Supreme Court and Congress can encourage or thwart progress to abolish the death penalty nationwide.

Nationwide and worldwide, public awareness and media coverage of the work of SCJP is at an all-time high—prompted in part by Joe Ingle's nomination to receive the Nobel Peace Prize.

This honor of an American abolitionist is born of tragedy, for it expresses the disgust of our allies that the United States stands with nations like South Africa and Iran in our persistent use of the death penalty, and reminds us that Canada, England, and European nations long ago discarded the death penalty as an uncivilized relic of a more primitive era.

Total victory over the death penalty in America will only come when the majority of citizens say "enough is enough," mean it, and force our elected officials to act. The leadership of SCJP—officers, staff members, and volunteers—invites you to help build that majority by joining with us today:

Your personal support will help accelerate our drive to abolish the death penalty nationwide by strengthening vital SCJP initiatives including:

- Testifying: We present testimony on death-penalty issues before state legislatures, at clemency hearings, and in trials.

- Providing Legal Aid: We track all death-penalty cases from indictment through trial to ensure that proper procedures are followed and representation is adequate.

- Visiting Prisoners and Assisting their Families: We make sure each state allows visits from family and friends and adequately meets each prisoner's religious, physical, and emotional needs.

- Lobbying: We actively advocate changes in death-penalty laws in face-to-face meetings with governors, state legislatures, and with lawmakers on Capitol Hill.

- Increasing Awareness: We teach community groups and churches how to effectively voice their opposition to the death penalty in the media and in direct meetings with political leaders.

Please help SCJP speed the day when our great nation no longer kills its own citizens in acts of government-sponsored vengeance. Please strengthen SCJP's commitment to abolish the death penalty in America by making your own personal commitment to help today.

Remember, right now more than 2200 men and women are on death rows in America. Almost all of them are poor and unable to obtain adequate legal help. At least 300 are mentally retarded. Close to 30 committed their crimes as children. And some will undoubtedly be proven innocent—either before or after they are killed.

You can send donations to help in the fight to abolish the death penalty to: SCJP, 1701 21st Avenue South, #423, Nashville, Tennessee 37212. Thank you for your support.

39

Southern Prisoners' Defense Committee

The Southern Prisoners' Defense Committee (SPDC) was created in 1976 by the Southern Coalition on Jails and Prisons, a grass-roots, prisoners-support organization, in response to the need for a regionally based program that provides prisoners with legal assistance. The Committee was modeled after the Mississippi Prisoners Defense Committee, which has successfully challenged conditions at Mississippi's only penitentiary. David Lippman, an attorney, was one of the founders of the Southern Prisoners' Defense Committee and continues to serve on the Board of Directors.

The Defense Committee's efforts on behalf of prisoners have brought about more decent and humane prison conditions, limits on the number of prisoners for certain facilities, creation or improvement of rehabilitation, vocational and educational programs, improved medical care, training for guards, fairer treatment for prisoners, and other reforms.

The Southern Prisons' Defense Committee has sought to enforce the constitutional prohibition on cruel and unusual punishment in jails and prisons of the South. It has raised various human rights issues regarding who should be in prison and for how long, whether certain forms of punishment are excessive, and what standards govern how prisoners are housed, fed, and treated. It has pressed for alternatives to incarceration.

SPDC's litigation has forced legislatures and executives to come to grip with the costs and dangers of sending so many people to prison for so long. It has required them to consider and implement alternatives to incarceration. Its capital punishment litigation has resulted in a number of death sentences being set aside and important precedents being established. The SPDC also raises the issues of race and poverty in the imposition of the death penalty in the courts, and in public forums as well. And the committee serves as a resource center for lawyers involved in any stage of capital litigation.

The Defense Committee attempts to respond to the urgent need for legal assistance to prisoners throughout the South, especially those facing execution. The South imprisons a greater percentage of its population than any other region of the country. The higher incarceration rate is not attributable to a higher crime rate. Persons are sent to prison for substantial periods for minor offenses ranging from writing bad checks to traffic offenses. In Alabama, a pregnant woman was sentenced to five years in prison for writing a bad check for $300. A 74-year-old man served a year in prison for driving without a license. Even the mentally ill are not exempt from this policy; they are often warehoused in jails or prisons after committing petty crimes.

The statistics speak for themselves: the length of actual time served in the South is almost 50 percent longer than in the rest of the country; more black people are in prison in the South than in any other region of the country; and the South sentenced more people to death than any other region.

There are only a handful of lawyers and programs that specialize in the defense of capital cases. "All that stands between the men, women, and children on death row and execution are two dozen dedicated attorneys," wrote one reporter.

Most of the Southern states have no public-defender programs and provide only the most minimal compensation for attorneys who take death cases. The result is, at best, lawyers who do not specialize in capital-punishment law and, at worst, lawyers who care nothing about the persons they are defending.

Tom Wicker, of the *New York Times*, has observed that "something near a pattern of inadequate or incompetent legal representation can be found in death penalty cases, particularly in the South, particularly for poor and uneducated persons."

The state is obligated to provide a poor person accused of a capital crime with a court-appointed lawyer only at trial and one appeal to the state supreme court. After that, a condemned person is on his own to obtain representation in order to seek review by the United States

Supreme Court or the lower federal courts. Many do not find assistance until execution is imminent.

The Defense Committee has repeatedly come to the rescue of inmates who are as close as a week to execution but without counsel. The Defense Committee has won new trials or sentencing hearings by showing fundamental violations of the Constitution. It has also counseled prisoners and their families, investigated correctional systems, obtained court orders prohibiting certain practices and setting standards for humane operations, vigilantly monitored the enforcement of those decrees, and helped establish support groups for incarcerated people.

For more information regarding the Defense Committee, write: Stephen Bright, Director, Southern Prisoners' Defense Committee, 185 Walton Street, N.W., Atlanta, GA 30303.

40

Legal Associates West

In 1984, Legal Associates West (LAW) was founded by W. M. Daniel Ravenscroft. It is now owned by Dan and his wife, Kay. Dan is a prison inmate (convicted of a white-collar crime), but don't let that disturb you. Sources indicate that even though Dan is not a licensed attorney, he has carved out a niche in the legal profession by his uncanny ability to take a case that no one wants, and prevail with a successful outcome. Primarily, LAW researches the issues, investigates factors relevant to the case, and in numerous instances, has been more successful than many attorneys.

LAW's primary function is the fair administration of justice, and to prevent the systematic application of injustice inflicted upon America's poor and incarcerated. LAW further publishes and distributes self-help booklets and other pamphlets and legal-information materials geared toward the criminal justice system. Ravenscroft also serves as a criminal justice consultant to attorneys, law firms, and other allied professionals in the legal profession.

LAW has created contracts with many organizations and carries memberships with California Attorneys for Criminal Justice (CACJ), Los Angeles; the American Civil Liberties Union (ACLU), nationwide; Prisoner's Rights Union, Sacramento; Citizens United for the Rehabilitation of Errants (CURE), Washington, D.C.; National Legal Services (NLS, Inc.), Atlanta, GA; National Coalition Against The Death Penalty (NCADP), Washington, D.C.; and a host of others too numerous to mention.

Ravenscroft has published extensively in legal publications, the *Daily*

Journal, Sacramento Recorder, and other tabloids pertaining to the criminal justice system and the legal profession.

LAW receives requests for information and assistance from all over the United States. Most requests are from prisoners, but many others are from attorneys seeking information regarding the issues they are researching, or just general information about the prison system.

An ancillary purpose of LAW is to involve and educate the communities both inside and outside of the penal system, and to employ their resources to develop further the funding bases needed to utilize political groups on the outside. They also aid in facilitating communication and education of the public regarding the plight of those inside, because they will eventually return to society. Dan believes in thinking before you speak, and by applying this in daily life he says one can begin to understand some of the struggles we have forced upon ourselves and undertake to correct them. Being separated from life in general does not solve the problem, says Dan. "Unity is the key to successful re-entry to the mainstream of normal life. . . "

LAW's administration is handled by Kay. Her experience includes business and personnel management, public relations, and involvement in political elections. Kay is also a Notary Public.

At present, LAW's primary funding is from legal research contracts, private donations, and other related revenue from allied services. One cannot help but categorize LAW's success with that of other larger firms, and while LAW is relatively new on the horizon, they will assuredly be around for many years to come. Their motto—"All for justice and justice for all!"

Those interested in further information, or in making a tax-deductible contribution, may write: LAW, P.O. Box 255784, Sacramento, CA 95865-5784. Telephone: (916) 920-5297.

41

U.S. Bishops' Statement on Capital Punishment

United States Catholic Conference*

In 1974, out of a commitment to the value and dignity of human life, the U.S. Catholic Conference, by a substantial majority, voted to declare its opposition to capital punishment. As a former president of the National Conference of Catholic Bishops pointed out in 1977, the issue of capital punishment involves both "profound legal and political questions" as well as "important moral and religious issues." And so we find that this issue continues to provide public controversy and to raise moral questions that trouble many.

We should acknowledge that in the public debate over capital punishment we are dealing with values of the highest importance; respect for the sanctity of human life, the protection of human life, the preservation of order in society, and the achievement of justice through law. In confronting the problem of serious and violent crime in our society, we want to protect the lives and the sense of security both of those members of society who may become the victims of crime and of those in the police and in the law-enforcement system who run greater risks. In doing this, however, we must bear in mind that crime is both a manifestation of the great mysteries of evil and human freedom and an aspect of the very complex reality that is contemporary society. We should not expect simple or easy solutions to what is a profound evil, and even less should we rely on capital punishment to provide such a solution. Rather, we must look to the claims of justice as these are understood in the current debate and to the example and teaching of Jesus, whom we acknowledge as the Justice of God.

Allowing for the fact that Catholic teaching has accepted the principle that the state has the right to take the life of a person guilty of an extremely serious crime, and that the state may take appropriate measures to protect itself and its citizens from grave harm, nevertheless, the question for judgment and decision today is whether capital punishment is justifiable under present circumstances. Punishment, since it involves the deliberate infliction of evil on another, is always in need of justification. This has normally taken the form of indicating some good which is to be obtained through punishment or an evil which is to be warded off. The three justifications traditionally advanced for punishment in general are retribution, deterrence, and reform.

Reform or rehabilitation of the criminal cannot serve as a justification for capital punishment, which necessarily deprives the criminal of the opportunity to develop a new way of life that conforms to the norms of society and that contributes to the common good. It may be granted that the imminence of capital punishment may induce repentence in the criminal, but we should certainly not think that this threat is somehow necessary for God's grace to touch and to transform human hearts.

The deterrence of actual or potential criminals from future deeds of violence by the threat of death is also advanced as a justifying objective of punishment. While it is certain that capital punishment prevents the individual from committing further crimes, it is far from certain that it actually prevents others from doing so. Empirical studies in this area have not given conclusive evidence that would justify the imposition of the death penalty on a few individuals as a means of preventing others from committing crimes. There are strong reasons to doubt that many crimes of violence are undertaken in a spirit of rational calculation which would be influenced by a remote threat of death. The small number of death sentences in relation to the number of murders also makes it seem highly unlikely that the threat will be carried out and so undercuts the effectiveness of the deterrent.

The protection of society and its members from violence, to which the deterrent effect of punishment is supposed to contribute, is a value of central and abiding importance; and we urge the need for prudent firmness in ensuring the safety of innocent people. It is important to remember that the preservation of order in times of civil disturbance does not depend on the institution of capital punishment, the imposition of which rightly requires a lengthy and complex process in our legal system. Moreover, both in its nature as legal penalty and in its practical consequences, capital punishment is different from the taking of life in legitimate self-defense or in defense of society.

The third justifying purpose for punishment is retribution or the restoration of the order of justice, which has been violated by the action of the criminal. We grant that the need for retribution does indeed justify punishment. For the practice of punishment both presupposes a previous transgression against the law and involves the involuntary deprivation of certain goods. But we maintian that this need does not require nor does it justify taking the life of the criminal, even in cases of murder. We must not remain unmindful of the example of Jesus who urges upon us a teaching of forbearance in the face of evil (Matthew 5:38–42) and forgiveness of injuries (Matthew 18:21–35). It is morally unsatisfactory and socially destructive for criminals to go unpunished, but the forms and limits of punishment must be determined by moral objectives which go beyond the mere inflicting of injury to the guilty. Thus we would regard it as barbarous and inhumane for a criminal who had tortured or maimed a victim to be tortured or maimed in return. Such a punishment might satisfy certain vindictive desires that we or the victim might feel, but the satisfaction of such desires is not and cannot be an objective of a humane and Christian approach to punishment. We believe that the forms of punishment must be determined with a view to the protection of society and its members and to the reformation of the criminal and his reintegration into society. This position accords with the general norm for punishment proposed by St. Thomas Aquinas when he wrote: "In this life, however, penalties are not sought for their own sake, because this is not the era of retribution; rather, they are meant to be corrective by being conducive either to the reform of the sinner or the good of society, which becomes more peaceful through the punishment of sinners."

We believe that in the conditions of contemporary American society, the legitimate purposes of punishment do not justify the imposition of the death penalty. Furthermore, we believe that there are serious considerations which should prompt Christians and all Americans to support the abolition of capital punishment. Some of the reasons have to do with evils that are present in the practice of capital punishment itself, while others involve important values that would be promoted by abolition of this practice.

We maintain that abolition of the death penalty would promote values that are important to us as citizens and as Christians. First, abolition sends a message that we can break the cycle of violence, that we need not take life for life, that we can envisage more humane and more hopeful and effective responses to the growth of violent crime. It is a manifestation of our freedom as moral persons striving for a just society. It is also a challenge to us as a people to find ways of dealing with criminals that manifest intelligence and compassion rather than power and vengeance. We should feel such confidence in our civic order that we use no more force against those who violate it than is actually required.

Second, abolition of capital punishment is also a manifestation of our belief in the unique worth and dignity of each person from the moment of conception, a creature made in the image and likeness of God. It is particularly important in the context of our times that this belief be affirmed with regard to those who have failed or whose lives have been distorted by suffering or hatred, even in the case of those who by their actions have failed to respect the dignity and rights of others. It is the recognition of the dignity of all human beings that has impelled the Church to minister to the needs of the outcast and the rejected and that should make us unwilling to treat the lives of even those who have taken human life as expendable or as a means to some further end.

Third, abolition of the death penalty is further testimony to our conviction, a conviction which we share with the Judaic and Islamic traditions, that God is indeed the Lord of life. It is a testimony which removes a certain ambiguity which might otherwise affect the witness that we wish to give to the sanctity of human life in all its stages. We do not wish to equate the situation of criminals convicted of capital offenses with the condition of the innocent unborn or of the defenseless aged or infirm, but we do believe that the defense of life is strengthened by eliminating exercise of a judicial authorization to take human life.

Fourth, we believe that abolition of the death penalty is most consonant with the example of Jesus, who both taught and practiced the forgiveness of injustice and who came "to give his life as a ransom for many." In this regard we may point to the reluctance that those

early Christians who accepted capital punishment as a legitimate practice in civil society felt about the participation of Christians in such
an institution and to the unwillingness of the Church to accept into
the ranks of its ministers those who had been involved in the infliction
of capital punishment. There is and has been a certain sense that even
in those cases where serious justifications can be offered for the necessity
of taking life, those who are identified in a special way with Christ
should refrain from taking life. We believe that this should be taken
as an indication of the deeper desires of the Church as it responds
to the story of God's redemptive and forgiving love as manifest in the
life of his Son.

With respect to the difficulties inherent in capital punishment, we
note first that infliction of the death penalty extinguishes possibilities for
reform and rehabilitation for the person executed as well as the opportunity
for the criminal to make some creative compensation for the evil he or
she has done. It also cuts off the possibility for a new beginning and
of moral growth in a human life which has been seriously deformed.

Second, the imposition of capital punishment involves the possibility of mistake. In this respect, it is not different from other legal processes; and it must be granted that our legal system shows considerable
care for the rights of defendants in capital cases. But the possibility
of mistake cannot be eliminated from the system. Because death terminates the possibilities of conversion and growth and support that we
can share with each other, we regard a mistaken infliction of the death
penalty with a special horror, even while we retain our trust in God's
loving mercy.

Third, the legal imposition of capital punishment in our society
involves long and unavoidable delays. This is in large part a consequence
of the safeguards and the opportunities for appeal which the law provides for defendants; but it also creates a long period of anxiety and
uncertainty both about the possibility of life and the necessity of reori-
enting one's life. Delay also diminishes the effectiveness of capital punishment as a deterrent, for it makes the death penalty uncertain and
remote. Death row can be the scene of conversion and spiritual growth,
but it also produces aimlessness, fear, and despair.

Fourth, we believe that the actual carrying out of the death penalty brings with it great and avoidable anguish for the criminal, for
his family and loved ones, and for those who are called on to perform

or witness the execution. Great writers such as Shakespeare and Dostoyevsky in the past and Camus and Orwell in our time have given us vivid pictures of the terrors of execution not merely for the victim but also for bystanders.

Fifth, in the present situation of dispute over the justifiability of the death penalty and at a time when executions have been rare, executions attract enormous publicity, much of it unhealthy, and stir considerable acrimony in public discussion. On the other hand, if a substantial proportion of the more than five hundred persons now under the sentence of death are executed, a great public outcry can safely be predicted. In neither case is the American public likey to develop a sense that the work of justice is being done with fairness and rationality.

Sixth, there is a widespread belief that many convicted criminals are sentenced to death in an unfair and discriminatory manner. This belief can be affirmed with certain qualifications. There is a certain presumption that if specific evidence of bias or discrimination in sentencing can be provided for particular cases, then higher courts will not uphold sentences of death in these cases. But we must also reckon with a legal system which, while it does provide counsel for indigent defendants, permits those who are well off to obtain the resources and the talent to present their case in as convincing a light as possible. The legal system and the criminal-justice system both work in a society that bears in its psychological, social, and economic patterns the marks of racism. These marks remain long after the demolition of segregation as a legal institution. The end result of all this is a situation in which those condemned to die are nearly always poor and are disproportionately black. Thus 47 percent of the inmates on death row are black, whereas only 11 percent of the American population is black. Abolition of the death penalty will not eliminate racism and its effects, an evil which we are called on to combat in many different ways. But it is a reasonable judgment that racist attitudes and the social consequences of racism have some influence in determining who is sentenced to die in our society. This we do not regard as acceptable.

We do not propose the abolition of capital punishment as a simple solution to the problems of crime and violence. As we observed earlier, we do not believe that any simple and comprehensive solution is possible. We affirm that there is a special need to offer sympathy and support for the victims of violent crime and their families. Our society should not flinch from contemplating the suffering that violent crime brings to so many when it destroys lives, shatters families, and crushes the hopes of the innocent. Recognition of this suffering should not lead to demands for vengeance but to a firm resolution that help be given to the victims of crime and that justice be done fairly and swiftly. The care and the support that we give to the victims of crime should be both compassionate and practical. The public response to crime should include the relief of financial distress caused by crime and the provision of medical and psychological treatment to the extent that these are required and helpful. It is the special responsibility of the Church to provide a community of faith and trust in which God's grace can heal the personal and spiritual wounds caused by crime and in which we can all grow by sharing one another's burdens and sorrows.

We insist that important changes are necessary in the correctional system in order to make it truly conducive to the reform and rehabilitation of convicted criminals and their reintegration into society. We also grant that special precautions should be taken to ensure the safety of those who guard convicts who are too dangerous to return to society. We call on governments to cooperate in vigorous measures against terrorists who threaten the safety of the general public and who take the lives of the innocent. We acknowledge that there is a pressing need to deal with those social conditions of poverty and injustice which often provide the breeding grounds for serious crime. We urge particularly the importance of restricting the easy availability of guns and other weapons of violence. We oppose the glamorizing of violence in entertainment, and we deplore the effect of this on children. We affirm the need for education to promote respect for the human dignity of all people. All of these things should form part of a comprehensive community response to the very real and pressing problems presented by the prevalence of crime and violence in many parts of our society.

We recognize that many citizens may believe that capital punishment should be maintained as an integral part of our society's response to the evils of crime, nor is this position incompatible with Catholic tradition. We acknowledge the depth and the sincerity of their concern. We urge them to review the considerations we have offered which show both the evils associated with capital punishment and the harmony of the abolition of capital punishment with the values of the Gospel. We urge them to bear in mind that public decisions in this area affect the lives, the hopes, and the fears of men and women who share both the misery and the grandeur of human life with us and who, like us, are among those sinners whom the Son of Man came to save.

We urge our brothers and sisters in Christ to remember the teachings of Jesus who called us to be reconciled with those who have injured us and to pray for forgiveness for our sins "as we forgive those who have sinned against us." We call on you to contemplate the crucified Christ who set us the supreme example of forgiveness and of the triumph of compassionate love.

42

A Letter from Italy on Abolition Day

To the People of the United States of America:

As persons deprived of everything but humanity, we hereby address condemned persons.

Unconditionally, always, everywhere and with all our strength we oppose the death penalty in order to cancel from the face of the earth this barbarity and have it buried in the past.

We humbly implore human beings not to dishearten themselves by cutting off the lives of unarmed hostages. Preserving in our hearts the destiny of every condemned person, particularly young people and the mentally disabled, we ask for general mercy.

We address nations worldwide. We trust they will welcome our message.

We address Americans first, towards whom we feel particular closeness. We are aware of the growing social and moral apprehension which your cities are facing. We also feel sorrowful for the increasing crime rate in the USA and for the violent crimes which are now being committed by young people as well. It is with a sound sense of friendship that we exort our American brothers not to respond to violence with violence, but to try to remove the social causes of criminality.

We entreat the American people to take responsibility for the destiny of some two thousand persons who have been abandoned to the executioner. You contradict the role played by the USA on the world stage in defense of human rights.

Americans! Save from death these fellow citizens of yours; stop executions immediately, starting with those juveniles now on death row.

Abolition in the western world must be a starting point for the extension of the abolitionist movement towards the east and south.

The abolition of the death penalty, this violence institutionalized to the highest intentional level, will be a sign of great strength for the moral progress of humanity.

Delivered to Ambassador Mr. Maxwell Rabb
on March 1, 1988

Part Five
Concerned Citizens

43

Mario M. Cuomo
Governor of New York

This speech against capital punishment was delivered at the College of St. Rose in Albany, N.Y., on March 20, 1989, when Governor Cuomo announced that he would veto a death penalty bill sent to him by the New York State legislature.

It is difficult to imagine a more important subject for consideration than the one that brings us together this morning. Together the legislature and the governor every year make thousands of judgments that are important.

But occasionally we are confronted with a question that has transcendent significance: one that describes in fundamental ways what we are as a people; one that projects to ourselves, and to the whole world, our most fundamental values—one, even, that helps configure our souls.

I have spoken my own opposition to the death penalty for more than thirty years. For all that time I have studied it, I have watched it, I have debated it, hundreds of times.

I have heard all the arguments, analyzed all the evidence I could find, measured public opinion when it was opposed, when it was indifferent, when it was passionately in favor. And always before, I have concluded that the death penalty is wrong, that it lowers us all, that it is a surrender to the worst that is in us, that it uses a power, the official power to kill by execution, which has never elevated a society, never brought back a life, never inspired anything but hate.

In recent years I have had the privilege of casting my vote on bills passed by the legislature to bring back the death penalty. And I have voted against it each time. On each occasion that I did, the legislature might have passed the bill despite my disapproval by obtaining a two-thirds vote. So far they have chosen not to.

Now the death penalty bill is before me again, and there can be another chance for the legislature of New York to speak on this subject in the name of the people they represent.

Because of the awesome significance of the matter, and the imminence of the decision, I sought a chance to speak directly to the public so that I could add my voice to and underscore the cogency of the arguments made by the bishop, the Assembly people, and so many of you—and made already so cogently, so forcefully, so eloquently.

Clearly there is a new public willingness to return to the official brutality of the past, by restoring the death penalty. And it is just as clear what has provoked this new willingness. Life in parts of this state, and nation, has become more ugly and violent than at any time I can recall.

Many, like myself, who have spent more than fifty years in this state are appalled at the new madness created by drugs and frustrated by what appears to be the ineffectuality of the federal, state, and local governments to deal with this new problem. Savage murders of young, bright, and committed law-enforcement people and other citizens enrage us all. Our passions are inflamed by each new terrible headline, each new report of atrocity. We know the people have a right to demand a civilized level of law and peace. They have a right to expect it.

When it appears to them that crime is rampant, and the criminal seems immune from apprehension and adequate punishment, and that nothing else is working, then no one should be surprised if the people demand the ultimate penalty. It has happened before, it will probably happen again. To a great extent it is a cry, a terrible cry of anger and anguish born of frustration and fear in the people. I know that, and I understand it.

I have been with the victims, too. I have felt the anger myself, more than once. Like many other citizens I know what it is to be violated, and even to have one's closest family violated, in the most despicable ways. I tremble at the thought of how I might react to someone who took the life of my son: anger, surely, terrible anger. I would not be good enough to suppress it. Would I demand revenge? Perhaps even that. I know that despite all my beliefs, I might be driven by my impulses.

So how could I not understand a society of people like me, at times like this, wanting to let out a great cry for retribution, for vindication, even for revenge, like the cry we hear from them now? I understand it. But I know something else. I know this society should strive for something better than what we are in our worst moments. When police officers are killed, violence escalates and lawlessness seems to flourish with impunity. It isn't easy for people to hold back their anger, to stop and think, to allow reason to operate. But that, it seems to me, is the only rational course for a people constantly seeking to achieve greater measures of humanity and dignity for our civilization.

We need to respond more effectively to the new violence; we know that. But there is absolutely no good reason to believe that returning to the death penalty will be any better an answer now, than it was at all the times in the past when we had it, used it, regretted it, and discarded it. There are dozens of studies that demonstrate there is simply no persuasive evidence that official state killing can do anything to make any police officer, or other citizen, safer. There is, in fact, considerable evidence to the contrary. Consider this: For the decade before 1977, we had the death penalty in New York State. In that period eighty police officers were slain. For the decade after, without the death penalty, fifty-four were killed. The argument for deterrence is further weakened by realization of how rarely and unpredictably it is applied.

For hundreds of years we have known that the effectiveness of the law is determined not by its harshness, but by its sureness. The death penalty has always been terribly unsure. The experts of the New York State Bar Association's Criminal Justice Section, and the Association of the Bar of the City of New York, have come out strongly against the death penalty after hundreds of years of cumulative lawyers' experience and study.

One of the points the state section made is that the death penalty must be regarded as ineffective as a deterrent, if for no other reason than because its use is so uncertain. Execution has occurred in only about five hundredths of 1 percent of all the homicides committed in America over the past decade.

Then, despite Ted Bundy, it seems to threaten white drug dealers, white rapists, white killers, white barbarians a lot less than others. Think of this: of the last eighteen people executed in this state, thirteen were black and one Hispanic. That seems an extraordinary improbability for a system that was operating with any kind of objective sureness. And there's more. Some of the most notorious recent killings, like the gunning down of the DEA Agent Everett Hatcher and the killing by Lemuel Smith, occurred in the face of existing death-penalty statutes.

Psychiatrists will tell you that there is reason to believe that some madmen, like Ted Bundy, may even be tempted to murder because of a perverse desire to challenge the electric chair.

For years and years, the arguments have raged over whether the death penalty is a deterrent. That used to be, frankly, the only argument when I first began debating it. But the truth is now that because the proponents have never been able to make the case for deterrence convincingly, they have moved to a different argument. It is phrased in many ways, but in the end, it all comes down to the same impulse.

The argument was heard in the debates in recent weeks on the floor of the Senate and Assembly, which I listened to and read with great care. Such things as this were said: "Whatever the studies show, the people of my area believe that the taking of life justifies the forfeiting of life." Or: "Our people have the right to insist on a penalty that matches the horror of the crime." And even this: "An eye for an eye, a tooth for a tooth." Where would it end? You kill my son, I kill yours. You rape my daughter, I rape yours. You mutilate my body, I mutilate yours. You treat someone brutally, and I, the established government of one of the most advanced states in the most advanced nation on earth, will respond by officially and deliberately treating you brutally, by strapping you to a chair and burning away your flesh, for all to see, so the barbarians will know that we are capable of official barbarism. We will pursue this course, despite the lack of reason to believe it will protect us, even if it is clear, almost with certainty, that occasionally the victim of our official barbarism will be innocent.

Think of it: at least twenty-three people are believed to have been wrongfully executed in the United States since the turn of this century. Twenty-three innocent people officially killed. But it is not called murder. And tragically, New York State, our great state, the Empire State, holds the record for the greatest number of innocents put to death over the years. We lead all the states in the nation with eight wrongful executions since 1905.

The proponents of the death penalty in this state assume that the criminal justice system will not make a mistake. They seem to be unconcerned about the overly ambitious prosecutor, the sloppy detective, the incompetent defense counsel, the witness with an ax to grind, or the judge who keeps courthouse conviction box scores. But that, ladies and gentlemen, is the human factor, and it's the deepest, most profound flaw in their argument.

In this country, a defendant is convicted on proof beyond a reasonable doubt, not proof to an absolute certainty. There's no such thing as absolute certainty in our law. The proponents of the death penalty, despite this, say we should pretend it cannot happen.

They do not discuss the infamous case of Isadore Zimmerman, who got so far as to have his head shaved and his trouser leg slit on the day of his scheduled execution in 1939, before Governor Herbert Lehman commuted his sentence to life imprisonment. And then twenty-four years later, Zimmerman was released from prison, after it was determined that the prosecutor knew all the time that he was innocent and had suppressed evidence. Zimmerman died a free man just a few years ago.

They do not discuss William Red Gergel, age 62, released in Queens just this year after spending 535 days in jail for a triple murder he did not commit. It was a case of mistaken identity.

They do not discuss a young man named Bobby McLaughlin of Marine Park, Brooklyn. Bobby McLaughlin was convicted of the robbery and murder of another young man in 1980. This was a one-witness identification case, the most frightening kind. In July of 1986, Bobby McLaughlin was released after serving six years for a murder he did not commit. Wrongly convicted by intention or mistake, take your pick of the facts, right here in the state of New York.

It all started when a detective picked up one wrong photograph: one wrong photograph, one mistake, one date with the electric chair. It could have been one more tragically lost life. It didn't happen, but it took an almost superhuman effort by his foster father and some aggressive members of the media to keep the case from falling between the cracks of the justice system. Bobby McLaughlin had this to say after he was released, "If there was a death penalty in this state, I would now be ashes in an urn on my mother's mantle."

Yes, it can happen. And it will happen if we allow it to. And what would we tell the wife or the husband, or the children or the parents, of the innocent victim that we had burned to death in our official rage? What would you say to them? "We had to do it"?

Then we would be asked, "But why did you have to do it, if you were not sure it would deter anyone else? Why did you have to do it?" And what would we answer? "Because we were angry"? "Because the people demanded an eye for an eye, even if it were to prove an innocent eye"?

What would we tell them? Should we tell them that we had to kill, because we had as a society come to believe that the only way to reach the most despicable among us was to lie down in the muck and mire that spawned them?

I hear all around me that the situation has so deteriorated that we need to send a message to the criminals and to the people alike, that we as a government know how bad things are and will do something about it. I agree. Of course we must make clear that we intend to fight the terrible epidemic of drugs and violence.

But the death penalty is no more effective a way to fight them than the angry cries that inspire it. We need to continue to do the things that will control crime by making the apprehension and punishment of criminals more likely. We've made a good beginning. Since 1983 we have increased funding for local law enforcement alone by 65 percent.

The legislature should finally vote for a real, tough, effective punishment for deliberate murder. And there is one: better, much better, than the death penalty; one that juries will not be reluctant to give; one that is so menacing to a potential killer, it could actually deter; one that does not require us to be infallible in order to avoid taking innocent life; one that does not require us to stoop to the level of the killers; one that is even, for those who insist on measuring this question in dollars, millions of dollars less expensive than the death penalty, millions—true life imprisonment, with no possibility of parole, none under any circumstances.

If you committed a murder at 20, and you live to be 81, you'll live 61 years behind bars. You'll go in alive, and come out only when you die. Now that's a tough penalty. Ask the people who know how tough this penalty would be, the people who know Attica or Auburn. Ask the people who know how hard such places are. They will tell you that to most inmates, the thought of living a whole lifetime behind bars, only to die in your cell, is worse than the quick, final termination of the electric chair.

Just recently in an article in the *New York Times Magazine,* a young man on death row named Heath Wilkins was asked whether people underestimated the deterrent power of life without parole.

"Absolutely," Wilkins responded. "Death isn't a scary thing to someone who's hurting inside so bad that they're hurting other people. People like that are looking for death as a way out."

For the six years I have offered it to the legislature, I have heard no substantial arguments in opposition to the proposal for life imprisonment without parole. I've heard none.

Finally, while we are fighting the criminals in the street with the relentless enforcement of firm laws and with swift, sure punishment, we must at the same time continue to provide all the things we know dull the instinct for crime—education, housing, health care, good jobs, and the opportunity to achieve them. The old fashioned effort to deal with root causes has never lost its relevance, even when it lost its popularity.

That, in the end, I think personally, may be the best antidote of all against the kind of terrible crime we are now experiencing. Certainly it offers us more hope than does the politics of death.

There will be few questions more difficult for us than the one we now face, and few opportunities as good as this to prove our commitment as a people to resisting the triumph of darkness, and to moving our society constantly toward the light.

For a politician, like the people from the Assembly who have joined us today, and myself, rejecting what appears to be a politically popular view can be troublesome. But I . . . make the same decision I have before. In my case, I make the same decison now that I have for more than thirty years, this time I believe on the basis of even more evidence and with a firmer conviction than before.

And I do it with a profound respect for the people who have raised their voices—and occasionally even their fists—asking for the death penalty. I have not as governor ignored those voices. I have listened intently to them. But after the sincerest effort, I have not been able to bring myself to agree with them. I continue to believe, with all my mind and heart, that the death penalty would not help us. . . . It would debase us: it would not protect us. . . . It would make us weaker.

I continue to believe, more passionately now than ever, that this society desperately needs this great state's leadership. We, the people of New York, ought now, in this hour of fright, to show the way. We should refuse to allow this time to be marked forever in the pages of our history, as the time that we were driven back to one of the vestiges of our primitive condition, because we were not strong enough, because we were not intelligent enough, because we were not civilized enough, to find a better answer to violence . . . than violence.

Today I will veto the death penalty bill sent to me by the legislature and return it with my proposal for life imprisonment without parole with the hope and the prayer that this time the legislature will once again choose the light over the darkness.

44

Toney Anaya

Former Governor of New Mexico

From an Interview with Toney Anaya

I've always been opposed to capital punishment. It was a small issue when I ran for governor. There were eight candidates, four Democrats and four Republicans, and my opponents were all adamant in their support for capital punishment. I stuck out like a sore thumb because I was the only one who indicated my opposition, so the voters of New Mexico knew my position before they elected me. It wasn't the principal issue in New Mexico at the time, although since then it has become a more heated one because of action I took. The voters elected me in an overwhelming majority, so I think that spoke well of what the real issues were in their minds.

During my term there were a couple of different times when I had to stay the execution of two individuals. These men were scheduled to die near the end of my term, and the attorneys representing them, knowing of my opposition to the death penalty, decided for political reasons to test Anaya and see if he would really do as he said he would do. I was critical of them for putting me in that position, because they did not exhaust all the legal remedies in behalf of their clients, and they knew they could wait until I left office to pursue the proceedings.

I did stay their executions until I left office in 1986. As a result, by the end of my term, capital punishment had become the big issue. Since I could not run again, because of New Mexico's constitution, the race was open to two candidates who were both in support of the death penalty; it was just a question of which one was going to enforce it. The Republican, who was the strongest on the issue, was elected.

Shortly after his election, Governor-Elect Gary Caruthers indicated that the first piece of paper he wanted on his desk after being sworn in was a death warrant. He intended to start executing the individuals who were on death row. Because of the way in which the issue had been raised in the campaign, and the Governor-Elect's adamant stand, I realized that I would have to come to grips with the issue.

I met with Governor-Elect Caruthers in a private meeting, where he and I discussed this issue. He made it very plain to me that he felt he had won the election partially on that issue and that, as he put it, I owed it to him to leave those people on death row so that he could execute them when he came into office. After that discussion, there was no question in my mind that I was going to take the steps that I subsequently took to commute the sentences, because I could not, in good conscience, leave those individuals there with that kind of an attitude on the part of the new governor coming in. Had there been some softening of his position, some indication that he would have treated each case on an individual basis, then I wouldn't have had to commute the sentences.

On the day before Thanksgiving, I informed the people of my decision. I purposely chose that time because of the symbolism of Thanksgiving Day itself. I had thought of waiting until Christmas time but that would have left me only about six days in office, and I felt that such a last-minute action would have created an even bigger uproar. I commuted the sentences of all five individuals on death row, and it did indeed create quite a political uproar in the state. In retrospect, I am glad I did what I did and I think that ultimately others who feel that way on the issue will be in the majority. Right now, the popular political position is to be on the other side.

My commutation statement read, in part, as follows:

Tomorrow we celebrate Thanksgiving Day in this country, a day we, as God-fearing Americans, have set aside to give thanks to our Creator for allowing us to live in a country as grand as ours: an enlightened country; a free country; a compassionate country; a capitalistic country; a country founded on religious principles; a country where we can practice, or choose not to practice, religious beliefs; a country whose constitution recognizes our belief in the unique worth and dignity of each person, even in the case of those who by their actions have failed to respect the dignity and rights of others; a country founded on the belief that we must strive to break the psychological, social, and economic patterns of racism; a country whose people are capable of solving any problem they make the commitment to confront, even the problem of breaking the vicious cycle of violence, of crime—a commitment for which to date this country has not shown the needed resolve.

On this day before Thanksgiving, as we reflect on gifts from God that we, as Americans, have been blessed with, as we prepare for the celebration of Christmas, the day when so many of us celebrate the birth of the one upon whose life many of our religious beliefs are based, I am dropping a pebble into a pond that will cause a ripple—a ripple which I pray will be joined by ripples in other ponds across this country, ripples that, coming together, will cause a rising tide, a tide of rationality, a tide of commitment, a tide of compassion, a tide of realism. . . .

I call for the abolition of the death penalty because it is inhumane, immoral, anti-God, and is incompatible with an enlightened society. . . .

While the clamor intensifies to "kill the killers," we ignore the real crime-fighting weapons mentioned earlier. In fact, because of the clamor for capital punishment, we as a society, crying out for effective law enforcement and meaningful crime-prevention measures, are perpetrating a cruel hoax on each other. We cry out in blood-curdling unison to "kill the killers," giving ourselves a false sense of security—a false sense of accomplishment, a hollow, empty, costly, temporarily satisfying, vengeful outburst of emotions. And, when the killers are killed, we have accomplished none of our crime-fighting goals as an enlightened society. Rather, we have lowered ourselves as an organized social order to the very rabble we seek to rid ourselves of.

The death penalty is applied in an arbitrary and disproportionate manner, is not swift and certain, and is costly. . . .

I have a few minutes ago signed five executive orders commuting the death sentences of the five men on New Mexico's death row to life sentences without the expectation of their ever setting foot on our streets again. . . .

It is my prayer that New Mexico can become the birthplace of an idea whose time has come—the elimination of the death penalty once and for all and the establishment of, and commitment to, a moral, just, and effective criminal justice system in its place. . . .

I've gone into private practice since leaving office, and I travel around the country speaking out on many issues that are of concern to me. The one issue that I have been asked by many groups to speak out on is capital punishment, and I've had the opportunity to address quite a number of conventions in many states.

45

Mike Farrell of "M*A*S*H"

Mike Farrell does many benefits to help raise money to fight the death penalty. He came to Nashville, Tennessee, to visit with the men on death row. He walked up and down the walks talking to all the men that are housed there and giving autographs to all who asked him. It was a welcome change for the men on the row who spend twenty-three hours a day locked in the small cell they call home. He spent a few minutes at each cell, shaking hands and giving encouragement to those there.

Mike really cares about the men on death row across the country. Not many people in the spotlight will confess their true feelings on this subject, for it certainly isn't the most popular stand to take. Mike made the following statement for this book.

The fact that I'm a celebrity is irrelevant when it comes to the death penalty. I'm a citizen and need to take responsibility for lending my efforts to creating this society in a way that works best for me and for all of us. In my opinion, the death-penalty question is one of basic human concern and it goes beyond race and class.

I have been in Australia where there is no death penalty, and most of the countries in Western Europe have no death penalty. They seem to have a lesser crime problem than we have in the United States. I favor finding alternatives to prison in many cases. Statistics show that the murder rate is just as high—and sometimes higher—in states with the death penalty as in states without the death penalty.

We need to establish a justice system in America that is not directed by passionate emotional responses. If we expect to be a just and humane society, we need certain safeguards, but executions should not be included.

If American society decides that executions are appropriate, I think they ought to be carried out in public. Americans could then see how horribly inhumane executions are, and on a personal level they would be able to see the brutality and injustice of inflicting that kind of punishment on someone. I've been opposed to the death penalty for as long as I can remember. I think it's important for all of us who believe in this country to keep it on the path we consider to be the right one.

46

Tom Wicker
Journalist

This article was originally published in the New York Times, *June 27, 1989.*

What a mockery these latest Supreme Court decisions make of this nation's pretensions to be the leading proponent of human rights!

Executing teen-agers and individuals with the mental capacity of children, putting indigent persons to death without exhaustive attention to their appeals, speeding state killings by short-cutting long established rules—these are procedures rightly to be condemned when they occur in the Soviet Union, China, South Africa, or anywhere. Yet the Supreme Court tells us that they are sanctioned by the Constitution of the United States.

Almost lost in the sound and fury resulting from the Supreme Court's flag-burning decision, for example, was another 5 to 4 holding of greater practical impact. States are not constitutionally required, the Court said, to provide counsel for penniless death-row inmates who continue their appeal in state courts.

Now the justices follow that ruling with further 5 to 4 decisions that youths who were only sixteen and seventeen years old when they committed crimes, as well as mentally retarded persons, may be executed. In their reach and effect, all these decisions dwarf the flag case, the primary impact of which is only on people's emotions, and which will have little effect on the course of actual events. The flag, after all, is only a symbol, cherished, of course, but a symbol nevertheless, and one desecrated and cheapened far more often by sleazy commercial and political exploitation than by some impassioned person burning it in protest.

A majority, unfortunately, does not exist among this court's nine members that is equally farsighted and courageous on the very real question of the state's power to take the lives of its own citizens. Instead, in several decisions, the court has narrowed the grounds on which defendants condemned to death can appeal and limited the means by which such appeals may be pursued.

A wiser Court found in 1972 that the death penalty was unconstitutional because of the arbitrary and capricious manner in which it was then administered. There's no evidence whatever that the new state laws that led the Court to reinstate capital punishment in 1976 have removed or even limited the caprice and arbitrariness; indeed, last week's ruling on appeals held one of these random inequities. Yet, the Court goes on devising or approving new procedures by which more people may be executed.

Even those who were legally children when the crimes for which they were convicted were committed now may be put to death constitutionally, along with the most hardened and irredeemable criminals. In the Court's view, a sufficient "national consensus" that such young people should be spared does not exist, because only fifteen states of the thirty-seven that sanction the death penalty, bar it for persons who were under eighteen when they committed a capital crime. Nor is there yet such a consensus, in the Court's opinion, for sparing the mentally retarded.

If nineteen states, just over half of the thirty-seven, banned the execution of under-age criminals, would that constitute a consensus? Would what is constitutional today become unconstitutional tomorrow, in that case? Is the Supreme Court of the United States a poll taker, or a head counter rather than a judicial body solemnly charged with the power to interpret the Constitution?

What a cruel document that Constitution must be, in the stony eyes of the court majority, the same five justices in all these cases. Last week, they said nothing in it required any state to provide counsel for indigent death-row inmates appealing beyond a first direct appeal in state court. Yet, more than 60 percent of later appeals from capital sentences in federal courts have been successful. Last year, the Supreme Court itself heard ten such cases and ruled seven times in favor of the appellant.

From so many successful appeals, the Court might logically have drawn the inference that death sentences in trial court often are improper. Instead, it chose to make it harder for the courts to hear, and in many cases to accept, the last desperate appeals of condemned persons, at least some of whom will have been wrongly convicted or sentenced.

Now the Court finds nothing in the Constitution, not even its prohibition of cruel and unusual punishment, to prevent the execution of teen-agers, or of adults with the mentality of children. What a harsh and merciless reading of a document written primarily to protect citizens against the power of the state!

47

Sister Helen Prejean
Director of Pilgrimage for Life

I'm going to be straightforward with you. I'm an abolitionist. It's my full-time work. I eat, sleep, and drink the death penalty. I give talks, write articles, and organize citizen action. My intent in this article is that by the time you get to the last paragraph you too will be an abolitionist, that your heart will be on fire about this human life and death issue, and that you will be moved to act.

I give a lot of talks to groups of all kinds, and if there is one thing I do know about the public and the death penalty, it is this: there are an awful lot of good people out there who, when polled, say they support the death penalty—housewives, teenagers, blue-haired, kindly grandmothers, churchgoing people. They say, "We've got to do something about all these murders, all this crime." And having the death penalty makes people feel we're serious about the crime problems, that we're really doing something.

We are now approaching 150 executions in this country since the reinstatement of the death penalty by the U.S. Supreme Court in 1976. So far, states have shot, gassed, drugged, or electrocuted to death 143 human beings. It has been done very selectively, only 1 percent are executed out of all the convicted murderers of the total homicides in this country, with nine Southern states doing most of the executing. Since 1976, 90 percent of all executions have taken place in the South, with Louisiana leading the pack, per capita, in its rate of killing citizens.

Before I deal any more with facts about the death penalty I want to share some of my personal experiences with you. I have accompanied three human beings to the electric chair and watched them die there. They were not heroes. In no way do I want to idealize them or condone their terrible deeds. But they were human beings. Each of them, in a last gesture from the electric chair while the guards strapped their arms and legs, offered me love and thanks as a parting gift.

It's one thing to read about an execution in the morning paper and quite another to go through that experience with the person. There is an incredible death ritual being practiced by the state of Louisiana. Killing someone in the electric chair is the most premeditated, calculated, systematic death you can imagine. When you witness an execution, you are asked to sign a paper saying that you will not exhibit emotion of any kind. "Clinical" was the word C. Paul Phelps, former head of Louisiana's Department of Corrections, used to describe the death process.

When the date of execution nears, the condemned man is moved to cell number one on his tier. That puts him closer to the guard's station so that every fifteen minutes or so a guard can look in on him to see how he's bearing up and make notes on a report.

A guard comes onto the tier around this time and hands a document to the inmate and asks him to read it and sign it. The inmate looks at the piece of paper and reads his own death warrant; the way he is to die (electrocution), the day and the hour, and a host of official signatures.

One day several guards arrive at his cell and tell the prisoner to come with them. They take him to a scale, weigh him, and one of the guards measures his length. The guards do not tell the inmates why they do this. The word among the men on death row is that they are being measured for their coffins. The real reason is that the penitentiary officers are going to perform a "dry run" of the execution. A guard of the inmate's build will sit in the chair, test the straps to make sure they hold, and try to escape. The guards participating in the execution want to avoid a Leandress Riley scene as described by Joseph Ferretti, a prison official at San Quentin:

"We had to carry the little colored guy in hollering. I never saw a guy so scared in all my life. His wrists were so damn small, he only weighed 80 pounds or so and he managed to get out of the straps three times."

Riley managed to undo his restraint just before the executioner lowered the cyanide into the vats of acid. He jumped up and frantically raced around inside the chamber, screaming in terror, beating wildly on the glass windows.

"We had to stop the process, open the chamber and strap him in again. Then he did it again but the third time they already gave him the gas. He kept right on screaming right up until he got that first whiff."

A couple of weeks before the execution, the family of the condemned man gets a telephone call. "Sorry to have to bother you with this, Mrs. _____, but your son _____ does have a date and if the thing does go down [I have never heard a prison official use the word "kill"], we just need to know if you have funeral insurance and will you send an ambulance to pick up the body or do you want us to see about the burial?"

The prison psychiatrist stops by the condemned's cell and asks if he wants "something for his nerves."

The captain at Camp F where the death house is located begins to get things in readiness. The electrician tests the chair. The Department of Corrections lines up twelve official witnesses.

The condemned man (hours or sometimes days before) is told to pack a couple changes of underwear, his Bible, and his address book (he will be allowed to make collect calls), and then he is taken in a prison vehicle to a green building which prison officials call "Camp F" and which inmates call "the death house." There in a holding cell a few short yards from the electric chair, guards now watching his every move 24 hours a day, he awaits his death.

His family and other loved ones come to visit with him for the last time. I watched Willie Celestine's family go through this. They sat in a room with Willie, his mother and father, his brother and sister, and his eleven-year-old nephew. Nobody looked at a watch and nobody looked at the white metal door behind which sits the electric chair. Conversation sagged and there were silences. Everybody was trying to be brave. At exactly 5:45 P.M. the warden told the family it was time for them to leave. They all kissed Willie and headed for the prison van waiting to take them to the front gates. His mother told me afterwards, "I just gave him a peck on the cheek and ran out. If I had put my arms around my boy, no prison guard could have pried them loose."

As soon as the family leaves, the condemned's last meal is brought in. Prison officials make a big deal out of this, going to special trouble to get the condemned man "anything he wants, steak, fried shrimp or oysters, crawfish . . ."

Then he goes back to the holding cell and he can hear a buzz of activities organizing his death. Top prison officials in three-piece suits start arriving. A secretary sets up a typewriter and begins typing the forms for witnesses to sign after the execution. A coffee percolator bubbles. The head of the security squad comes to "check the man out." The prison mental health official drops by to assess the man's mental state. (Earlier in the process this same department will have had an interview with the inmate to assure that he is indeed sane and can, therefore, be executed.)

At 10:00 P.M. several guards go into the cell of the inmate and prepare his body for execution. They shave his head, including his eyebrows, cut his left pants leg below the knee, shave around his ankle, diaper him, and put a clean white T-shirt on him.

Exactly at midnight the warden, accompanied by five guards, announces to the condemned that it's time to go. They escort him with shackled hands and feet to the room where the chair awaits him. He is allowed to say his last words. The witnesses sit very close behind a glass panel to protect them from the smell of burning flesh.

He is strapped into the chair and a mask is placed over his face. Everyone steps back. The Warden raises his hand. The executioner pulls the switch three times. The first surge is 1,900 volts, followed by a pause of a few seconds to let the body cool. Then 500 volts is given, and finally another 1,900 volts.

The prison doctor checks the pupils and the heart. The Warden looks at the big clocks on the wall and announces the official time of death. The witnesses silently file out and sign the forms.

And everybody goes home.

Now let's talk about the victims. When I'm giving a speech, this is usually the time that someone says, "You want us to feel sorry for this guy because the state is putting him through this death ritual, but what about what he did to the victim and what about the victim's family?"

There is a "see-saw" principle that people seem to imply about abolitionists: if you're against executions, you're against victims. Or, the converse: if you're loyal to the victim, you're for the death penalty.

Through my personal experiences, first with death-row inmates, then with murder victims' families, I have become an advocate of both. Vernon and Elizabeth Harvey, whose daughter, Faith, was cruelly tortured and murdered eight years ago, have helped me understand the plight of victims' families. They have taken me to meetings of Parents of Murdered Children. There I heard mothers and fathers trying to deal with grief beyond all telling. I was in for a few surprises. I didn't know that there was in Louisiana a Victims' Reparation Fund to help families get counseling, unemployment benefits, funeral expenses. I also didn't know that often when families go to sheriff's offices to apply for these funds they are treated with insensitivity and bureaucratic run around. "Don't know about any funds," one deputy said. "Why don't you write to Ann Landers? She helps people."

I also didn't know that victims' families often feel abused by the criminal justice system. They often don't know their rights or what they can expect or how to make sense of court proceedings and schedules. And to top it all off, often after the trial, after the initial crisis is over, they are left to themselves by friends and relatives. "If I try to bring up my daughter's death, friends change the subject," one parent told me.

I do not believe it is accidental that when 95 percent of the energies of the state are poured into death and recrimination so little is left for the healing process.

Look at the gamut of pain in store for a victim's family when pursuing the death penalty. First, their loved one is violently torn away. Then, at the trial they relive every detail of that death. (When the prosecutor goes for the death penalty, he wants the victim's family in the courtroom.) After this, if the murderer gets a death sentence, the appeals begin. Every time a date of execution for the murderer is set, it is announced by the media. Often there are stays of execution until the appeals process is completed. Finally, after three, five, even ten years the murderer is executed and the family gets to elect a family representative to watch him die. When, in this process, can the healing begin?

In July 1988, a Mennonite volunteer arrived in this state to begin full-time work for victims. It's a first for Louisiana. The irony is that abolitionists have been the ones raising the funds and recruiting the personnel for the much needed service.

Let me now share with you facts about the death penalty. Generally, people don't get to see the death penalty close up. Being chosen for death is a highly selective process and there is no evidence anywhere in this country that shows a wealthy person has ever gone to death row.

The death penalty is a lottery. Who gets death isn't necessarily related to how heinous the murder is. It is intricately related to three factors: Are you poor? Did you kill a white person? And did you do it in a Southern state? Of those executed since 1976, eight out of ten had white victims. There has yet to be a white person executed in Louisiana for killing a black person. Of the forty-two persons presently on death row in Louisiana about half are black and half are white, but over-whelmingly, when you look at the race of the victim 7.5 of every 10 killed a white person.

The chief reason wealthy persons don't go to death row is that they get excellent legal defense. After the celebrated murder trial of Aaron Mintz in New Orleans several years ago, his son stood on the courthouse steps the day his father was acquitted and said, "If my father had only spent $100,000 he probably would have gone to prison." Mintz spent $200,000 on his defense. In Louisiana indigent defenders can spend $1,000 maximum on behalf of his or her client.

Let's talk about locale and the death penalty. In which DA's district was the murder committed? Was the DA running for re-election at the time? Most people have no idea that the DA has complete discretion regarding whom he indicts for first-degree murder (for which you can get death) and with whom he plea-bargains (which reduces the charge). That kind of arbitrary power hopelessly skews any possibility of equitable and even-handed justice. You can circle in red the districts in Louisiana where the DAs go for the death penalty and where they don't.

Add to all of this the fact that there is virtually no evidence to suggest that executing people deters future murders. In Louisiana, during the summer of 1987, eight people died in the electric chair in eight and a half weeks. In that same quarter, the murder rate in New Orleans rose 16.9 percent. "Domestic quarrels and drugs," the police super-intendent said when asked the reason for the increase.

And add still further that evidence is mounting that executions are far more costly than life imprisonment. For death there is a more involved legal process because "death is different," as the U.S. Supreme Court has said. There are three to five times more pretrial motions. It takes longer to select a jury. The attorney, whose client's very life is at stake, uses every niche in the appeals process. On April 1, 1988, there was a story about a plea bargain in a murder trial in Hahnville, La., partially because the parish (a civil district of Louisiana corresponding to a county) was having difficulty mustering the $150,000 for the trial.

We do not have to keep executing people in this country. There is a way for us to protect ourselves from dangerous murderers without imitating the very violence we seek to eradicate. Since the late 70s in Louisiana, because of citizen concern, a life sentence was changed by legislative stature to a real life sentence, "without benefit of pardon, probation, or suspension of sentence."

"Yeah," you say, "then you have some bleeding-heart, liberal governor who can commute their sentences and let them go free." Maybe. But given the political climate of this issue and that governors are pretty savvy fellows, I suggest that we will hear about such cases if and when they do happen precisely because they will be so rare.

A coalition of organizations—Amnesty International, The National Coalition to Abolish the Death Penalty, and the National Interreligious Task Force on Criminal Justice—are sponsoring the campaign under the name "Lighting the Torch of Conscience." The main effort is to encourage people in the churches to be studying and discussing the death penalty. By studying and discussing capital punishment in Sunday school programs and sermons, church members can base their opinion of the death penalty on Scripture and religious tradition and not so much on a knee-jerk response.

Many of the country's major Protestant denominations, including the Episcopal Church, the United Methodist Church, and the Presbyterian Church U.S.A., have passed resolutions opposing capital punishment, as have the American Jewish Committee and the United States Catholic Conference.

To abolish the death penalty is going to require the clergy's becoming actively involved. Denomination after denomination has made statements against the death penalty. What's missing is the people who attend church on Sunday.

For more information on the death penalty in Louisiana or elsewhere contact:

Pilgrimage for Life, Peace Center
916 St. Andrew Street
New Orleans, LA 70130
(504) 522-5519

48

Harmon Wray

Death Penalty Resistance Project

The execution of drifter and condemned killer John Spenkelink in Starke, Florida, on May 25, 1979, occasioned a great deal of controversy and public attention and took place only after intense legal and political efforts to stop it on the part of many people in Florida and elsewhere.

I happened to be one of eight people from outside Florida who went there a few days before the scheduled execution to support those struggling against the death penalty in Tallahassee, the state's capital city. We called ourselves People Against Executions, and despite our diversity of faith and perspectives, we agreed to assume the role of seeking to dramatize the moral and spiritual dimensions of the struggle by engaging in nonviolent acts of civil disobedience. Our appeal throughout was for the governor to exercise his legal authority to grant executive clemency to John Spenkelink and commute his sentence from death to life imprisonment.

We failed, of course, to prevent the execution, and, as we feared at the time, there have been many others who have been executed since then in this country. A few of those have almost certainly been innocent; some have been mentally ill; at least one was a child at the time of his crime; and one was a woman. Tennessee hasn't executed anyone since 1960, but we aren't too far away from a situation in which the only chance for one or more condemned men to live will be for Governor McWherter to choose the legal option of commuting their sentences from death to life in prison.

In my years of working against capital punishment, I have read the following excerpt from Jesus's Sermon on the Mount (Matthew 5: 21–22, 38–39, 43–44, 48; 7: 1–2) and other Bible passages to many church groups:

> You have heard that it was said to the men of old, You shall not kill; and whoever kills shall be liable to judgment.
>
> But I say to you that everyone who is angry with his brother shall be liable to judgment. . . .
>
> You have heard that it was said, An eye for an eye and a tooth for a tooth.
>
> But I say to you, Do not resist one who is evil. . . .
>
> You have heard that it was said, You shall love your neighbor and hate your enemy.
>
> But I say to you, Love your enemies . . . and pray for those who . . . persecute you. . . .
>
> You must be perfect, as your heavenly Father is perfect. . . .
>
> Judge not, that you not be judged.
>
> For with the judgment you pronounce you will be judged, and the measure you give will be the measure you get.

I have received many interesting reactions to the biblical words from church folks who believe in the death penalty. The following is just an example.

"Where would Christianity be if Jesus had gotten off with 8 to 15 years, with time off for good behavior?"

"Jesus must have believed in capital punishment, because he allowed himself to be executed. If it's good enough for Jesus, it's good enough for Charlie Manson."

"I don't care what Jesus says. Sometimes you have to put your religion in a drawer. I say we ought to fry the bastards."

"Didn't Jesus say, 'An eye for an eye and a tooth for a tooth'?"

Some of these responses are so absurd that it's hard to respond to them at all, except with despair. What I've discovered is that church folk are adept at indulging in convenient rationalizations on the issue of capital punishment, basically stemming from the fact that most American Christians don't seem to have the foggiest idea of the dif-

ference between our American citizenship and our Christian disciple-
ship. That is to say, we don't know the difference between Christ and
Caesar.

In our society, it has become, in one sense, far too easy to be
a Christian, or at least to pass for one, especially in the South. The
faith has lost its radical, unique meaning for too many of us, allowing
us to compartmentalize our lives, to put our religion in a drawer when
it threatens our prejudices and what we believe is our self-interest.

I am afraid that I have to agree with Daniel Benson, a lawyer
in Texas, when he says that he is growing increasingly impatient with
Christians who seek to rationalize and explain away the clear, radical,
and threatening words of Jesus, especially in the Sermon on the Mount.

"No amount of tortured reasoning, exegesis, interpretation, and
logic-chopping can harmonize the commands of Jesus in Matthew 5:38–
39, 43–45, with the practice of shooting, hanging, gassing, or electrocuting other human beings. But we have become so accustomed to
turning aside from these commands, and ignoring them, that our practice of legalized killing seems right and normal, while the words of
Jesus appear to be abnormal, wholly unrealistic.

Perhaps the question we ought to be asking ourselves is not why
do we continue to use the death penalty, but why do we continue to
call ourselves Christians? In my judgment there is a fundamental im-
passe here; one cannot have it both ways. One either follows the command to love even one's enemies, and in that case does not kill those
enemies, or one resolutely kills one's enemies, as needed from time to
time, and in that event, of course, does not and cannot love them.

Benson also says that he thinks that Jesus meant exactly what he
said, and that sometimes there is no other choice but to take the Scriptures pretty straight, pretty literally. Jesus really does mean that we
who claim to follow him should not kill people—period, that we should
not even indulge our anger at our brother or sister, that we should
not resist an evil person with more evil, that we really are supposed
to love our enemies and pray for them, and that we are commanded
not to judge other folks by any standard other than that by which
we wish to be judged.

Along with a small group of others, I read these words from the
Sermon on the Mount to Governor Graham, who was about to order
the legalized murder of John Spenkelink in his state's electric chair.

As we read these words in a loud voice, over and over again, for three or four days, our voices grew increasingly desperate and hoarse. I do not know how much Bob Graham listened to the Word of God contained in these words, but he should have been listening very carefully, because, as I have suggested, I am convinced that the Lord Jesus really meant very literally that Bob Graham was commanded not to judge John Spenkelink, not to resist his evil with more evil, to love John and pray for him, and not to kill John.

I believe that Jesus also meant very literally that all those people in Florida and elsewhere whose financial and electoral support Bob Graham was courting were supposed to have the same loving attitude toward John and were commanded by God not to participate in hating him, condemning him, and killing him.

For years I have believed that the issue of capital punishment is not just another issue for Christian people to be concerned about. As Karl Barth once pointed out, the first Christian community was the crucified Jesus and the two criminals being executed on either side of him. I think the issue and the practice of capital punishment capture and symbolize many of the central themes and elements of what the Christian faith is all about: creation in the image of God, the universality of human sin, the execution of Jesus at the hands of the political and religious establishment of his time and place, God's forgiveness and reconciliation of all people through Jesus's death and subsequent resurrection, and the Christian churches' responsibility for liberation of the captives and healing of the broken. And I think that the death penalty can illumine many other theological and ethical issues.

What we were saying to Governor Graham, what we will say to Tennessee's governor and to others, is that we understand the feelings of fear, anger, and revenge that people have about violent crime and about the criminals who perpetrate it. We understand these feelings because we share them. To this extent, we are called into question by Jesus's statment that to be angry at our enemy is to come under God's judgment. But what we as abolitionists want capital-punishment advocates to realize is that as a society we ought not to construct public policy, and we ought not to act, on our violent, vengeful feelings.

We are called to something higher. Even some people we know who have had close loved ones murdered are able to rise above their feelings of revenge and to ask that murderers not be executed, and even to forgive them. Surely if they can do it, Bob Graham, who never knew John Spenkelink or the man he killed, can do it too.

Very early on Friday morning, May 25, a few hours before John Spenkelink was killed, I was touched and moved by God in a way I have never before experienced. I was kneeling in the grass before the governor's mansion with three good friends who had shared with me that agonizing week. We all knew that, barring a miracle, Bob Graham and the people of Florida were going to kill John in about nine hours, at about 10 o'clock, and we were trying to pray.

I began to talk to God, to give thanks for my friends, and to ask God to give John strength, to give us strength, and to give Bob mercy in his heart. Gradually I began to realize that I was also asking God to give us mercy in our hearts for Bob Graham. I became aware that now I was really praying, for the first time all week. I began to weep, again for the first time in that immensely painful week.

It came to me that whatever happened late that morning, one of these days John Spenkelink was going to die, that someday Bob Graham was going to die, and even that I would die, as well. It struck me with the force of revelation that all flesh is as grass, that, like the moths, we are not long for this world. In some way that I cannot understand, for a few moments I knew with absolute certainty that after we died, in the mystery and beauty of God's love, we were all going to love one another—the killer John, the killer Bob, and all the rest of us sinful, pitiful, frightened, and violent people. For a moment, with my eyes closed, I saw with utter clarity an image of John and Bob embracing each other, with God looking on.

I knew then with a depth of insight that transcended any previous awareness, that we are all in the same boat—all afraid to live and scared to die, unable really to love one another or ourselves very well, living and dying in sin and in pain, but, somehow, each loved by God in a very personal and special way, and all, every last one of us, forgiven and promised a new, joyous life by God. Sometimes we get a taste of this new life, but it comes to us fully only beyond our present experience in this world of human history.

A few hours later, even in my grief and outrage that John Spenkelink was murdered, I realized that he was at peace now, that he was free at last, after thirty years of suffering and violence, six of them spent on death row. And I also knew that Bob Graham, my brother in sin and, I believe, in Christ, would not know peace and freedom for a very long time. For this reason I suddenly felt sorry for Bob. I am still mad as hell at him and at what he is doing, but now I feel sorry for him, too.

Not for a minute would I take back what we tried to do in Florida as witnesses, what hundreds of people all over the country are trying to do. I would not acquiesce in the deliberate, cold-blooded, premeditated killing, in our names, with our tax money, and by our elected and appointed officials, of those who have killed. I would not let Bob Graham, or the governor and legislators of Tennessee, or any of the rest of us who intend to kill God's children, off the hook, just as those on death row should not be let off the hook for what they have done. I am utterly convinced that Christians, and everybody else, for that matter, are called by God to resist killing and to choose life. Actively fighting the death penalty is one way in which I personally seek to do that; you all have your own ways of doing it in your life.

Beyond this, I still feel the anger and the outrage at legalized murder—so futile, so cruel, so costly. I believe that, from the biblical standpoint, there is an important place for prophetic moral outrage and for righteous indignation at evil. I am persuaded that, whatever he may have done to wind up on death row, John Spenkelink was standing on solid biblical ground in his active resistance to his own death and to the executions of others condemned by the state, even those who are tempted to give in to the state's power to kill them.

A good example of this can be seen in a letter John wrote about a year before his own death from his cell in Florida to John Evans, a man on death row who had decided to let the state go ahead and kill him. The letter was addressed to "Dear Brother in trouble":

> . . . I don't fully understand your reasons for wanting to let the government go ahead and immediately kill you. The government here in Florida has me as their number one to be executed and I'll fight them with every breath I have. And it's not just for me, it's because the death penalty is unconstitutional and two wrongs do not make a right. There's many, many people who do not want our government to take such a strong control on life. It's no secret that parts of our government have murdered before in this country and in other countries.
>
> Please don't let them get away with killing you. Maybe you may

feel that I don't have any right for asking you what to do with your life. But I care about you, too. I just can't see myself giving in to these blood thirsty politicians. Parts of our government care and parts don't. I guess people in this world will always be this way. We never know what tomorrow will fully be like. I'll hang in there as long as possible, they'll have to kill me, cause I sure won't let them get their blood thirsty way with me. Take care. Help us too.

Truth and understanding,

John Spenkelink

I believe that Christians, like John Spenkelink, are called to live and to act out of a posture of appropriate moral outrage to resist nonviolently evils such as deliberate killing of human beings, whether by an individual or by a government. The tension is a difficult one. We are called to righteous indignation, not to self-righteousness, to hate the sin but to love the sinner, to resist evil, but to love those who do evil, to speak the truth, but to speak it in love, to love life but to accept death when it has come. And finally, as the Sermon on the Mount reminds us so starkly, we are called to be nothing short of perfect, but we are also called to realize that we are far from it, and to beg God to have mercy on our souls and to forgive us—every last one of us—over and over again, for our falling short.

May God have mercy on John Spenkelink and on all those on death row throughout this land and the world. May God have mercy on Bob Graham and on all those who want to continue killing God's children. May God have mercy on all of us.

49

Peter Gabriel
Rock Musician

Killing solves nothing. It does not work as a deterrent. Show me the drop in violent crime since the death penalty was brought back. It is not a deterrent.

The death penalty kills innocent people. It has been proved that, since 1900, twenty-three people have been wrongly executed. Can you look in the eyes of their mothers, wives, and children and tell them that their men died in the name of justice?

The death penalty discriminates against racial minorities and those without power and money. If you are a black man, and you are convicted of murdering a white man, you are four times as likely to receive the death penalty as a white man convicted of murdering a black. What sort of society can call that justice? Where are the principles on which this great nation was built?

The death penalty creates voyeuristic media events that excite the sadistic elements in our nature. It breeds violence.

The death penalty provides a human sacrifice for a sick society.

The death penalty is the cry of politicians who buy votes with fear.

The death penalty has no place in a civilized world.

The death penalty has no place in the United States of America.

THE DEATH PENALTY MUST GO.